INSIGHT ⊙ GUIDES

SHANGHAI
CITY GUIDE

www.insightguides.com

◉ Walking Eye App

YOUR FREE DESTINATION CONTENT AND EBOOK AVAILABLE THROUGH THE WALKING EYE APP

Your guide now includes a free eBook and destination content for your chosen destination, all for the same great price as before. Simply download the Walking Eye App from the App Store or Google Play to access your free eBook and destination content.

HOW THE WALKING EYE APP WORKS

Through the Walking Eye App, you can purchase a range of eBooks and destination content. However, when you buy this book, you can download the corresponding eBook and destination content for free. Just see below in the grey panels where to find your free content and then scan the QR code at the bottom of this page.

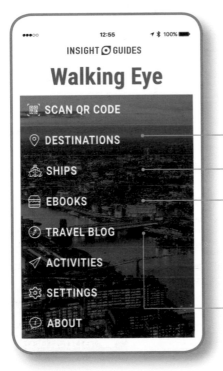

Destinations: Download your corresponding essential destination content from here, featuring recommended sights and attractions, restaurants, hotels and an A–Z of practical information, all for free. Other destinations are available for purchase.

Ships: Interested in ship reviews? Find independent reviews of river and ocean ships in this section, all available for purchase.

eBooks: You can download your free accompanying digital version of this guide here. You will also find a whole range of other eBooks, all available for purchase.

Free access to travel-related blog articles about different destinations, updated on a daily basis.

HOW THE DESTINATION CONTENT WORKS

Each destination includes a short introduction, an A–Z of practical information and recommended points of interest, split into 4 different categories:
• Highlights
• Accommodation
• Eating out
• What to do

You can view the location of every point of interest and save it by adding it to your Favourites. In the 'Around Me' section you can view all the points of interest within 5km.

HOW THE EBOOKS WORK

The eBooks are provided in EPUB file format. Please note that you will need an eBook reader installed on your device to open the file. Many devices come with this as standard, but you may still need to install one manually from Google Play.

The eBook content is identical to the content in the printed guide.

HOW TO DOWNLOAD THE WALKING EYE APP

1. Download the Walking Eye App from the App Store or Google Play.
2. Open the app and select the scanning function from the main menu.
3. Scan the QR code on this page – you will then be asked a security question to verify ownership of the book.
4. Once this has been verified, you will see your eBook and destination content in the purchased ebook and destination sections, where you will be able to download them.

Other destination apps and eBooks are available for purchase separately or are free with the purchase of the Insight Guide book.

Contents

Thanks to the Information Office of Shanghai Municipality
for their support with this project.

THE BEST OF SHANGHAI: TOP ATTRACTIONS

Here, at a glance, are the city's must-see sights, from iconic attractions like the Bund and the Oriental Pearl Tower to the charming former French Concession and the Yu Garden Bazaar.

△ **The Bund.** This architectural cocktail of pre-1949 buildings, once hailed as Asia's Wall Street, is one of the most enduring symbols of Old Shanghai. Take in the spectacular night-time view from one of the restaurant or bar terraces along the Bund itself (like M on the Bund, Bar Rouge or The Peninsula) or gaze across the river from the Park Hyatt or the Pudong Shangri-La. See page 101.

▽ **Lu Xun Park.** Grab a spot at this pleasant green space in the Hongkou area and watch Shanghai's older citizens at play – graceful ballroom dancers, tai chi exponents, budding opera singers and strollers among the lakes. See page 209.

△ **Shanghai Urban Planning Centre.** For a sense of where Shanghai is heading as a city and for a good overview of the metropolis, visit this museum on People's Square. Its interesting exhibitions and scale models will give you an idea of Shanghai's future. See page 121.

▷ **Oriental Pearl Tower.** The best time to visit this rocket-like structure is on weekday mornings (when it's infinitely less crowded). You can ride all the way to the top bubble, but the best views are from the second tier. On a clear day, you can see all the way to the Yangtze River. See page 217.

△ **Shanghai Museum.** China's best collection of prized Chinese arts and crafts is housed in a building shaped like a giant ancient bronze cooking vessel called a *ding*. See page 128.

△ **Xintiandi.** Shopping, dining, drinking and entertainment with character, set in a "village" of refurbished old *shikumen* (stone-gate) houses. See page 147.

△ **Former French Concession.** The plane-tree-lined streets of Fuxing Road and Wukang Road in the former French Concession area make for a lovely walk with their chic boutiques, stylish cafés and charming old houses. See page 163.

▽ **Shanghai Natural History Museum.** This vast collection of more than 280,000 exhibits has been rehoused in a sparkling new building in Jing'an Sculpture Park. Highlights include a 4000-year-old mummy and some towering recreated dinosaur skeletons. See page 180.

△ **Yu Garden and Bazaar.** For a taste of Shanghai's Chinese heart and soul, the Yu Garden area offers temples, a classic Chinese garden, atmospheric teahouses and busy, narrow lanes full of street life, shopping and food, glorious food. See page 137.

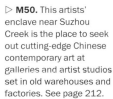

▷ **M50.** This artists' enclave near Suzhou Creek is the place to seek out cutting-edge Chinese contemporary art at galleries and artist studios set in old warehouses and factories. See page 212.

THE BEST OF SHANGHAI: EDITOR'S CHOICE

Here are our top picks of Shanghai's dazzling sights, plus some tips and tricks even the locals don't always know.

ONLY IN SHANGHAI

Customs House. Listen to its landmark clock play the Chinese Communist tune *The East is Red* every 15 minutes. See page 109.

Hairy crabs. Feast on these delicacies when they are in season (Oct–Nov) at any of Shanghai's fine Chinese restaurants. See page 67.

Huxinting Teahouse. Savour a cup of green tea at this century-old teahouse in the middle of a lake. See page 139.

Site of the First National Congress of the CPC. This is where Communism first sank its roots in China. See page 148.

Maglev train. The fastest train in the world, the Maglev is a mind-blowing ride. Its top speed? A mere 431km (267 miles) an hour. See page 258.

Inside the Jade Buddha Temple.

TRADITIONAL SHANGHAI

Jade Buddha Temple. Primarily known for its two Buddha statues crafted in jade, one in a seated position and the other lying on its side. See page 210.

Longhua Temple. Incense-filled courtyards, giant urns of joss sticks, imposing Buddha images and jostling crowds make this one of the city's most popular temples. See page 187.

Longtangs. Venture into the narrow alleys leading off the tree-lined streets of the former French Concession to catch a glimpse of residential lane life, where goods are sold, meals are cooked and gossip is exchanged. See page 160.

Shanghai Arts and Crafts Museum. See fast-disappearing crafts from yesteryear Shanghai at this grand old mansion. See page 155.

Shikumen Open House Museum. Recreates life as it was once lived in a traditional *shikumen* house. See page 149.

Yu Garden. A classic Chinese garden in the Old City with pools, pavilions and rockeries. See page 139.

Hairy crabs, a Shanghai delicacy.

Shanghai's modern skyscrapers: the Shanghai World Financial Center, Jin Mao Tower and the Shanghai Tower.

SHANGHAI FOR FAMILIES

Changfeng Ocean World. Tanks full of tropical fish, a shark tunnel and even a dolphin show in a park-like setting with a lake for boat rides. See page 199.

Fuxing Park. Lush green space for romping around in. A playground with slides, a mini Ferris wheel and dodgem cars. See page 149.

Shanghai Natural History Museum. Inspiring building housing recreated skeletons of Asia's largest dinosaurs, including the 26-metre (85ft) -long Mamenchisaurus. See page 180.

Shanghai Acrobatic Troupe. See amazing feats of contortion at the Shanghai Centre Theatre. See page 50.

Shanghai Disney Resort. The Chinese mainland's first Disney Resort features the mammoth theme park, 40-hectare (99-acre) Wishing Star Park, a shopping and dining district, plus two themed hotels. See page 224.

Shanghai Natural Wild Insect Kingdom. Live bugs in a rainforest setting, and a pond for fishing. See page 218.

Expect fireworks at the new Shanghai Disney Resort.

UNIQUE ARCHITECTURE

Shanghai Tower. You might just get neck strain looking up from ground level at the tallest building in China, shaped like a twisting dragon's tail. Ascend to the world's highest observation deck for staggering views across the metropolis. See page 220.

Jin Mao Tower. This pagoda-like structure which fuses Chinese design with Art Deco elements stands out in the Pudong skyline. See page 219.

Hengshan Moller Villa. This fairytale Gothic fantasy once owned by a British shipping tycoon is now home to a small hotel and restaurants. See page 174.

Park Hotel. Concession-era Czech architect Ladislau Hudec's finest Art Deco masterpiece is a landmark along busy Nanjing Road (W). See page 123.

Shanghai Exhibition Centre. A wedding cake of a building incorporating a mishmash of architectural styles but striking nonetheless. See page 176.

Tomorrow Square. Its soaring pincer-like roof stands out in the busy People's Square area. See page 123.

Road intersection in front of the impressive Shanghai skyline.

The Bund Sightseeing Tunnel.

Yu Garden at night.

Shanghai lights up at night.

CHINA'S FUTUREWORLD

Bold and vibrant Shanghai is where the faded glory of the 1930s and China's visions for a warp-speed future meld into one.

Shanghai surprises – no shocks – on first contact, with images that could only have come from the pages of a sci-fi novel. Walking out of gleaming Pudong Airport, the world's fastest train, harnessing electromagnetic levitation technology, will whisk you to downtown Pudong in eight minutes flat.

Located at the estuary of the Yangtze River in eastern China and facing the Pacific Ocean, Shanghai is vast – covering an area of 6,340 sq km (2448 sq miles) and boasting a heaving population of 24.2 million in 2016.

Shanghai is the spearhead of the country's programme for economic reform and has flourished as a result of overseas investment. The city is China's largest economic centre, with a per capita GDP similar to that of a medium developed country – US$17,105 in 2016.

The China (Shanghai) Pilot Free Trade Zone was created here in September 2013. A total of 580 multinational companies subsequently established their regional headquarters in Shanghai, and 411 foreign-funded R&D centres were also set up.

Shanghai is one of the world's leading financial centres and an important shipping centre. Shanghai's financial markets generated a total transaction volume of 1,364.66 trillion yuan in 2016, with trading volumes of several products ranked top among global markets. The city does a bustling trade with more than 500 ports around the world, handling 701.77 million tons of goods in 2016. On top of that, its international container volume has been ranked top in the world for seven consecutive years.

Shanghai might dazzle with its newly minted superstructures, but it retains slivers of its rich history too, making it a rewarding tourist destination and international cultural-exchange centre. Indeed, Shanghai received 8.5 million overseas tourists in 2016, in which year 741,900 flights were processed at Shanghai Pudong and Hongqiao international airports. Shanghai handled 164.6 million outbound and inbound travellers in 2016.

As the host city of the 2010 World Expo, Shanghai is constantly striving towards the motto, "Better City, Better Life". Propelled by a 2040 target, when Shanghai aims to be an innovative, cultural and ecological city with global influence, the city is busy reinventing itself into a sophisticated, international and extraordinary metropolis.

People on Nanjing Road.

THE SHANGHAINESE

With high living standards, innovative fashion trends and a propensity to look towards the future, the Shanghainese are rightly proud of their cosmopolitan city and outlook.

The Shanghainese are very much like their cutting-edge city: smart, hip and – often – pleased about it.

A migrant town

Greater Shanghai sprawls over 6,340 sq km (2,448 sq miles) with a population of 24.2 million in 2016. Like New York, it is a port and an immigrant town, with the forefathers of its residents mostly hailing from other cities and districts of East China.

Shanghai was already a thriving city in the 18th century, but it was only after the Sino-British Opium Wars in the early 1840s when Shanghai became a treaty port that the city developed into Asia's biggest and most progressive metropolis. Shanghai's foreign Concessions witnessed fast economic growth as the surrounding areas of East China were torn apart by war and famine over the following decades.

Historically, migrants have had an enormous impact on Shanghai: the southern port city of Ningbo, whose bankers dominated Shanghai's financial industry until the 1940s, was a big influence on the development of Shanghai's language, cuisine and personality. There was also a prominent Cantonese community in 19th-century Shanghai, which had followed the British in as compradors. The foreigners, too, left an indelible imprint on 19th- and early 20th-century Shanghai, occupying different enclaves of the city during the Concession years and creating a generation of foreign children who called Shanghai home.

The migration process continues today. Shanghai's economic boom of the past decade has attracted a new wave of immigrants

It is common to see groups doing exercise outside in Shanghai.

– ambitious young people from the rest of the country and small-time businesspeople from the surrounding provinces.

Reversing the flow that saw immigrant Shanghainese leave for Hong Kong in the 1940s and 50s, Hong Kong residents – many with Shanghainese roots – have now moved north to seek their fortunes.

Except for a half-century respite after 1949, Shanghai has always had a strong foreign presence. Today, the number of Europeans, Americans, Koreans, Japanese and other nationalities continues to grow dramatically. Exact figures

> The one-child policy, in effect from 1979 to 2015, has restricted Shanghai's population growth, but the huge influx of migrants has offset this: in 2014 the population rose above 24 million, up from 16 million in 2000. In 2016, government regulations to control excessive urbanisation saw the city's population shrink for the first time in a century.

are hard to come by, but there are around 170,000 foreigners. As Shanghai moves to take its place in the pantheon of world-class cities, the authorities are encouraging the influx of foreigners wanting to participate in the new China boom.

Changing lifestyles

China's one-child policy, implemented in 1979 to slow down an explosive population growth rate, has had a huge impact on the life of the Shanghainese. Most young people in Shanghai today are the product of a one-child family. Children are encouraged to view cousins as siblings. The policy was quietly relaxed in 2013, when offspring from one-child families who married a partner who was also an only child were allowed to have two children. The policy finally ended in 2015 when it was declared that all couples were free to have two children. However, many young urban families still opt for a single child, citing reasons such as economic pressures and busy lifestyles.

Until the 1990s, Shanghai was one of the world's most densely populated cities. Then began the biggest construction project China has ever attempted – the reconstruction of central Shanghai and the development of vast housing estates around its perimeter. More than

MIGRANTS

As in any international city, poorly educated labourers who come chasing dreams of prosperity often end up doing the menial work. Most of the jobs Shanghainese deem too lowly – construction, factory jobs, garbage collection and massage – are filled by Chinese from other regions. The majority of migrant labour comes from nearby provinces like Jiangsu, Anhui and Jiangxi.

Magnolia, Shanghai's city flower.

2 million people have been shifted out of the old housing in the central districts since 1995, a process which continues to this day. The new standard for Shanghai living today is an apartment in a high-rise block on a housing estate, with a small pet dog yapping to be taken for a run on the small piece of grass outside.

In this new Shanghai, people have something that they have never had before – privacy. In the old alleys, everyone knew everything about everyone else; the walls were paper-thin and gossip spread quickly when women washed out the chamber pots in the morning. In the new estates, people tend not to know their neighbours. Life has moved from one extreme to the other.

The young and restless

Young people in Shanghai enjoy an independent urban lifestyle, both native Shanghainese and young migrants who come for university and jobs. They rent – and very quickly buy – their own apartments, live together before marriage, spend more time with their parents and increasingly behave like young people in any major city in the West.

There is a lot of pressure on children to excel.

There is a technology gap as well, as Shanghainese embrace the world of iPhones and e-commerce, obtaining most of their information online and engaging with the outside world in an unprecedented way, one that leaves their parents and grandparents behind.

Still, because the trajectory is upward and optimistic, there is little adolescent angst or alienation in Shanghai – there is simply too much opportunity.

What makes a Shanghainese?

When they get together, Chinese people love to discuss regional differences in character – and Shanghai people are a favourite topic.

The Shanghainese are good at business and they understand the art of compromise – qualities that help make this city the commercial capital of China and a magnet for foreign investment.

In Shanghai, some locals are often too ready to make assumptions about others, either seriously or in jest. Indeed, calling someone a country bumpkin is one of their most potent put-downs – it means they are not smart enough, too slow on the uptake, too unsophisticated, too… un-Shanghainese.

The Shanghainese are typically more open to new ideas. It began in Old Shanghai with something called Yangjingbang Culture, "Yangjingbang" being the name of the creek that separated the French Concession and the Chinese city. The term refers to the amalgam of Chinese and Western ideas and influences into something that was uniquely Shanghainese, in terms of language, clothes, food, lifestyle and attitudes. The trend is visible again today

THE SHANGHAINESE DIALECT

Most Shanghainese prefer to speak the local dialect called Shanghaihua instead of Mandarin (or *putonghua*), the official language of China, even though they are conversant with the latter. Although both are written using the same Chinese characters, the Shanghainese dialect is almost completely incomprehensible to Chinese from many other parts of the country.

The government has been actively promoting the Shanghai dialect to avoid it slowly disappearing in an increasingly diverse city. There is now a Shanghainese-language radio show and bus announcements are made in Mandarin, English and Shanghainese.

> *People from other parts of China see Shanghainese fashion and lifestyles as something to emulate. Such is the cachet of this premier Chinese city.*

(although other parts of China are becoming equally cosmopolitan).

Conspicuous consumerism

Shanghainese value quality and follow trends, but are highly price-conscious. As incomes rise, though, the old mode of shopping – to go to a major department store to identify an item, then head for the local knock-off market to buy a copy of the same thing at a tenth of the price – has given way to an insistence on buying the genuine article. Even office girls save up for the real Vuitton, and boutiques in Paris these days employ Chinese-speakers to handle the crowds of Shanghai shoppers who descend on the French capital during the summer sales. Shanghai shoppers are unsurprisingly at the forefront of the e-commerce revolution, too. Home-grown e-commerce sites – such as Taobao, Tmall and JD.com – are popular for purchasing everything from shampoo to Chanel, often delivered to your doorstep within 24 hours.

A key feature of the consumerist lifestyle is fads, and Shanghai follows the latest trends in clothing, mobile phones and nightclubs. Central Huaihai Road, one of the city's key fashion shopping streets, is the epicentre of chic fashion in China. But as quickly as people try to emulate the Shanghai look, it morphs into something else.

Shanghainese girls are now fashion leaders rather than followers – the rest of the country looks here for trends, and Shanghai women

Basketball is popular.

seem unconcerned as to what the rest of the world is doing.

Shanghai people are regarded as being highly ambitious. They are less satisfied with comfort, more likely to fight for luxury.

While a conversation with a Beijing taxi driver can cover vast territories, it's difficult to get a tight-lipped Shanghai taxi driver even to tell you how business is going.

Thanks to the Shanghainese, the city will undoubtedly become the powerhouse that drives China through this century, becoming once again the dominant East Asian, if not world, metropolis.

TRENDY FASHIONISTAS VS PYJAMA POWER

Shanghainese women are China's fashion trendsetters. They have everything necessary to be so: increasingly sophisticated tastes, high disposable incomes, and an insatiable thirst for international trends. Shanghainese women were China's first to start perming their hair after the Cultural Revolution, and it's no coincidence that fashion magazine *Vogue* started its China edition in Shanghai. Shanghainese women fly to Paris for the summer sales, keep an eye on Japanese fashion, and change their hairstyle with the season.

But it's not all Gucci and Prada. The old Shanghai trend of wearing nightclothes outside on the street can occasionally still be spotted. Men and women venture out sporting anything from a frilly nightie to warm flannel PJs – usually to the market for their morning shopping – which dates from the era when pyjamas were a luxury product and warranted showing off, and is part of the traditional Shanghai *longtang* dweller's sense that the immediate neighbourhood is their living room.

Nanjing Road was already a bustling thoroughfare by the 1930s.

DECISIVE DATES

4000 BC
Prehistoric hunter-gatherers settle in the Yangtze Delta.

1000 BC
A tiny farming and fishing village is established on the banks of the Huangpu River.

AD 500
Shanghai grows in size and importance, and it develops a trading 1300 culture during the Southern Song Dynasty (1127–1279).

1400s
The Huangpu is dredged several times, setting the stage for commercial success.

1554
Shanghai builds a wall to protect itself from

Japanese pirates; the circular edges of the wall still define the borders of the Old Town.

1685
The Qing Dynasty opens a customs office, and Shanghai grows in commercial importance, with cotton, silk and tea the key exports.

1839–45
The British Army invades China and forces it to sign the Treaty of Nanjing, which gives Britain a foreign concession in Shanghai. France and America soon establish concessions of their own.

1851–4
The Taiping Rebellion rages across China, and Chinese residents pour into Shanghai.

Shanghai's ancient city walls.

1850s
Shanghai's boisterous Golden Age begins, and it becomes one of the fastest-growing and most famous cities on earth. It is rife with crime, but rich in opportunity for both Chinese and Westerners.

1911
The Qing Dynasty collapses, and a weak and fragmented Nationalist government takes over the Republic of China.

1921
The Chinese Communist Party is founded in Shanghai; Mao Zedong attends the meeting.

1923
The Hongkong and Shanghai Bank Building opens on the Bund.

1931–2
Japan bombs and invades Shanghai, but withdraws under the weight of international pressure.

Shanghai traded with Britain in the 19th century.

1933–41
Shanghai becomes a safe haven for some 23,000 Jews fleeing persecution in Europe.

1937
Japan bombs and invades Shanghai again, destroying many buildings and driving scores of residents out of the city.

1949
The Communists win the Chinese Civil War and the People's Republic of China is founded.

1978
Deng Xiaoping launches the "openings and reforms" era.

1992
Deng takes his famous "southern tour" to

Shanghai Tower.

encourage commerce in Shanghai, which he calls the Dragon's Head of the Yangtze Delta.

1994
Former Shanghai mayor Jiang Zemin becomes president of China. Metro line 1 opens, as does the Oriental Pearl Tower in Pudong, symbol of the new city.

1998
The Jin Mao Tower opens in Pudong.

1999
Pudong International Airport opens, and the city's elevated highway system is finished.

2001
Shanghai Cooperation Organisation is founded.

Shanghai hosts the 9th APEC Summit.

2002
Shanghai hosts the first Tennis Masters Cup in China.

2003
Hu Jintao succeeds Jiang Zemin as president of China.

2004
Shanghai hosts the first Formula One Grand Prix in China. The high-speed Maglev rail line opens.

2008
The World Financial Center building opens in Pudong.

2010
Shanghai hosts a successful World Expo, attracting 73 million visitors over the six-month period and completing a host of infrastructure projects that have considerably improved city living: extended subway lines, additional tunnels to Pudong and widened highways.

2016
The Shanghai Tower usurps its lofty predece-ssors and becomes the second tallest building in the world at 632 metres (2,073ft), with the world's highest observation deck. Also in Pudong, Shanghai Disney Resort opens on 16 June. A decade in the making, it's the largest international resort Disney has ever built.

Boating down the Yangtze River.

THE SHANGHAI STORY

In its transformation from fishing village to bustling trading port and now business centre, Shanghai has survived wars, foreign takeovers and the Cultural Revolution to emerge as China's leading city.

Located near the mouth of the Yangtze River, Shanghai was destined for glory. Its history as a trading port can be traced back to the Song dynasty (960–1279), a period of rapid urbanisation for China, especially in the south. In 1074, the provincial bureaucracy elevated Shanghai from a *hudu* (fishing village) to a *zhen* (commercial town), and in 1159, to that of a *shi* (market town). By 1292, during the early Yuan dynasty (1279–1368), the population of the region around Shanghai had grown so rapidly that officials created a *xian* (county), with Shanghai as its capital. From then on, Shanghai served as a seat of government and eventually became one of the most productive counties in China.

In 1404, Ming-dynasty (1368–1644) officials rerouted the Wusong River into the Huangpu, helping to turn the latter into a navigable waterway. From the 15th century onwards, the Huangpu gradually widened and deepened to become Shanghai's main river. The neglected Wusong meanwhile withered to its present proportions as Suzhou Creek. With the Huangpu flowing directly into the Yangtze River and out to the sea beyond, Shanghai's fortunes soared.

The walled city

In the 1550s, a wall was built to protect Shanghai from pirates. Most of Shanghai's residents lived outside the city walls, but its wealthy families built their homes inside the walled city, surrounding them with grand gardens. Within the walls were Buddhist and Taoist temples, as well as government offices, charity halls, guildhalls and private academies where members of the rich families could study for the Confucian examinations.

Yu Garden's Huxinting Teahouse.

During pirate attacks, guards would sound the alarm and people would flock through one of six gates to enter and seek refuge within the high walls of the city.

At the heart of the old walled city were Yu Garden and the Temple of the Town God (see page 137), which became the focal point for public gatherings. In the 15th century, a temple was built at this site by the Ming emperor. Called Jinshan Miao, it was reconstructed in 1726 as the Temple of the Town God and

In the 14th century, cotton growing (and weaving) was a key trade in Shanghai.

dedicated to the spirit of Huo Guang, a famous Ming general. The temple served as a locus of worship for the Shanghai folk, who believed that their Town God possessed the power to ward off pirates, bandits and other marauders. It was also a popular site for festivals, and like today, was a thriving marketplace. The garden that surrounded the temple was originally

EARLY CHRISTIAN INFLUENCE

Italian Jesuit missionaries converted many educated Chinese, including a Shanghai-born scholar Xu Guangqi (1562–1633) to Christianity. Matteo Ricci (1552–1610), an astronomer for the Ming court, was responsible for exposing the young Xu to Western scientific knowledge.

Over the next few decades, with the aid of the Jesuits, "Paul" Xu promoted Christianity and Western learning in Shanghai. Xu attracted many local scholars into his intellectual circle, with whom he published a number of important Chinese and Western books on agriculture, astronomy, religion and philosophy.

The imprint of Paul Xu and his Jesuit friends on Shanghai may be seen today in the Xujiahui district, where the St Ignatius Cathedral, more popularly known as Xujiahui Cathedral (see page 184), stands tall.

privately owned by the Pan family. During the Qing dynasty, when the family fell on bad times, it was sold to a group of merchants who turned it into a public space, which it remains today.

Early economy

The key to Shanghai's growth during the Ming dynasty (1368–1644) was the cotton industry. Cotton originated in India but found its way into China in the 13th century. The fertile Jiangnan region surrounding Shanghai provided the ideal environment for growing cotton. Cotton cloth became a major cottage industry for villagers throughout the region. By the late Ming period, merchants imported raw cotton to spin and weave into cloth, which was then exported to other parts of China.

By the Qing dynasty (1644–1911), many other industries had grown around the cotton boom. These included the cultivation of indigo for producing *nankeen* (blue cotton cloth), and soybean cake for use as fertiliser in the cotton fields. Soybeans grown in north China were brought to Shanghai, where merchants distributed them to the hinterlands.

In 1684, the Qing emperor lifted restrictions on ocean transport. Although the effect was not immediate, by the mid-1700s merchant

A high wall and moat was built around Shanghai in the 1550s to save it from pirates.

ships plying the China coast with beans, grain and other supplies on board were a common sight. Shanghai became a major distribution centre for both maritime and river trade. With thousands of dockworkers towing cargo off the docks to be stored in warehouses, and restaurants and street vendors hawking food to hungry travellers, it must have been quite a sight to walk along the banks of the Huangpu. Adding to the colour, alongside the many merchant and trading ships, sampans and barges, were "flower boats" or floating brothels, carrying girls from Suzhou and other nearby towns.

The opium trade

In 1760, the Qing emperor restricted all foreign trade to the southern port of Canton (Guangzhou). By 1800, the British were importing into Canton opium that was grown and processed in Bengal. The British exchanged opium with the Chinese for silver, some of which they used to buy Chinese tea. In 1796, the Qing emperor banned the import of opium, but it was too late. By the early 1800s, millions of Chinese

> *"The expense of a war could be paid in time; but the expense of opium, when once the habit is formed, will only increase with time."* – Townsend Harris

had become opium addicts, and silver flowed out of China by the tonne. In 1839, a Chinese official declared a ban on opium and destroyed the British opium supply in Canton, heralding the start of the First Opium War.

Over the next three years, the British Navy attacked and occupied several port cities, including Shanghai. The British also forced China to open these cities to international trade.

Treaty port Shanghai

In 1842, the Qing government signed a treaty with the British to end the First Opium War. Among other things, the Treaty of Nanjing designated five "treaty ports" – including Shanghai – where British nationals could reside in "Concessions" and conduct trade with the

Zui Bai Chi, a traditional Chinese garden in Songjiang district.

Chinese. Other foreign powers soon joined the system with treaties of their own.

The original British settlement was at the confluence of the Huangpu River and Suzhou Creek. The French settled just south of the British along the Huangpu, while the Americans occupied the area north of Suzhou Creek. A series of grand buildings lining the river were erected and the stretch became known as the Bund (see page 101). Then, in 1863, the British and American settlements merged to form an enclave called the International Settlement. Both the International Settlement and the French Concession had their own municipal governments, run respectively by British and French nationals. Over the next 50 years, both expanded westward to encompass several square miles of choice real estate south of Suzhou Creek.

At first, the settlements were off limits to Chinese. With the advent of the Taiping Rebellion (1850–64), the rules were relaxed to allow thousands of Chinese to flood into the settlements.

Lane housing

During and after the Taiping Rebellion, row-house neighbourhoods with *shikumen* (stone gate) or *longtang* (lane) housing sprang up in the settlements, displaying a mixture of Western and Chinese architectural forms. In later years, these spacious lane houses were built smaller and closer in order to accommodate the city's growing population.

In a span of 50 years, Shanghai's population grew ten-fold, making it one of the world's fastest-growing cities. The job opportunities in Shanghai attracted both Chinese from neighbouring provinces and foreign nationals from all over the world. By 1930, the total population of Shanghai surged to 3 million, placing it among the top five most populous cities.

A cauldron of revolution

By the early 20th century, Shanghai was a major manufacturing centre. Hundreds of thousands of Chinese men, women and children laboured day and night for pitiful wages in the foreign-owned cotton and silk textile factories. These workers were the most visible sign of the exploitation of China by foreign imperialists.

In 1912, the ailing Qing dynasty gave way to a fledging republic, which soon fell to rapacious warlords. Sun Yat-sen's Nationalist Party (Kuomintang or KMT) headquartered itself in Canton, but Sun spent much of his time in Shanghai.

Shanghai, with its large worker and student population, was considered the perfect breeding ground for a Communist revolution. In 1921, the CPC held its first congress in Shanghai's French Concession. During the 1920s, the CPC led workers' strikes and student movements, including the famous May 30th

> During the 1930s, Shanghai was home to refugees from all over the world. Two of the largest groups from abroad were the White Russians and European Jews.

Movement in 1925. Sparked by the murder of a Chinese worker by a Japanese factory foreman, and further inflamed by the shooting of student protestors by Shanghai's Municipal Police, this anti-imperialist movement gathered force throughout the country.

The White Terror

In 1927, Chiang Kai-shek's Northern Expedition made it to Shanghai. The CPC organised a citywide strike. But Chiang had other plans. After sending delegates to meet with Du Yuesheng (or "Big Ears" Du), one of the leaders of Shanghai's notorious Green Gang, Chiang ordered a purge of the Communists in Shanghai. On 12 April, 1927, Green Gang members and Kuomintang soldiers rounded up and executed thousands of Communists operating in Shanghai. Over the next decade, the Green Gang continued to terrorise the city and extorted millions from its wealthy bourgeoisie to fill the coffers of Chiang's government. In return, they were given a virtual monopoly over the city's opium racket.

World War II Shanghai

China had a vast depository of resources – mineral and agricultural – that Japan needed to fuel its industrial expansion. In 1931, Japan took Manchuria (which they renamed "Manchukuo") by force, and in 1932 provoked a war in Shanghai's Zhabei district, killing thousands of Chinese civilians and moving Japanese military personnel into China.

In 1937, Japan finally launched a full-scale invasion of the country from its power base in Manchuria, rapidly occupying the eastern seaboard of China. In December 1937, forces reached the then-capital, Nanjing (Nanking), where they carried out the horrific Rape of Nanking, brutally torturing, raping and murdering the city's population in a bloodbath that remains an unhealed wound for China. Chiang's government was chased to the interior, Wuhan and Chungking, where they were to spend the ensuing years of war.

The period between 1937 and 1941 was a strange one for Shanghai: the Japanese surrounded the city, operating from their bases in Zhabei and entering the old Chinese city, but

Shanghai Jewish Refugees Museum. Shanghai received about 23,000 Jewish refugees during 1933–41.

Imposing architecture dominates the Bund.

they dared not enter the French Concession or the International Settlement, which would have been an act of war against Britain, America and France. Nonetheless, they made their ambitions known, bombing KMT bases in Zhabei and moving in the warship *Udzumi*. Many of the foreigners living in Shanghai took this as a signal to leave, but others – notably Jews fleeing the Nazi threat in Europe – arrived in numbers to replace them.

The Chinese, of course, had no such escape route, but those who were able to fled to the Concessions. For the rest, it was a horrific time as the Japanese were cruel. Untold numbers of prominent Chinese were called up to "731", the Kempitai (secret police) headquarters where they were tortured, sometimes to death.

When Pearl Harbor was bombed, in December 1941, the Japanese took possession of the International Settlement. Vichy France, already part of the Nazi collaborationist government, gave up the French Concession to Japanese military control. Foreigners in the International Settlement were enemy nationals, and were made to wear armbands to identify them as such.

It took the Japanese a year to set up the internment camps such as Longhua and more than a year to set up the Jewish ghetto in Hongkou. Prior to 1941, Jews – both refugees and long-time Shanghai residents – could live throughout the city, but after the occupation were restricted to the Hongkou "ghetto". They had to apply for permission to enter and depart, even for regular jobs, from a disagreeable Japanese soldier named Goya.

Food was always scarce, and the invaders were unspeakably cruel to the Chinese, torturing and killing with little mercy.

In 1943, the Allied powers signed an agreement returning Shanghai to Chinese sovereignty. In one fell swoop, 100 years of semi-colonialism came to a sudden, crashing end.

The liberation

In 1949, following a four-year civil war between the KMT and Communists, fought mostly in

Street in Shanghai's Old City.

the northeast of China, the People's Liberation Army (PLA) marched southward, taking China's coastal cities. Chiang and his cohorts fled to Taiwan, vowing to return. But they never did.

In May 1949, the PLA liberated Shanghai, and, on 1 October, Mao Zedong triumphantly declared the founding of the People's Republic of China (PRC).

After its liberation by the CPC, Shanghai continued to play a leading role in rebuilding the nation. Despite the exodus of many of the city's most talented business managers to Hong Kong and Taiwan, Shanghai still had the greatest concentration of technical know-how, the most diverse and effective educational system, and the most productive workers in China.

The dragon rises

In the late 1970s, Shanghai emerged from the nightmare of the 1960s and early 70s. The 1980s were marked by gradual improvements in living standards and a heightened sense of optimism. In 1992, following the success of economic reforms in Shanghai and other cities in southern China, the CPC began the long process of removing the shackles of a planned economy. With the opening of Shanghai to foreign investment in the early 1990s, the stage was set for an economic and infrastructural boom that was unprecedented in world history.

In 1990, Shanghai's Pudong (see page 215) was set up as a Special Economic Zone (SEZ), and became the showcase for the city's modernisation scheme. Through tax incentives,

Aerial attack on Shanghai by the Japanese Air Force.

Shanghainese calendar girl.

Tower, which was the second tallest building in the world when it opened in 2016. All three of Pudong's buildings tower over the colonial edifices along the Bund across the Huangpu River.

A global metropolis

The 2010 World Expo was declared a huge success, surpassing its goal of 70 million visitors over the six-month period. The Expo helped Shanghai clean up and invest in infrastructure, and the result is a vastly expanded and improved transportation system. By 2014, Shanghai had the longest metro network in the world, and it is still growing.

Today, Shanghai continues to transform itself into a cosmopolitan metropolis. The government has built dozens of new public parks throughout the city, but at the same time, hundreds of old, decrepit *shikumen* neighbourhoods have been torn down to make way for new high-rises, while others, like the Xintiandi entertainment complex, have been gentrified. Foreigners from Asia, Europe and the Americas have flocked to the city by the thousands to work, bringing with them their cultures, their cuisines and their creative energies.

Despite challenges, the city continues to exude a powerful sense of optimism and a creative energy unrivalled in the world. The Shanghai Disney Resort in Pudong, which opened in June 2016 – Disney's biggest and most expensive international resort to date – is the latest testament to Shanghai's global importance. For those with the means and the moolah, Shanghai is *the* place to be.

lowered tariffs and other benefits, the municipal government encouraged foreign enterprises and banks to move into Pudong.

In 1990, the Shanghai Stock Exchange moved to Pudong's Lujiazui financial zone. New housing and offices in Pudong were built from the mid-1990s onwards, and have lured many residents and businesses to move across the Huangpu River.

Meanwhile, during the 1990s, the city government constructed an elevated highway system to ease urban traffic, built four suspension bridges spanning the Huangpu River, expanded many of the city's clogged streets, dug a metro line running north–south and another east–west, and constructed the futuristic Pudong International Airport. Two new icons arose in Pudong to dominate the skyline: the Oriental Pearl Tower in 1995, and the Jin Mao Tower in 1999 – the tallest building in China at the time. This title was usurped by the Shanghai World Financial Center when it opened in 2008, and then again by the 632-metre (2,073ft) -high Shanghai

SHANGHAI FORTUNES

During the 1920s and '30s, Shanghai was famously a place where fortunes could be made, and often lost, with blinding speed.

The richest men in Old Shanghai were the property developers, buying up swathes of real estate in what were often outlying rural areas, and watching the city grow out to them. These prosperous men included Silas Hardoon, who arrived penniless from Baghdad and become Shanghai's richest man; Sir Victor Sassoon (see page 111), whose signature buildings still stand (the Peace Hotel, Cathay Cinema, Grosvenor House, the Embankment Building); and Sir Elly Kadoorie, with his portfolio of hotels.

The China Pavilion for the 2010 Expo,
which was a roaring success.

Looking up the Shanghai Tower.

Oriental Pearl Tower.

BUSINESS AND ECONOMY

With ready access to an educated workforce and impressive
physical and digital infrastructure, Shanghai is playing
a central role in China's ongoing economic growth.

Prospective buyers surveying a scale model of a condominium – property is much sought after in boomtown Shanghai.

From the incessant clatter of construction that fills the gleaming metropolis of Pudong and the old downtown in Puxi, to the clink of glasses toasting a steady stream of closed deals in conference rooms and restaurants all over the city, Shanghai is hopping with a high-voltage buzz and energy that screams out economic development.

Shanghai has been one of China's most important commercial cities for the past 150 years, and it's hard to overstate the importance of this city to the national economy.

Shanghai beats other major Chinese cities as a destination for investment. For information on what's hot, check the Shanghai government's business website at www.investment.gov.cn.

Since its latest bout of growth began in the early 1990s, Shanghai's economy expanded by at least 10 percent every year until the global recession hit in 2008–9, and has since stabilised.

China has become a global player, with Shanghai as its financial and business heart.

Shanghai's thriving retail business forms a sizeable chunk of the service sector. The Shanghainese are China's most style-conscious people; the city is filled with packed malls, screaming billboards and sidewalks that sometimes look more like catwalks. Visitors may wish to purchase Chinese silk or porcelain as gifts for family and friends back home, but they can just as easily opt for Ferragamo on Nanjing Road, Versace on Central Huaihai Road or Graff on the Bund – or any one of the top-flight international designer brands.

Shanghai renaissance

Over the years a centrally planned economy was instituted, and all production was set by the state and distributed by the state. In return for labour and loyalty, a citizen's needs were provided from the cradle to the grave by the government.

Several decades after the founding of New China from the ruins of a vast but mostly rural land torn apart by years of wars, Shanghai, as the new nation's economic forerunner thanks to its rich portfolio of light industries, had to contribute a big chunk of its annual fiscal income to the state purse, only to be paid out to other provinces as part of the central economic planners' blueprint to pull off a nationwide balance of socialist wealth. And nearly half of the central government's pool of merchandise to be rationed out came from Shanghai. Meanwhile, the city had to relocate more than 300 of its factories to China's hinterlands from 1949 up to 1980, taking with them about 1 million technicians. This scenario didn't end until Deng Xiaoping orchestrated the reform and opening-up policies.

When Deng Xiaoping agreed to loosen Shanghai's reins after 1990, the city reacted like an orchard exposed to warmth after a long winter. Forty years was not long enough to extinguish Shanghai's commercial instincts: the stage was set for the intensive development that began in the 1990s and continues today.

COMMERCIAL CULTURE

The intangible factor in Shanghai's economic success is the confident, urbane and commercial-minded character of the typical Shanghainese. The parents of most of today's Shanghainese moved to the city decades ago to seek their fortunes – hardworking people with an appetite for risk and the brains to make the best of opportunity. To this day, Shanghai is the lodestone that attracts the most ambitious Chinese from all corners of the country.

Economic pillars

Shanghai products have maintained their reputation as the best made in the country. Over recent years, the government has placed emphasis on the six so-called "pillar industries": information technology, automobiles, chemicals, steel, machinery and biotechnology. Production in these six areas constitutes about 70 percent of Shanghai's total industrial output.

With wage levels continuing to rise, Shanghai manufacturers have moved up the technology curve – and relocated to technical and industrial parks on the fringes of the city. With the encouragement of both the municipal and central governments, the city has become a production centre for high-tech items like semiconductors and telecommunications equipment. These industries rely on educated workers with good language skills, and this is where Shanghai excels.

Shanghai is the world's busiest container port. With China's best highway, rail and inland marine infrastructure, and two vast modern airports, Shanghai serves as the logistics centre for

Stereotypical Chinese business meetings focus on gradual relationship-building, but in fast-changing Shanghai, it's likely that your business partners will want to get down to brass tacks as quickly as you do – and, in many cases, even faster.

much of the country. It is little wonder that the Yangtze River Delta continues to attract high-end manufacturers from all over the world, who know that business in Shanghai is not built upon low wages and sweatshop labour.

Financial centre

Shanghai's evolution as the financial centre of China is another driver in the city's economic miracle. China's rapid move towards a market-oriented economy over the past two decades has required the development of modern financial institutions. Pudong's Lujiazui (see page 215) is home to China's most powerful banks and insurance companies, as well as the Shanghai

High-tech industry is the mainstay of Shanghai's thriving economy.

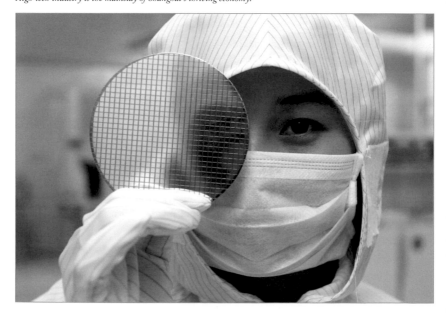

Shanghai's shoppers.

Stock Exchange. In 2013, the Shanghai Free-Trade Zone was also launched in Pudong. The first of its kind in China's mainland, the zone is a testing ground for economic and social reforms, and its success has resulted in similar free-trade zones being opened in other large Chinese cities.

China has a good grasp of the reforms necessary to make Shanghai competitive as a financial centre, and are implementing them in a methodical and measured manner. Banks have received government bail-outs, sold stakes to overseas investors and raised additional capital from global markets.

The number and types of financial instruments offered in both the consumer and institutional financial markets are on the rise, and both companies and individuals are able to invest in a whole new class of assets, such as gold and foreign equities. With the domestic retail banking industry now open following China's entry to the World Trade Organization,

consumers have more financial choices than ever before.

Future directions

China's most cosmopolitan city was in the global eye during the 2010 World Expo, which saw public investment continue at a sustained rate, virtually guaranteeing the city's targeted 10 percent annual growth. In tandem with China's subsequent economic slowdown, Shanghai's GDP growth slipped to 6.9 percent in 2015. The city's economy is relatively balanced, however, and driven by numerous sectors – including services, exports, logistics, domestic and international finance and high-tech manufacturing – and it remains a strong driver of China's growing economic influence.

Investors who accept the unique risks presented by China's business environment are betting that its rapidly growing economy will bring them profits on a scale not possible in smaller markets.

Scene from the Kunju opera's staging of
The Peony Pavilion.

PERFORMING ARTS

Chinese opera, music, drama, dance and cinema are all experiencing a renaissance in Shanghai, and the city looks set to claim its former glory as a world cultural centre.

The Shanghai Grand Theatre (see page 121) is a gleaming glass and steel structure, with an aluminium roof that arcs gracefully toward the heavens. The city's first world-class theatre set the standard for performing arts venues across China when it opened in August 1998. And if that wasn't enough, a second and equally impressive facility opened in 2005. Located in Pudong, the Shanghai Oriental Arts Centre (see page 223), with its dramatic tinted-glass exterior, resembles a butterfly orchid when viewed from above. Designed by French architects and featuring state-of-the-art technology, both theatres have succeeded in luring the world's top performing arts companies to Shanghai.

> *It is appropriate that Shanghai should have two of China's best performing arts theatres. It was in this city that many Chinese art forms were incubated, refined and born.*

Glory days of the arts

In the 1920s and 30s, Shanghai was the undisputed performing arts capital of China, a magnet for aspiring and established artists from around the country. The greatest Chinese opera stars dazzled audiences with their interpretations of classic operas. Professional storytellers mesmerised crowds in teahouses, relating tales so long they took months to finish. Acrobats, jugglers and contortionists cavorted before crowds in the narrow streets around the Yu Garden. The Shanghai

Shanghai Acrobatics Troupe – not to be missed.

Municipal Orchestra performed the works of classical and contemporary European composers at the Lyceum Theatre, and films were so popular that it was front-page news when a new cinema opened.

After 1949, private opera troupes were disbanded and reorganised under government auspices. Itinerant performers were obliged to stop their wanderings. The foreigners who comprised the bulk of the Shanghai Municipal Orchestra left. Yet, somehow, many art forms have withstood the odds and are still being performed today.

A Beijing opera star takes centre stage.

Chinese opera (Beijing-style)

Chief among the traditional performing arts is Chinese opera, a broad term for sung drama that includes more than 360 different varieties. This is a highly demanding art: actors, who begin training as children, must learn to sing and dance, acquire an extensive repertoire of highly stylised gestures and perform acrobatics. It is equally challenging to watch. Few props are used, which means the audience must use their imagination to fill in considerable blanks; characters are role types recognisable only by their make-up and costumes; and interpretative differences are highly nuanced. With so many less challenging modern diversions, Chinese opera today is losing its fans, especially in the cities.

For the past century, Shanghai has been home to four kinds of Chinese opera: Peking, Kunju, Yueju and Huju. Peking opera is the best known, recognisable by its falsetto singing, vivid make-up, percussion-based music, striking acrobatics and librettos based on the exploits of legendary heroes. In Old Shanghai, Peking opera was king, with great stars such as Mei Lanfang, renowned male interpreter of women's roles, who was enticed here from Beijing by wealthy patrons.

So seductive was the profusion of performing arts in Shanghai that Peking opera troupes began to borrow from other art forms and a Shanghai school of Peking opera developed. Called *haipai*, which is characterised by a willingness to experiment, it was the first to use mechanical scenery and special effects, and to adapt scripts from outside the traditional repertoire. This willingness to innovate is criticised by purists, but it has helped Shanghai's Peking opera company maintain its vitality and remain one of the strongest in the country.

Kunju, Shaoxing and Huju opera

Kunju, named after nearby Kunshan, is sometimes known as the mother of Peking opera. Its music is gentle and melodic, dominated by the bamboo flute, and its librettos are long and lyrical, read to this day as literary classics. The Shanghai Kunju Company has sparked renewed interest in this dying genre, most recently with *The Peony Pavilion*.

Written by Tang Xianzu in 1598, *The Peony Pavilion* has 55 acts, a cast of 100 and still packs a punch.

Yueju opera, which originates in Zhejiang province, has a repertoire of mainly tragic love stories like *A Dream of Red Mansions*, with music augmented by violins and cellos. Interestingly, it is performed almost exclusively by women. It first became popular in the 1920s – when fans would throw gold and jewellery on stage to their favourite actresses – and has a large cult following of housewives to this day.

Huju is a strictly local opera form sung in the Shanghainese dialect. Rarely performed in theatres, it's sometimes still staged outdoors near the Temple of the Town God, a gathering place for itinerant performers since the Ming dynasty.

Pingtan

Though the wandering performers of Old Shanghai are gone, a few of their arts have survived, notably Pingtan and acrobatics. A

Pingtan storytelling is accompanied by traditional string instruments like the pipa and sanxian.

respected art form of storytelling with close links to music, Pingtan is usually performed by a man and a woman who use only a fan or a teacup as props but keep audiences spellbound with animated facial expressions and virtuosic musical accompaniment on Chinese string instruments like the *pipa* and *sanxian*.

Contemporary drama

Westerners began introducing their own performing arts and forming acting clubs as early as the 1860s, but their plays had little reach beyond the foreign community. The first spoken drama performed by the Chinese was a 1907 adaptation of Harriet Beecher Stowe's *Uncle Tom's Cabin*, staged by leftist students. In the 1920s, young authors like Tian Han began writing plays and, in 1933, the China Travelling Dramatic Troupe was founded to take spoken drama from Shanghai to the rest of the nation. Its greatest moment was the 1936 première of Cao Yu's *Thunderstorm*, a tragedy that remains a classic on the Chinese stage.

An increasing number of international theatre troupes, whose performances range from Shakespeare to contemporary Asian drama, tour Shanghai more frequently these days, giving audiences a new perspective.

Shanghai Symphony Orchestra.

Le coup de cœur du Jury !

PRIX DU JURY - À L'UNANIMITÉ

SHANGHAI DREAMS

UN FILM DE
WANG XIAOSHUAI

Movie poster of the award-winning Shanghai Dreams.

Orchestral music

The Shanghai Symphony Orchestra dates to 1879, when it began as a town band for the International Settlement. Over the years, the band became a symphony, comprising mainly foreigners and, after 1938, Chinese musicians.

ACROBATIC ARTS

Acrobatics did not originate in Shanghai but was so popular pre-1949 that the city became a centre for acrobatic troupes from around the country, and the first port of call for circuses and magic shows from overseas. After 1949, acrobatics was promoted heavily by the government as a proletarian art form. It was also one of the few arts permitted during the Cultural Revolution.

The audience in Shanghai is comprised primarily of overseas tourists. The Shanghai Acrobatic Troupe, which performs nightly at the Shanghai Centre Theatre, is one of the best of its kind in the world.

The presence of so many foreign musicians in Shanghai attracted aspiring Chinese musicians from around the country and led the great music educator Xiao Youmei to establish the country's first music school – now the Shanghai Conservatory of Music – in 1927.

Graduates of the Conservatory were instrumental in persuading authorities that classical music could "serve the people"; many indeed went on to be key forces in the post-1949 development of Western music and opera. Western classical music in turn became a major influence in the reform of Chinese music – traditional instruments were modernised, new instruments were created and Western-style orchestral ensembles were formed. Both the Shanghai Symphony Orchestra and Shanghai Conservatory are strong institutions. The city also supports two other major orchestras, the Shanghai Philharmonic Orchestra and the Shanghai Broadcast Symphony Orchestra.

Ballroom dancing is popular in Shanghai, with couples twirling on pavements and parks in the early morning hours.

Ballroom and ballet dancing

Dance was wildly popular in Shanghai, but more as a participatory activity than as an art form which people watched in a theatre. Dance was closely linked with jazz and – together with films – was the prime means through which jazz was introduced. In the 1920s and 30s, Shanghai had enough dance halls to support over 500 jazz bands, mostly comprising Filipino musicians. Ballroom dance remains popular among the Shanghainese today. Jazz too has made a comeback, and once again many of the musicians are foreign.

Ballet and contemporary dance were brought to Shanghai by the White Russians in the 1920s – Dame Margot Fonteyn in fact began her studies with a Russian ballet teacher in Shanghai (see page 158). After liberation, the Soviet Russians continued to develop the art form, and the Shanghai Ballet School and Shanghai Ballet were founded. Russian classics dominated their repertoire up until the mid-1960s, when the creation of a proletarian ballet with Chinese characteristics was encouraged. Classic poses from Peking opera were integrated into ballet and the choreography was made more "revolutionary", meaning that ballerinas danced with clenched fists and rifles, their eyes ablaze with the fire of class hatred.

The Shanghai Ballet today performs primarily European classics, although they still stage the classic piece *The White-Haired Girl*, and are moving into experimental East-West collaborations with international ballet companies and choreographers, such as Derek Deane. There is also the Shanghai Song & Dance Ensemble, which combines elements of contemporary, classical and traditional Chinese dance, and has several rising young stars.

Shanghai has a well-respected modern dance company founded by the renowned dancer Jin Xing, a Beijing transplant. Jin Xing – who used to be a colonel in the People's Liberation Army – is a strong choreographer whose work is shaking up Shanghai's modern dance scene.

Shanghainese cinema

Cinema also got its start in Shanghai, where the first film ever shown in China was screened in 1896 – as an interlude between magic tricks

Shanghai Ballet dancers in a contemporary piece.

Jin Xing is a modern dancer and TV personality.

Shooting a film in Shanghai.

and a fireworks display in a vaudeville show. The first films made in China were produced by foreigners in Shanghai and the first Chinese-produced films were also made here.

By the 1930s, movies were the biggest form of entertainment, with first-run Hollywood films shown in lavishly decorated auditoriums that could seat nearly 2,000 people. The first Chinese "talkie" was produced in Shanghai in 1931, starring the legendary actress Butterfly Wu, and the industry soon prospered despite the popularity of Hollywood movies.

The Communist Party gave the film industry much support after 1949. Filmmakers like Wang Xiaoshuai, whose *Shanghai Dreams* won the Prix du Jury at Cannes in 2005, are gaining international acclaim.

Shanghai is also marketing itself as a cheaper, more exotic movie-making locale for Hollywood. *Mission Impossible III*, *The White Countess*, *The Painted Veil*, *Her* and *Skyfall* were all filmed in Shanghai, with many more in the making.

What the future holds

The government recognises that performing and other arts are essential to Shanghai's

> Critically acclaimed Chinese films like *Crouching Tiger, Hidden Dragon* and *Lust, Caution* (set in Shanghai and Hong Kong) have gone mainstream, while Chinese film stars like Zhang Ziyi, Fan Bingbing, Gong Li and Chow Yun-fat have made a name for themselves in Hollywood, and directors such as Zhang Yimou, Chen Kaige and Wang Kar-wai are globally admired.

drive to be a major global city, and has built first-rate performance venues and imported popular shows, from the musical *Cats* to high-octane pop acts like Queen and Adam Lambert. At the Shanghai Disney Resort, the 1,200-seat Walt Disney Grand Theatre shows the first-ever Mandarin production of Disney's *The Lion King*.

Old Shanghai was the nation's performing arts capital because it was open, cosmopolitan and relatively free. Shanghai is fortunate in that so many of its stellar performing arts companies survived a century of war, revolution and chaos.

Writing in Shanghai

So important is Shanghai in the history of modern Chinese literature that nearly every great writer of the first half of the 20th century lived here at some point.

Shanghai's famous inhabitant writers have included Lu Xun, Guo Moruo, Ba Jin, Mao Dun, Xu Zhimo, Qian Zhongshu, Cao Yu, Tian Han, Ding Ling – the list goes on. They came for different reasons, but all found themselves in a city primed to support a literary revolution. The Shanghai region had, for centuries, produced great poets, painters and calligraphers – arts that are intertwined in traditional Chinese thinking. When Westerners settled here after the Opium Wars, they spread their own literature and ideas through missionary schools and universities. In time, graduates of these schools began to study overseas and returned with new world views. When the "old culture" of the traditional literati met the "new culture" of the Western-influenced students, great literary ferment was inevitable.

Shanghai became a nucleus of literary experimentation, a role made easier by its commercial base as a printing and publishing centre. The pinnacle of the written word in China had always been poetry, but in Shanghai the novel – written in the vernacular, rather than classical Chinese – became the vogue. Famous examples include Mao Dun's *Midnight*, Ding Ling's *Miss Sophie's Diary*, Ba Jin's *Family* and Qian Zhongshu's *Fortress Besieged*.

Poetry, too, became a form of experiment. New-style bards such as Guo Moruo tossed aside the strict technical rules for writing Chinese poetry and immersed themselves in the flowing verse of poets like Whitman and Tagore. Xu Zhimo wrote of love, ideals and freedom, and he lived his life as passionately as he wrote his poetry.

The essay also held an important place in Shanghai's literary world, its greatest practitioner the legendary Lu Xun, who lived and wrote here from 1927 to 1936. He wrote with an acid-tipped pen, criticising the entire fabric of Chinese society. Many of his essays revolved around political or revolutionary topics. He is best known in the West, however, as the author of *The True Story of Ah Q* and *Diary of a Madman*, which lampooned Chinese character and culture.

Statue of Ding Ling.

In China, a new generation was finding its voice; in recent years, young writers have published passionate accounts of characters struggling to find love or meaning in the modern city.

Jin Yucheng is one of Shanghai's most treasured contemporary writers. In 2015, his best-known novel, *Blossoms*, won the prestigious Mao Dun Literary Prize. The novel follows 100 characters and flips between two time periods – exploring the Shanghai of the old and the new.

Even the body is a canvas for Shanghai's artists.

VISUAL ARTS

A stimulating mix of both traditional and cutting-edge contemporary art forms has made Shanghai an exciting centre of artistic expression.

Shanghai's progress in transforming itself into a cultural centre is nowhere more apparent than in the visual arts. Indeed, in less than a decade, the city has become the nation's standard-bearer for museum design and management, and a key centre for contemporary art.

Old Shanghai was an important arena of artistic experimentation, a meeting place for methods and philosophies from China and the West. Its booming economy enabled it to support artists, patrons and collectors, and its cosmopolitan atmosphere made them feel at home. In traditional China, the arts had long been looked upon as a gentleman's pursuit rather than a professional's *métier*, but in Shanghai it has become acceptable to combine culture with commerce – and still be respected.

Chinese painting

Painting is traditionally considered the greatest of the traditional arts in China. It is intimately related to calligraphy, which holds a similarly exalted status, and seal-carving. In Old China, some facility in painting or calligraphy was a virtual requirement for any self-respecting member of the literati.

Shanghai was heir to a tradition of highly accomplished gentlemen painters. Painting was a meditative and philosophical art that was considered as much a reflection of the artist's inner moral being as his artistic skill. Brushwork was of paramount importance, its intent to reflect the essence of whatever was portrayed rather than its true appearance. Tradition reigned supreme; a painter who wished to portray a

Liu Haisu's work is reminiscent of Impressionism.

mountain was as likely to study a past master's representations of mountains as to go and look at one himself. Though many Chinese painters were aware of such Western techniques as perspective and shading, they eschewed them.

Western influence

However, as Shanghai became more cosmopolitan in the late 19th and early 20th centuries, a new school of painting called *haishang* developed. *Haishang* is essentially a combination of different styles and techniques, its most distinctive feature being openness to new ideas – it

The Joe Camel cigarette is a recurrent motif in Zhou Tiehai's work.

> In recent years, Shanghai has become a centre for Chinese contemporary art. There are big bucks to be made, too – although the stratospheric sales volumes have fallen since the heady days of the market peak in 2010 and 2011. In the first six months of 2016, Sotheby's, Christie's, Poly and Guardian sold US$45.4-million worth, a decline of 21 percent from the same period in 2015.

is the visual arts equivalent of Chinese opera's *haipai* (see page 48). This *haishang* broad-mindedness grew to encompass Western art when the printing industry blossomed at the turn of the 20th century and painters could see reproductions of Western masterpieces. Art students began to paint still lifes and nude models, and to take their easels outdoors and sketch what they saw – methods that were a departure from traditional Chinese art.

Shanghai soon became the destination of choice for students interested in Western painting, including renowned painters such as Liu Haisu and Xu Beihong. Liu Haisu studied in Paris and Japan and later founded the Shanghai Art School. A great admirer of such artists as Van Gogh and Cézanne, Liu sparked a scandal when he organised an exhibition of nude

MUSEUMS APLENTY

When the Shanghai Museum (see page 122) built its striking building in People's Square in 1996, it was seen as proof that the city was serious about improving its cultural standards. Often cited as one of the best museums in China, its success fuelled a plan to refurbish and build many more museums in Shanghai, both public and private. Shanghai's must-visit art museums include the China Art Museum, Power Station of Art and MoCA (Museum of Contemporary Art). On the West Bund 'art corridor', don't miss the Long Museum West Bund, Shanghai Centre of Photography and Yuz Museum. Aurora Museum in Pudong showcases a magnificent collection of ancient Chinese art and artefacts. The Shanghai Natural History Museum, Shanghai Urban Planning Exhibition Centre (see page 121), Shanghai Film Museum and Shanghai Museum of Glass are also well worth a visit.

paintings, which was quickly shut down by the police. Liu eventually returned to brush-and-ink painting, but his traditional-style works still reveal the influences of his Western education.

Xu Beihong studied in Paris and Berlin and spent much of his career moving between Western- and Chinese-style painting. At its best, his work combines elements of both, as seen in his famous galloping horses, which seem ready to run off the scroll with their flowing brush-strokes and bulging muscles.

The vivacity that characterised painting in Shanghai largely ended with the Sino-Japanese War. After 1949, Soviet-style Realism became the main influence, and the subject matter of both traditional and Western-style painting tended to be revolutionary. Traditional paintings often included trains and tractors, and the practice of drawing people dwarfed by landscape ended – workers, peasants and soldiers had to dominate nature, not be overshadowed by it.

After the Cultural Revolution ended, artists quickly picked up their brushes and began to paint in both traditional and Western styles.

Galleries at M50.

The contemporary art boom

In recent decades, Shanghai has become known as a centre for abstract art, often inspired by traditional painting. Chinese contemporary art has, in fact, become one of the hottest commodities in the art world, and Shanghai has cleverly combined culture with commerce to become a major art centre. Chinese avant-garde artists who struggled to scrape a living now sell paintings for millions of dollars. In April 2016, contemporary paintings by Wang Huaiqing, Liu Wei and Xu Beihong sold for a combined US$16.9 million at a Sotheby's auction in Hong Kong.

The works of Shanghai's artists range from Yue Minjun's beaming sculptures to Zhou Tiehai's famous variations on the Joe Camel cigarette ad, and from Ding Yi's vibrant geometric abstracts to Zhong Biao's realist oils

that often feature Shanghai as a backdrop. The artists come from all over the country, but are drawn to the Shanghai galleries, where, they say, they get both exposure and top dollar for their work.

Artist Yue Minjun.

Shanghai's reputation as a centre of art is so well known globally that both the Guggenheim and the Pompidou Centre are thinking of opening museums there.

Modern sculptures like this are frequently found in parks all over Shanghai.

Sculpture, bronze and jade

In Old China, sculpture was primarily seen in temples and at royal tombs. Sculpture grew with Buddhism during the Tang dynasty and many of the greatest examples are Buddhist in character. The Shanghai Museum has an excellent collection of stone Buddha sculptures while the Jade Buddha Temple is home to the exquisite Jade Buddha statues. Interestingly, modern Shanghai is a major producer of Buddha statues; its foundries can cast the huge metal figures that are so favoured these days by monasteries.

The city is also heir to a tradition of Western sculpture that grew up alongside Western-style architecture in the old days. It has public sculptures of famous figures from arts – the writer Tian Han, the composer Nie Er, and even the Russian poet Alexander Pushkin. The government oversees the creation of sculpture for public areas, such as the many life-size bronze sculptures of typical Shanghainese going about the business of daily life – a young woman talking on a mobile phone, a couple pushing their child in a stroller, a man on a bicycle. Sculpture is also a growing genre for contemporary artists, who create both abstract and realist pieces.

Cast bronzes, carved jades and porcelain were produced by artisans and collected by emperors, literati and wealthy merchants. In addition to beauty and age, bronzes were also prized for their inscriptions and supposed ability to drive away ghosts and evil spirits; jades because they were thought to embody every virtue and to contain much *qi*, the vital life force; and porcelain for its lustre, feel and melodious ring when struck. Shanghai was not a major production centre for any of these crafts, but many wealthy collectors lived here and the Shanghai Museum in Puxi and Aurora Museum in Pudong have excellent galleries devoted to each of these.

Embroidery and folk crafts

The Jiangsu-Zhejiang region was the nation's key producer of silk, with imperial silkworks located at Suzhou, Hangzhou and Nanjing until they were closed in 1894. Sericulture is linked with embroidery, and Suzhou became an important centre of this craft. Of the four nationally recognised styles of embroidery – which include Hunan, Sichuan and Guangdong – Suzhou's was considered the most elegant, and was used for the embroidered gowns worn by the emperor and his family. Suzhou was also the main supplier of the embroidered insignia,

SUZHOU EMBROIDERY

Embroidery is a craft that has been passed from mother to daughter in rural Suzhou for centuries. At the end of the Qing dynasty, there were 100,000 "embroidery girls" in the area, but the number has since fallen to 10,000, and most of the "girls" are now quite elderly.

Embroidery girls work in their homes on pieces assigned to them by the Suzhou factories. A complex piece – like a dragon robe that might be worn by an emperor – could take one woman stitching alone at least five years to complete. To speed up the process, the girls often work together, stitching towards each other from opposite sides of the frame. They also work together when doing Suzhou's famous two-sided embroidery, in which each side of the cloth is identically embroidered – usually with a cute kitten surrounded by flowers and butterflies.

Although there is great demand for hand-embroidered goods, the craft is slowly dying because peasant families have become prosperous and no longer need the work.

The magic of shadow puppetry lives on in exquisite puppets made from donkey or water-buffalo skin. The Shanghai Art Museum has an excellent collection.

or rank badges, worn by the nine different levels of civil and military officials in imperial China. The market for such robes and insignia ended with the demise of the imperial system in 1912, but the embroidery industry stayed alive because of demand for opera costumes, household items and export goods.

Woodblock printing is an ancient craft that fell into decline after the introduction of mechanical printing in the 19th century, but was revived in Shanghai in the 1920s and 30s by the renowned writer Lu Xun. He hired a Japanese artist-engraver and organised a class for young artists at which he acted as interpreter. Lu encouraged students to depict society as they saw it. The results are often bleak – starving children, downtrodden refugees, industrial landscapes – but nonetheless beautiful; samples from his collection can be seen at the Lu Xun Memorial Hall (see page 209). The craft has remained alive in

Shanghai, as have silkscreening and other related methods of artistic printing.

Experimental art

But if attempts to revive folk arts have been less than successful, the government's support of painting, calligraphy, sculpture, photography and even video and performance art is of great significance. This backing is generally indirect and largely a corollary of efforts to ensure that showcase projects like the Shanghai Art Fair and the Shanghai Biennale, which was launched in 1996, become respected international events.

Nonetheless, the result is that Shanghai now has dozens of private galleries that sell local and national works and a burgeoning community of artists. It has frequent shows of experimental art and photography, the Shanghai Biennale has grown into an important international exhibition, and major retrospectives by classic and contemporary global masters are helping to popularise art to a new, younger audience. Once again, Shanghai's winning combination of culture and commerce, creativity and connoisseurship has enabled it to emerge as a key centre of the visual arts.

Contemplating contemporary art at the Shanghai Art Museum.

Xiao long bao – a Shanghainese speciality.

CUISINE

Shanghainese cuisine is best described as earthy and hearty comfort food – peasant fare, as some call it. But the city is also home to scores of sophisticated eateries that tout celebrity chefs from the major capitals of the world.

From crispy fried crullers for an early-morning breakfast to a late-night snack of plump steamed dumplings, it is obvious that Shanghai is a city that loves to eat – 24 hours a day. At first light, cooks begin crowding the astounding produce markets, starting the cycle of shopping, preparing food, eating and endless conversations about food that is central to the Chinese way of life.

For sheer variety alone, Shanghai is one of the best places to eat in China. Dining choices range from itinerant street vendors where take-out is the only option, to swanky celebrity chef eateries like Jean Georges and Joël Robuchon. The geographical diversity is just as breathtaking, with culinary offerings from Africa to Brazil, India to the Mediterranean, the Americas, Europe and Southeast Asia, and styles ranging from the simple to the sublime, fast food and fusion, as well as an impressive array of Chinese regional cuisines.

Lunch at Din Tai Fung.

Comfort food

Shanghai's own cuisine has its roots in hearty peasant cooking, without the grand flavour statements and enormous variety or subtle complexities of Cantonese food. With its long-simmered stews and sauces, sweetened for the child in all of us, this is comfort food not haute cuisine. An insistence on seasonality and freshness lifts it from the ordinary, although Shanghai gourmands say that increased fish farming and hot-housing of fruits and vegetables have irrevocably changed the original flavours of classic Shanghainese dishes.

Shanghai cuisine is a subset of Huaiyang cuisine, which is the lush region located between the Huai and Yangtze rivers. It encompasses both Zhejiang and Jiangsu provinces, a place so rich and fertile that it's known as the land of fish and rice.

Seafood staples

The sea and rivers that feature so prominently in Shanghai's history play an equally important role in shaping its largely seafood-based cuisine. The most famous dish is Shanghai's signature *dazha xie* or "hairy crab". More popularly known in Asia as "Shanghai hairy crab" (see page 67), the finest versions of this autumn delicacy come from Yangcheng Lake in nearby Jiangsu

Seafood features prominently in Shanghainese cooking.

are cooked with soy sauce and chilli. The classic Shanghai prawn dish is "crystal prawns", marinated in egg white and brine and stir-fried, while the hilsa herring (*shiyu*), now rarely prepared, is renowned for its succulent scales. Fish head, when stewed with *fenpi* (bean starch jelly sheets), soy sauce and red chilli in a clay pot, makes another favourite dish.

Pork, poultry and veggies

Turning inland, pork plays a more prominent role in the cuisine than poultry: the rustic *tipang*, a great hunk of pork rump on the bone stewed to melting tenderness, is a Shanghai classic, as is *hong shao rou* or "red-cooked" pork, fatty cubes of pork stewed in a soy sauce marinade until they practically melt in the mouth.

Poultry also plays a role, featuring in the classic appetiser *zuiji* or "drunken" chicken

Tipang, or stewed pork rump, is another Shanghai speciality.

province. The crustacean gets its name from the black hair-like filaments found on its legs. To retain their exquisite taste, the crabs are steamed and served with a black vinegar and ginger dip.

The city that grew up on the banks of the Huangpu River is especially fond of its denizens. River fish like carp (crucian carp, variegated carp and black carp) are typically "red-cooked", ie prepared in a sauce of soy and sugar. River eel is cooked in casseroles, clams are stir-fried with ginger and scallions, and mussels

CLASSIC SHANGHAINESE DISHES

Most local food aficionados will agree that the following dishes constitute classical Shanghainese cooking: *dazha xie* (hairy crab); *tipang* (pork rump); *hong shao rou* ("red-cooked" pork); *shizi tou* ("lion's head" meatballs); *shui jing xia ren* (crystal prawns); fish head with *fenpi*, a jelly made of bean starch; *hong shao huang yu* ("red-cooked" yellow croaker fish); *suji or suya* (vegetarian chicken or duck); *zuiji* ("drunken" chicken); *shi yu* (hilsa herring); *jiaobai* (wild rice stems); *kaofu* (wheat gluten); *paofan* (rice dregs made into porridge); xiao long bao (pork dumplings); and *shengjian mantou* (pot-stickers).

(chicken marinated in Shaoxing rice wine), *fengya* or "wind-dried duck", which is dried outdoors and preserved for the winter, and duck and taro soup. There is also Jinhua processed ham, from Zhejiang province, often sliced and steamed with rock sugar and added to fish dishes and soups, or stir-fried with vegetables.

Traditionally, the vegetables of Shanghai cuisine – either cooked with meat or as dishes on their own – are fresh from the farm and seasonal, such as fat spring bamboo shoots or their more delicate-tasting winter counterparts, baby lima beans, lily buds, Chinese broccoli, *jicai* or "shepherd's purse", asparagus lettuce, leafy *mixian*, and the quintessential Shanghai vegetable dish, *jiaobai* (wild rice stems).

Shanghainese cooking styles

With its country roots, the preparation of Shanghai cuisine is far less complex than that of its Cantonese or Beijing cousins, with only three major methods of preparation: *hongshao* or red-cooked (with sugar and soy sauce), stewed or

For the sweet-toothed.

> The words "gan bei" or "bottoms up" are uttered when making a toast at hard-drinking and more informal social gatherings. These days, people are more likely to use the more health-conscious phrase "sui yi", which means "drink as much as you want" (or not at all).

simply stir-fried with ginger and scallions. Garlic is rarely used in Shanghainese cooking.

Nonetheless, Shanghai's famous style is revealed in its cold dishes, artistically arranged hors d'œuvres of dazzling variety: plates of julienned vinegary pickles, tiny raw crabs marinated in rice wine called *zuixie*, spiced broad beans, "drunken" chicken marinated in wine, and sweet marinated wheat gluten (*kaofu*), all laid out in picturesque arrays at street stalls.

Bakeries and bortsch

The international influence on Shanghai's design, architecture and fashion also left its culinary footprints. Many of the first-generation state leaders, notably Deng Xiaoping and Zhou Enlai, spent time in Paris, and it was their

passion for croissants, say the Shanghainese, that perpetuated the Euro-style bakeries that were first brought to Shanghai by the French. Shanghai's neighbourhood bakeries today number in the thousands. Their shelves are filled with croissants, brioches, jewel-like teacakes and lighter-than-air sponge cakes.

About the same time that the French were baking croissants, Shanghai's White Russian population, which swelled after the 1917 Russian Revolution, was brewing bortsch. Those Russian restaurants are long gone, but *luo song tang* (literally "Russian soup") is considered by many locals to be a Shanghainese dish.

Shanghai continues seamlessly to incorporate new influences into its cuisine. Not to be outdone by the likes of McDonald's and Burger King which line the streets of Shanghai, the street vendors who fry spring rolls in great bubbling woks of oil now also slice up potatoes into french fries, accompanied by a watery ketchup, for young schoolchildren.

Seasonal specialities

Shanghai home cooks still define their menus by the season. Each seasonal speciality is eagerly anticipated and then deftly incorporated into dishes – until the next delicacy arrives at the markets.

Shanghai's fat spring bamboo shoots, called orchid bamboo shoots because of their lovely fragrance, come from nearby Sheshan in Songjiang county. The bamboo shoot is sliced and often "red-cooked" on its own, as well as used in other dishes. Wintertime brings a more subtly flavoured shoot.

With early springtime come the small, succulent and intensely flavoured strawberries, mulberries, the apricot-like pipa fruit and red cherries, and a brief, glorious season of yellow cherries. The itinerant pedlars in Old Shanghai who would crush the juicy summer *yangmei* berry, a cousin of the bayberry, into a thirst-quenching drink have disappeared, but sugarcane juice vendors still ply the streets, the long mottled stalks of succulent green sugarcane balanced precariously on their bicycles their calling cards.

The Barbie-pink peach blossoms of spring, more substantial and pinker than their famous cherry blossom cousins, yield to summer's Nanhui honey peach, a delicate and juicy thin-skinned white peach with a subtle yet distinctive flavour. The peach has both a round and flat variety, the latter sold as "designer fruit" in the US. Along with the autumn hairy crab, November brings fresh figs from Baoshan, while the winter months see deliciously sweet miniature oranges from the offshore islands.

Street food and snacks

The street food (see page 68) in Shanghai primarily comprises snacks, and while it cannot compete with places like Malaysia or Singapore, one can still eat extraordinarily well on street food alone. Expect everything from

Ci fan gao, a fried rice cake, is a classic street snack.

WET MARKETS

The wet markets of Shanghai make fabulous theatre as well as a fascinating introduction to Shanghai food: the philosophy of freshness is encapsulated here, where everything is just-picked and fresh-killed, and cooks shop daily, tailoring their menus to the seasons' constantly changing produce. The mind-boggling display of items includes vegetables, fruit, live poultry and seafood, tofu and noodles, and even clothes and household sundries.

Muslim-style Xinjiang mutton kebabs to Shanghai dumplings, at all hours of the day and night.

Breakfast is almost always eaten on the run, with *youtiao*, the long fried *dough* cruller, a favourite. The classic Shanghai way of eating *youtiao* is to wrap it in a sticky rice cake and eat the two together – experiencing both soft and crunchy sensations in one bite – and wash it down with freshly brewed soybean milk. That same mix is found in rice cakes (*ci fan gao*), deep-fried squares of compressed rice that make a filling breakfast. Another favourite is *paofan*, the ricepot dregs which are steeped, then made into a *congee*, or porridge. And then there's the very popular *jianbing pancake*, cooked on steaming griddles with a fried egg, crispy beancurd sheet, preserved vegetables, coriander and chilli sauce, then rolled up for takeaway.

Snacks and street food are available on virtually every corner of Shanghai, but the best selection of Shanghai snacks is found at Yu Garden Bazaar (see page 137). Such is the fame of Shanghai street food and snacks that hordes

Trays of steaming hot xiao long bao at a restaurant in Yu Garden Bazaar in the Old City.

of Chinese tourists patiently wait in line at Yu Garden's Nanxiang Mantou Dian, purportedly the best place for *xiao long bao*, the tiny pork-stuffed dumplings with translucent skins for which Shanghai is famous.

The lines are just as long for the so-called potstickers, *shengjian mantou*, pan-fried in giant crusty black pans and sprinkled with scallions, and for *anchun jiaozi*, soft, sweet "pigeon-egg" dumplings made with glutinous rice flour and filled with osmanthus flower and mint. *Tang yuan*, glutinous rice dumplings with a sweet filling in a soup of fermented rice, is a traditional New Year delicacy, as is *nian-gao*, literally "New Year cake". Other favourite snacks include crisp-crusted *meimao su* or "eyebrow" shortcake, a pastry named for its arched shape and filled with sweet or savoury stuffing, and *chou doufu*, or smelly bean curd, more politely known as fermented bean curd and an acquired taste, from Fengxian on the outskirts of Shanghai.

FESTIVAL FARE: FROM RICE DUMPLINGS TO ICE-CREAM MOONCAKES

Shanghai's festivals and the special food associated with them are undergoing a renaissance, with more foodie options than ever before. Chinese New Year, the biggest and most important festival (in Jan or Feb according to the lunar calendar) is a great excuse for the fish-loving Shanghainese to eat fish dishes. Yu, or fish, is a homonym for prosperity in Chinese, and is considered an auspicious New Year's dish, along with *tangyuan*, the soft glutinous rice dumpling that always ends the meal. *Qingming* or the springtime tomb-sweeping day is mostly observed with ceremonies at the gravesites of family members, and by eating the *qingtuan* cake, made of glutinous rice paste and stuffed with a sweet filling. Summer's Dragon Boat Festival is the time to eat *zongzi*, the lotus-leaf-wrapped glutinous rice dumplings. The Mid-Autumn Festival is an occasion to gorge on mooncakes. These heavy pastries are traditionally filled with sweet lotus-seed or red-bean paste and salted egg yolk, but these days creative options like Häagen-Dazs ice-cream mooncakes and gourmet chocolate adaptations are preferred among the younger Shanghainese.

Dine on fusion French at Jade on 36 restaurant.

Unrivalled dining scene

Shanghai's international culinary scene is so spectacular that the city is the only one in China's mainland to have its own Michelin Guide. New restaurants open every month, and one local publication lists 35 different types of cuisine in its restaurant directory. Add to that the enormous variety of eateries, from hole-in-the-wall digs to haute cuisine by celebrity chefs, and you have a dining scene that is unrivalled in all of China.

As a city of immigrants, Shanghai's restaurants represent a veritable microcosm of China. Along with the major cuisines – Cantonese, Beijing, Sichuan – are endless variations in between. Sichuan hotpot (*huoguo*) restaurants, at which a pot of chilli-laced bubbling soup, sitting over a flame, is used for dipping and cooking vegetables and meats, are popular, as are dim sum buffets. Sensing opportunity, well-known restaurants have opened branches in Shanghai, including Beijing's famous Da Dong for Peking duck, Hong Kong's legendary Fook Lam Moon, Taiwan's Din Tai Fung and Singapore's Crystal Jade chain of restaurants.

Chinese cuisine trends sweep Shanghai every couple of years or so: first, it was the food of the ethnic Yunnan minority, then came the cuisine of lakeside Hangzhou, followed by spicy Hunan food from Mao Zedong's home province and hearty cumin-spiced dishes from the northwestern Xinjiang region.

Local Shanghainese restaurants run the gamut from the tiny four-table Chun, serving home-style Shanghainese cooking in a studiously unpretentious setting, to Shanghai Uncle's authentic dishes in a glittering banquet hall. Restaurants like Ye Shanghai and Yongfoo Elite serve updated versions of old classics in luxurious surroundings (with prices to match). Meanwhile, locally-born Michelin-starred chef Tony Lu is giving his hometown's cuisine a welcome dose of creativity and refinement at his four Shanghai restaurants, including 2-Michelin-star vegetarian restaurant Fu He Hui.

Shanghai is becoming quite the international dining hotspot, drawing celebrity-chef and Michelin-starred franchises as well as homegrown restaurants manned by tal-

> *Among the A-list celebrity chefs who have opened restaurants in Shanghai are Jean Georges Vongerichten, brothers Jacques and Laurent Pourcel and Joël Robuchon.*

ented chefs from around the world. Some are world-class and some are neighbourhood bistros, each adding to the depth of dining out in Shanghai. Perennial local favourite M on the Bund started it all, and its European-Mediterranean menu, well-selected wine list and views of the waterfront are still hard to beat. Across the road, celebrity chef Jean Georges Vongerichten serves *haute* French, Italian and Korean at three dazzling restaurants within Three on the Bund, while down the street Joël Robuchon, Shanghai-based French favourite chef Paul Pairet and the Hakkasan team from London are among the tasteful inhabitants of luxury landmark Bund 18. Pairet also helms Shanghai's most avant-garde table (yes, just one!) at Ultraviolet, which serves an interactive 20-course menu to 10 diners a night at a secret location and is booked out months in advance. The Shanghai dining options are as endless as they are exciting.

A feast of hairy crabs

The signature dish for "the city above the sea" comes – of course – from its waters. Ancient poets wrote of savouring "hairy crabs" and sipping wine under a ripe harvest moon, and the tradition endures.

The *dazha* crab, which is indigenous to the lower reaches of the Yangtze River, begins its journey in May, when millions of the migratory crustaceans swim eastwards to the mouth of the river to spawn. The baby crabs swim into connecting rivers and lakes, where they are caught and reared in crab farms. The immense popularity of the hairy crab has instigated the development of crab farms throughout the region, but connoisseurs still insist that the crabs from Yangcheng Lake are beyond compare. The unique ecology of this lake – clean and so clear that the sunlight fills its depths – helps to nurture such delectable creatures. (Predictably, there is an industry specialising in fake Yangcheng hairy crabs – so much so that genuine sellers are now developing special crab ID tags.) Genuine Yangcheng Lake crabs all sport distinctive shiny green shells, pearl-white bellies, golden legs covered with long, thick hair – hence their name – and spit foam continuously.

The female crab with her rich, flavourful roe becomes available in October, while the male crab reaches maturity in November. The petite hairy crab is an expensive delicacy and crab gourmands have strict criteria when it comes to selecting the perfect specimen. The crab should be alive and alert. The legs and the hairs should be long, and the crab's apron should be white. Preparation is focused on preserving the prized flesh and the fragrant natural crabmeat flavour: crabs are steamed to a gorgeous shade of vermilion, sometimes

with ginger, and are served with a dipping sauce of raw minced ginger, black vinegar and sugar.

To eat the crab, the apron and carapace are taken off first, and the roe extracted (or saved until last, depending on your preference). Next, the legs are pulled off, and the meat inside mined with a chopstick or fingers. A nutcracker is then used for the claws. Finally, the succulent chunks of meat inside the main body of the crab are tackled. Everything but the lungs is eaten, and particularly adept crab-eaters can put the

A stack of Shanghai hairy crabs.

entire crab back together after eating it, as if it had never been touched.

Hairy crabs are considered to be "cooling" to the body, so the sherry-like Shaoxing wine or *huangjiu* is served to rebalance the body's yin and yang. Like those crab gourmands who can put the shell of a whole crab back together again after tearing it apart, the human body, too, needs to return to its pre-crab-eating state.

STREET SNACKS

Shanghai's street food provides more than mere sustenance – it's a chance to experience a fast-disappearing way of life.

Shanghai's massive restaurant boom notwithstanding, most locals probably have at least one snack a day. It might be something substantial, like the big and yummy *jianbing* omelettes, or just a piece of fruit on a stick – all sold by the city's itinerant street vendors. The best variety of snacks can be found in the Yu Garden Bazaar, but they can also be found around town, sold by street vendors who are perfectly in tune with the rhythms of Shanghai's hunger pangs: they appear in doorways and on street corners early in the morning, outside schools, metro stops and big office buildings at the end of the day, and even on side streets late at night. These vendors, who often come from neighbouring provinces, are carrying on an important Shanghai tradition – sharing the foods of their villages with Shanghai, where they will eventually become absorbed into the melting pot that is Shanghainese cuisine.

Meat and seafood kebabs.

Fried dough sticks called youtiao are a breakfast staple throughout China.

Fried dumplings are one of the most ubiquitous street snacks in the city.

An array of vegetable-based dishes.

Streetside cafés serve simple, delicious dishes such as freshly made noodles in soup for just a few kuai.

One of the advantages of street food is that, like these spring rolls, it is cooked to order and served piping hot.

A speciality of the Muslims who live in China's far west province of Xinjiang are lamb kebabs, grilled over hot coals and served with a sprinkling of chilli powder.

SHOPPING

Bold, brash and confident, Shanghai appears to be on the verge of sidelining glitzy Hong Kong and reclaiming its former role as China's fashion and design hotbed.

Shoppers outside Metro City shopping mall in Xujiahui.

Shopping in Shanghai has evolved to encompass luxury brands, funky boutiques, couture and just about anything custom-made. China, after all, was once the world's factory, and Shanghai is its showcase.

Between the two World Wars, Shanghai's shopping culture burgeoned when the "Big Four" department stores (see page 124) were built to cater to the city's cosmopolitan citizens.

Something for everyone

Today, the Big Four stores have been revamped and stocked with more stylish goods. Other department stores have joined them, both in the traditional shopping areas of Nanjing Road (E) and Central Huaihai Road and in new areas like Pudong, Xujiahui and the Bund. International brand names are well represented in Shanghai, reflecting the city's increasingly sophisticated tastes – and strong purchasing power.

Local and foreign entrepreneurs – inspired by Chinese tradition and Shanghai's cosmopolitan atmosphere as well as the easy access to raw materials – produce high-quality goods with unique one-of-a-kind designs. Bespoke clothing, shoes and even fine china and table linens are an affordable luxury in Shanghai. There are also plenty of adventures for intrepid shoppers who venture from the main thoroughfares and into local markets, backstreets and private showrooms. Here you can expect a slice of Shanghai life, with the added bonus of unique goods and bargains. The warren of shops around Yu Garden Bazaar (see page 137), for instance, is where battery-powered Panda bears, fake chirping crickets and the like abound.

Chinese furniture and curios

Most old-style Chinese furniture shops are in the vicinity of Hongqiao Road (see page 192) and Wuzhong Road (see page 194). All the

> *The world's über-luxury brands, from Armani to Zegna, are all vying for a piece of Shanghai, and shiny new malls are constantly being built to keep up.*

Good purchases include traditional Chinese clothing.

shops stock restored and unfinished pieces. Ask to visit the warehouse area, where you can stroll among dusty piles of rickety trunks, kitchen cabinets, calligraphy tables, chairs and wedding chests. Once you have chosen your piece, the store's craftsmen will restore and refinish it to your specifications. Most of the furniture here is newly made of old wood, or has been aged to give it an "antique" look. Shop owners will usually tell you the real provenance of the piece. But, as with all Shanghai shopping, buyer beware. The warehouses will also help ship your purchases home.

In downtown, several boutique furniture shops sell original Shanghai Deco – the uniquely Shanghainese take on Art Deco – pieces from the 1920s and 30s. For smaller curios and more typical Shanghai items from the 1920s and 30s such as opium pipes, cigarette-girl retro posters, lanterns and porcelain, visit the five-storey Cang Bao Building (see page 140) near Yu Garden, filled with kitsch as well as rare books and maps, Cultural Revolution memorabilia, vintage furniture and clothing. Weekend mornings are the best time to go.

Fabrics and pearls

The sprawling Shanghai South Bund Fabric Market at Lujiabang Road offers a dazzling array of silks, cashmeres and linens. The on-site market tailors are usually not the best with cut and fit, but can generally create decent copies of your own clothing or of one of their own designs (you'll see these on display at the stalls). Normally, the stallholders will speak enough English to facilitate communication.

The Silk King stores (there are branches around town) are another option for fabric and clothing. These emporiums offer quality silk as well as a variety of excellent (but pricey) fabrics like cashmere; the tailors on the premises can custom-make clothing for you. As a bonus, they can also create shoes to match your outfit.

The Yangtze River Delta and the network of canals and ponds surrounding Shanghai is home to China's thriving freshwater cultured pearl industry, making cultured pearls one of the best buys in Shanghai. Round, lustrous gem-quality pearls as well as multicoloured Baroque, seed- and coin-shaped pearls are sold at boutiques and at the Hongqiao Pearl Market; jewellery can also be custom-made.

Shanghai chic

The unmistakable Shanghai style is back in the chic boutiques that line the former French Concession streets, where creative minds marry Chinese and Western styles (see page 74) with highly successful results. Fumin Road, Xinle Road, Anfu Road and Maoming Road are treasure troves of boutiques, featuring every-thing from local clothing designers to *qipao* tailors. The trendy shopping and dining area of Xintiandi runs the gamut from hip malls like K11 with luxury brand boutiques, stylish acces-sories and an art museum in the basement, to indie outlets in the side lanes. Xintiandi Style Mall stocks a well-curated collection of shops by established and rising Chinese and Asian designer brands, including Uma Wang, Content and The Thing.

Shanghai is home to plenty of trendy boutiques.

Window dressing along Central Huahai Road, another of the city's shopping drags.

Tianzifang mushroomed from a single fac-tory building used as a design incubator for young artists into a bustling enclave of bou-tiques and cafés encompassing the surround-ing tangle of narrow residential lanes. Amidst the souvenir tat, there are still some gems to be found. A hotspot for art is M50 (see page 212). Some of the city's best-known galleries and art studios are clustered here.

THE LURE OF CHINESE SILK

Since ancient times, China has cornered the world's silk market. Legend has it that the concubine Lei Zu discovered the silk-making process when she acci-dentally dropped a silkworm cocoon into her tea over 3,000 years ago. By 200 BC, the precious "woven wind" fabric was being dispatched to Western mar-kets via the fabled Silk Road. China is still the world's largest exporter of silk, with most of the fabric pro-duced around Shanghai. Peasants raise silkworms less than 100km (60 miles) away in mulberry tree-carpeted Deqing County, near Hangzhou, the heart of China's silk producing region. Naturally, Shanghai is home to all varieties of silk, from stiff brocades to slinky materials.

SHANGHAI CHIC

Many shops sell one-of-a-kind designs, made in Shanghai and fiercely proud of it, that marry the best of East and West.

Shanghai's cosmopolitan soul makes for fresh and interesting design work, and in recent years Shanghai's local design scene has flourished. Invariably, the creations here take traditional Shanghai as their inspiration, and then update, update, update – sometimes far into the future. It's retro style, re-imagined, reinvented and re-made for modern Shanghai. Some of these pieces are original, often handmade, and each one is a work of art. Their creators, too, are often a fusion mix – Westerners living in (and inspired by) Shanghai, or Shanghainese with a global world view.

Shopping for made-in-Shanghai items is a happy adventure as well: most shops are located in the former French Concession, in spaces and places as varied as the designs are – charming vintage ateliers and contemporary chic boutiques in style havens such as Xintiandi, Fuxing Road, Taikang Road and Fumin Road.

Many Shanghai fashion designers have expanded to capture overseas markets. Taoray Wang (www.taoraywang.com) designs are particularly popular in the US.

Local designer Leaves Fashion (72 South Mao Ming Road) sells Shanghai-style haute couture, including this hand-made Chinese qipao dress.

A-Zenith Art Gallery (433 West Yan'an Road) presents collections of Shanghai-style housewear and furnishings by talented local designer Gao Wei, a fusion of elegant Oriental details and Western classic.

Getting measured for a new suit. Shanghainese tailors are known for their deft needlework and tailoring skills.

CUSTOM-MADE ANYTHING

One of the great things about Shanghai is that it is possible to get almost anything custom-made. Many a visitor has taken a shine to the city's fabric markets – like the Shanghai South Bund Fabric Market at 399 Lujiabang Road – entering like a gleeful child let loose in a sweet shop and walking out with a completely brand new wardrobe at bargain prices. Virtually anything in Shanghai can be custom-made: shoes, furniture, bed linen, coats – at a fraction of the cost of similar ready-made items.

It sounds too good to be true, and maybe it is. While there are true artisans among those who create Shanghai's custom-made items, they are few and far between. Fabric-market tailors may not give you exactly the couture cut you want (several fittings may be required); the furniture you ordered may not be put together to the highest standards; and the sweater may seem as if it's been knitted for someone else's body. Vendors will fix the problem, if they can, but visitors often don't have the time for repairs. The best course of action is to go only to those who have been personally recommended, or whose work you have seen. And never pay the entire bill until you have collected the goods and are satisfied with them.

Llludeco hand produces lamps and lanterns to order, mixing Chinese and Middle Eastern themes.

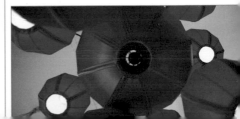

Yang House has created a high-tech suitcase using Audi's ultra-lightweight car-body technology. With a charging port and biological fingerprint recognition, Shanghai design is looking firmly to the future.

Dancing the night away.

SHANGHAI NIGHTS

Shanghai is once again staking its claim to be considered the "Paris of the Orient". Whether one's taste inclines to classy lounge bars, elegant dance clubs, all-night karaoke or just late-night supper, the city can cater for it.

The classic 1930s pop song *Ye Shanghai (Night-Time Shanghai)* trilled the tribute, "You really are a city that never sleeps."

The bar and club scene

Like much of modern Shanghai's revival, its nightlife renaissance in the early 2000s owed a large debt to foreign investment. Most of Shanghai's successful bars were opened and run by either Chinese "returnees" who had lived or studied abroad, or by foreigners. This scenario is changing, however, as young, affluent and well-travelled Chinese entrepreneurs are taking their own stake in Shanghai's after-dark lifestyle boom.

Appearances count for a lot in Shanghai, including its bars. Other Chinese cities are dominated by earthy and unpretentious dives, but in Shanghai even the casual is carefully crafted – and sky-high terrace views to accompany a glass of chilled bubbles are often preferred. Its most famous bars, like the Long Bar at the Waldorf-Astoria and Bar Rouge, hug the riverfront, with elaborate decor to rival the best nightspots in the clubbing capitals of the world – and prices to match.

Shanghai's bar denizens are as varied as the city itself. Local and foreign students usually congregate at the cheap and cheerful Windows Too in Jing'an Plaza or graffiti-clad Perry's, which has a few rowdy locations including one in the former French Concession. Slightly more stylish but still good on a budget (especially during the long happy hours), are Le Café des Stagiaries, run by French hospitality interns, and Spanish haunt, Malabar.

The opulent Long Bar at the Waldorf-Astoria.

Shanghai's upwardly mobile and college-educated yuppies, or "Shuppies", who enjoy mid-management positions and salaries their parents never dreamed of, are generally a bored bunch eager for new experiences. Many Shuppies are also eager to assert their sophistication, which in Shanghai translates to enjoying an "international lifestyle", often accompanied by fine wines, oysters by the dozen, cigars and live music.

The moneyed Hong Kong, Taiwanese and local residents like to spend extravagantly at clubs like intimate Monkey Champagne tucked away behind Donghu Road, M2 on Central

Huaihai Road and Fusion in Xintiandi. Expect glamorous groups gathered around private tables drinking bottles of champagne and various other alcohols – often delivered to the table with flaming sparklers sticking out of the spout for additional extravagant effect.

The new hotspots

Given such conflicting demands, opening a bar in Shanghai is a Darwinian undertaking – most have the shelf life of an open can of club soda. Trend-obsessed barflies follow the "hot new thing", currently high-end gastro lounges and craft-beer pubs.

Continental house- and techno-lovers converge in droves at Lola for all-night dance sessions. Bar Rouge, located at 18 on the Bund, with its fabulous views across to the Pudong skyline, is a jaw-dropping stunner, as is Latin-themed Unico at Three on the Bund and M1NT, with shark tanks and a rooftop terrace.

For more relaxed lounging on the Bund, Shanghai's style set head to The Nest, a Nordic vodka bar with low-slung armchairs and a sophisticated menu, and Glam, an artsy cocktail lounge by the folks behind Bund pioneer M on the Bund. Local cocktail connoisseurs will recommend El Ocho, just off West Nanjing Road,

On the dance floor.

Shanghai's abundance of characterful nightspots will leave you spoilt for choice.

Live music at the Cotton Club.

Senator Saloon and Speak Low. The latter, a four-storey Japanese-style speakeasy hidden behind a secret door in a bartending equipment shop, was voted No. 2 on Asia's 50 Best Bars list in 2016.

DJ clubs

Shanghai's booming DJ scene offers mainly hip-hop, R 'n' B, techno, garage and house, mixed by both Chinese and foreign DJs. Recent years have also seen a long list of internationally renowned spinmasters at the decks of Shanghai's top clubs, which attract an edgy subsection of Shuppies and foreigners.

Live rock and jazz

Shanghai has a small but growing live rock music scene, led primarily by Yuyintang and MAO Livehouse. Both venues feature mainly Chinese bands, playing anything from electronica to heavy metal and hip-hop. As the music scene has grown, so has the demand for foreign acts to play in Shanghai. Recent foreign performers on the Shanghai stage include Metallica, Queen & Adam Lambert, and the Rolling Stones – to name a few.

Shanghai's jazz and blues scene is best encountered at the Cotton Club, JZ Club, Heyday, and the House of Blues and Jazz. Both local and foreign jazz acts take centre stage. The Peace Hotel's Jazz Bar, a nostalgic favourite with its octogenarian jazz players, reopened in 2010 as part of the renovated 1920s hotel. Intimate 1960s-style supperclub Shake, by the people who run Heyday, offers up-tempo jazz and soul music from Thursdays to Saturdays.

Local pastimes

While the hipsters live it up at chichi bars, dance clubs and music dives, their elders and their lower-income peers opt for more time-tested activities. The karaoke parlours, or KTVs (Karaoke TV), draw a steady flow of Shanghainese of all ages and classes.

Moneyed business types also congregate at posh bathhouses like Sea Cloud Garden on

Karaoke remains popular in Shanghai.

Panyu Road. In glaring marble and crystal, these luxurious complexes feature elaborate bathing options: along with the sauna, steam room and jacuzzi are special pools containing pearls or rose petals for purported medicinal benefits.

Ordinary Shanghainese with limited means are resourceful at concocting budget forms of entertainment. Ballroom dancing was the rage in the 1980s and remains popular among retirees. Shanghainese toting mini-stereo sets often gather in downtown parks like Xujiahui Park and Fuxing Park and also the Bund at dawn and dusk, playing music that sends the dancers twirling merrily.

Shanghai is famous for its insular communities contained in its traditional *longtang* (lane) housing, where Shanghainese pass their days and nights socialising with their neighbours, often outdoors in the lanes. Children play football and badminton, teens strum guitars and elderly men compare their pet songbirds. After dinner, the lanes fill with a clacking sound like an invasion of locusts from mah-jong games.

Regardless of season, older men prop up tables and carry out stools to play cards. Even as the lanes disappear, some people still hold on to their traditions, shifting the setting of their outdoor games to bustling city pavements.

After-hours entertainment

Most of Shanghai's bars and clubs ebb in the wee hours as the revellers stumble homewards. Street kitchens start wheeling up their carts, unloading tables and stools, and firing up the coal brickets from 9pm onwards every evening. Shanghai does not have one central area for after-hours street food; instead, stalls are scattered around the downtown area – usually within stumbling distance of popular clubs. The traditional staples are wonton soup (*yuntun*), fried noodles (*chaomian* or *chao hefen*) and fried rice (*danchaofan*). Many noodle and dumpling shops downtown close late at weekends, while franchises like the Soy Milk King chain serve breakfast dim sum items like soy milk and *youtiao* (fried dough sticks) around the clock.

Shanghai rocks

Gone are the days when the only visible alternative music scene in China was rock. Nowadays, hip-hop, breakcore, breakbeat, dance and electronica, folk as well as rock are all part of the scene in Shanghai.

Shanghai's rock developed mostly independent of the rest of China, taking its musical influences from abroad rather than from within. Its earliest roots lie in the streetside guitar bands of the early 1980s. With often home-made instruments, groups of neighbourhood youth reinvented tunes by 1970s Taiwan's pop icon Teresa Teng or composed ribald ditties, hoping to outshine rival groups down the block. Shanghai also produced China's first nascent rock star, Zhang Xing.

For 15 years, Shanghai rock stewed underground, with only a handful of bands around at any given time, and playing only at obscure dives and underground rock parties. By the late 1990s, however, a few young, ambitious bands such as Crystal Butterfly had secured gigs at more mainstream bars, and their names and songs started to infiltrate public awareness. At the same time, rock parties were being held more often and more publicly. Now that the city has a number of regular venues, like MAO Livehouse and Yuyintang at Yan'an Road (W), Shanghai has the infrastructure needed to nourish its growing rock scene.

Folk music is creeping into the Shanghai scene, mainly thanks to Bandu Music, a café-cum-bar (as well as record label) in Shanghai's Moganshan art district. Tiny café-bar Wooden Box in a quiet lane off West Nanjing Road also has a regular roster of folk, jazz and bluegrass most evenings, and a suitably chilled-out bohemian vibe.

The DJ scene is big in Shanghai, with both local and foreign DJs and musicians

organising music parties at various venues in town, with bars, clubs, art galleries, museums and concept stores hosting these events. Dada is a small club stalwart managed by a Shanghai-based independent promoter featuring local DJs spinning house and underground dance music every Thursday, Friday and Saturday. Its unpretentious crowd tends toward younger Chinese and expats.

The Mixing Room is the smaller club/ live-music portion of the huge Mercedes-Benz Arena in Pudong. Its world-class stage and sound system hosts big-name

Getting the crowds worked up at Yuyintang.

international and Chinese DJs and bands, including DJ Shadow, Howie B, Diplo and Neon Trees. French club Le Baron attracts DJs, producers and tastemakers from the international clubbing circuit. Unico on the Bund also regularly hosts big DJs like Questlove between its regular Latin musicians, percussionists and jazzy house beats.

Pudong at sunset.

ARCHITECTURE

Mixing Art Deco, Postmodernist, Song-dynasty
Chinese, neoclassical, über-modern and just
plain kitsch, Shanghai is a stimulating
showcase of architectural treasures.

Even world-weary visitors from the globe's most sophisticated urban centres catch their breath the first time they see Shanghai's skyline. The city is in the middle of the biggest urban building boom the world has ever known, and the sheer size, scale and speed of its reconstruction is astounding. Shanghai's juxtaposition of avant-garde glass and steel structures and its old-world brick and mortar historic buildings is visually arresting – the result is an almost visceral tension between the ultra-modern and the traditional.

Nowhere is this tension as palpable as on the Bund (see page 101) along the Huangpu River, where the neoclassical Bund buildings face off against the soaring mirrored towers of Pudong. The futuristic Oriental Pearl Tower (see page 217) is, for better or worse, now the most recognised structure in the city. Before it was built, the Bund was the indisputable symbol of the city.

1920s mansion in Xintiandi.

East meets West

Today, many sections of the city have been replaced with modern high-rises and green open spaces. Shanghai has always been about being modern. In the 1920s and 30s, that meant Art Deco (see page 88), the streamlined, then-futuristic architectural style that is as easily identified with Shanghai as it is with Miami Beach. Well known for its ability to weave outside ideas into the local culture, Shanghai adapted the born-in-the-West Art Deco to China, and it became a symbol of the cosmopolitan, hybrid city. After the recent frenzied building of imported modern designs, the next decade may, similarly, see the emergence of a new architectural style that Shanghai can call its own.

The Shanghainese are slowly coming to terms with their architectural identity. They still want the latest the world has to offer, but they are also confident enough to celebrate, however subtly, the unique history of their city. So some buildings include design references to lane neighbourhood architecture, and many new office towers are blatant paeans to the Art Deco splendour of old. The city is enjoying a rich architectural environment in which themes from all over the world contribute to Shanghai's dramatic skyline.

Pudong skyline.

Shanghai modern

Shanghai's most successful modern buildings include allusions to Chinese architecture, or push the high-design envelope in some way. The Shanghai Grand Theatre (see page 121) on People's Square does both. Designed by Frenchman Jean-Marie Charpentier, it resembles a hyper-modern transparent temple to the arts – until you realise that the convex curvature of the roof is a clear homage to the heavy roofs and upturned eaves of traditional Chinese palace architecture.

At the time of its completion in 1989, the Shanghai Centre (see page 176) on Nanjing Road (W) was the only tall building for miles. Its obvious nod to traditional motifs is seen in the simple, strong red columns that support the entrance portico. Less obvious is the monumental reference that architect John Portman designed into the building – it is in the shape of the Chinese character for mountain, *shan* (山).

Next to the Shanghai Centre is Plaza 66, a building that is successful despite its lack of

REACHING FOR THE SKY

In the international quest to build the world's tallest buildings, Shanghai is at the forefront. The Lujiazui skyline in Pudong now features a triptych of dominant megatowers, crowned by the 632-metre-high (2,073ft) Shanghai Tower, which opened in 2016 as the world's second-tallest building. It usurped the sleek Shanghai World Financial Center, which was completed in 2008 and stands 492 metres (1,614ft) tall, as China's tallest building. Just next door, the architecturally elegant Jin Mao Tower, which was completed in 1999 and stands at 420 metres (1,378ft), now seems rather diminished in stature.

The three tallest buildings west of the Huangpu River are midgets by contrast: Shimao International Plaza on People's Square sits at 333 metres (1,093ft); Sinar Mas Centre on the North Bund was completed in 2016 at a height of 319 metres (1,048ft); and Wheelock Square at Jing'an is 297 metres (974.5ft). The Huaihai Road business district has K11, formerly the Hong Kong New World Tower (278 metres/912ft), while Xujiahui sports the Grand Gateway Plaza (262 metres/860ft).

any attempt at traditional architecture. Plaza 66 architects Kohn Pederson Fox Associates of New York also designed Wheelock Square on Yan'an Road (W), which has overtaken Plaza 66 as the tallest building west of the Huangpu since its 2008 completion. East of the Huangpu River, the soaring pagoda-like Jin Mao Tower (see page 219) is another impressive architectural creation, although it has been usurped as Shanghai's second-tallest building.

Postmodern European architects have been equally popular in Shanghai. The seagull-inspired Pudong International Airport – a 2000 landmark in glass and brushed aluminium – was designed by Paris-based Paul Andreu, who also designed the National Theatre in Beijing. Andreu also designed the ceramic and glass Shanghai Oriental Arts Centre in Pudong (see page 223).

Lane houses

The most typical Shanghainese architectural form is the *lilong or longtang* (lane) neighbourhood, which, until the latest building boom began 20 years ago, was common throughout the city. Lane neighbourhoods (see page 160) typically cover a city block, and have a few entrances from the street that can be locked by iron gates. Within the neighbourhood, lanes are arrayed in a regular matrix pattern, the stone-framed doors *(shikumen)* facing south.

A view across the rooftops of the Old City.

Shanghai Grand Theatre.

First built by foreign entrepreneurs, the lane houses mutated slowly over 80 years in response to economic forces and changes in architectural taste. Rising land prices impelled developers to shrink each dwelling, while the advent of reinforced concrete enabled the building of three- and four-storey houses. In the final stages of its evolution, lane dwellings lost their courtyards and came to resemble modern urban apartment buildings.

But adaptive re-use projects such as Xintiandi (see page 147) have had a strong impact on public perceptions of the value of the old lane houses. More and more Shanghainese now feel that their native architecture is worth preserving.

The magnificent Bund

No visit to Shanghai is complete without a stroll along the Bund (see page 101), with its striking panorama of European-style buildings. About half of the 24 structures on the Bund were built during the 1920s, and nine during the first two decades of the century. Most incorporate the neoclassical themes that influenced the design of public buildings during that period. The queen of them all is the regal 1923 Hong Kong

A lane-house doorway – called shikumen – is formed by three pieces of solid stone with rounded upper joints and an inward-opening set of wooden doors leading to a courtyard.

The Shanghai Arts and Crafts Museum was once a private home.

& Shanghai Bank building at No. 12 (now the Shanghai Pudong Development Bank), but the most famous is the Art Deco 1929 Cathay Hotel (renamed as the Peace Hotel in 1956, and now operating as the Fairmont Peace Hotel and the Swatch Art Peace Hotel). The 1937 Bank of China, next door, is the only Bund building to incorporate Chinese themes into its design.

Built in 1947, the former Bank of Communications at No. 14 is the youngest building on the Bund, with a stripped-down Art Deco

CHINESE ARCHITECTURE

For a Chinese city, there isn't that much Chinese-style architecture in Shanghai. A few examples of Ming dynasty Yangtze River Delta style (Jiangnan) architecture can still be found. These are distinguished by their whitewashed walls, distinctive rooflines, undulating "dragon walls", latticework and keyhole windows. The structures inside Yu Garden are also in the Jiangnan style; be sure to visit the gardens if Suzhou is not part of your itinerary. At nearby Shanghai Old Street (Shanghai Laojie), the newly built buildings mimic the Jiangnan style. Other notable Chinese structures are the Longhua Temple and Jade Buddha Temple, both built in the Southern Song dynasty style.

style, while the 1874 neoclassical former British Consulate at Nos 33–53 is the oldest.

Former French Concession homes

The International Settlement was considered *the* place to do business in Old Shanghai, but from the 1920s onwards, the nouveaux riches of all nationalities preferred the tree-lined streets of the French Concession for their homes. Stroll down Fuxing Road, Wukang Road or Xinhua Road and you'll see the lovely Mediterranean, Tudor and Art Deco homes that set the architectural fashion some 70 to 80 years ago.

Many are private residences, but some are commercial enterprises, such as the magnificent Shanghai Arts and Crafts Museum (see page 155). Close by is Taiyuan Villa (see page 156), a French Provincial mansion built for the Comte du Pac de Marsoulies. An Art Deco masterpiece on Lane 18, Gao'an Road is now the Xuhui District Children's Palace. The former

> Old Shanghai's cosmopolitan character is reflected in its places of worship, many of which are both architecturally and historically intriguing. Catholic, Protestant, Muslim, Jewish and Russian Orthodox monuments dot the city.

residence of a British businessman on Shaanxi Road (S) is now the Hengshan Moller Villa (see page 174), a boutique hotel.

Apartment living was the height of modernity in the 1920s and 30s, and architects were given free rein to use the latest ideas in their designs – like the Normandie apartments (see page 165). Art Deco styles, with their emphasis on linearity, verticality and functionality, were perfectly suited to these structures, which dot Frenchtown.

The Shanghai of tomorrow

The pace of change in Shanghai over the past 20 years has been exhausting, and shows few signs of decelerating. The largest urban redevelopment spans 144 sq km (55 sq miles) of land along the banks of the Huangpu River. Much of the area is now devoted to green public space, set far from the river's edge, and buildings with heights limited to 30 metres (98ft) to protect precious water

Peace Hotel (with the green roof) and the Bank of China beside it.

views. The South Bund is rising as a fancy new business and residential quarter, and Shiliupu Wharf has been transformed from a no-man's land of dingy warehouses into a waterfront marketplace inspired by Sydney's Rocks area. Further upstream, the West Bund is being established as a "cultural corridor" of museums and galleries housed in former factories and aircraft hangars. A landscaped riverside promenade linking these areas is wonderful for cycling or running.

Northeast of the Waibaidu Bridge, an international cruise-ship terminal and shopping and entertainment projects have replaced the rundown shipyards and warehouses of the Hongkou and Yangpu districts. And on Chongming Island, a rural district within the Shanghai city limits, a huge "carbon-neutral" satellite city is emerging.

Recent Shanghai urban planning has reflected an almost stereotyped Modernist vision of vertical skyscrapers and landscaped greenbelts crisscrossed by wide avenues and superhighways. Hopefully, cutting-edge architectural concepts like "designing for density" and "green design" will help Shanghai confront today's daunting urban realities and enable the city to emerge with an architectural style identifiably its own.

Interior of the Moller Villa, now a hotel owned by Hengshan Group.

SHANGHAI DECO

Art Deco was Old Shanghai's signature style – both in its pure form, and fused with Chinese characteristics.

Art Deco: the streamlined, elegant look, born at the Exposition for the Decorative Arts in Paris in 1925, was a metaphor for the new age of skyscrapers, steamships, trains and all things *moderne*. Progressive Shanghai embraced it eagerly, but made it her own by adding Chinese elements to Art Deco, and Art Deco elements to Chinese styles.

Art Deco defined Shanghai's skyline between the late 1920s and late 1940s: the Park Hotel (the tallest building of its day), the Grosvenor House and – most famous of all – the iconic Peace Hotel. Even traditional lane houses were modernised with the addition of Art Deco exterior details.

So completely did Shanghai embrace this style that it permeated virtually all design: furniture, graphic art, even fabric. And so completely did Art Deco become associated with Shanghai that, even today, contemporary architects wanting to add a bit of Shanghai style to their skyscrapers invariably use Art Deco features.

Shanghai still has one of the largest collections of Art Deco buildings in the world. And the city's passion for the style continues unabated, with Shanghai hosting the 13th World Congress on Art Deco in November 2015, which attracted more than 200 experts and connoisseurs from around the world.

A Shanghai institution and erected in 1929, the Peace Hotel (then the Cathay) was tycoon Victor Sassoon's jewel in the crown – and perhaps the epitome of Shanghai's Art Deco architecture and design. The octagonal, skylit atrium has been restored to its former glory.

Art Deco used geometric forms liberally, but whereas Western Art Deco used modern materials like steel, Shanghai artisans preferred the traditional dark wood to craft their furniture.

Art Deco was everywhere – even in the details. Tycoons like Robert Morriss, owner of the North China Daily News, hired artisans to create decorative ironwork with Art Deco motifs – this was to complement the architecture of his sumptuous mansion, now the Intercontinental Shanghai Ruijin, also the former Ruijin Guesthouse.

The 1930s and 40s were the golden age of film – and of cinemas. The Cathay Cinema, with its classic Art Deco lines and tapered tower, screened both Hollywood films and those made in Shanghai's booming movie studios.

A classic Art Deco beauty, with its central tower opening out to stepped wings, Grosvenor House was another Sassoon property, built in 1929.

This advertisement poster, dating back to the 1930s, is a vignette of the good life in Shanghai: here, the mah-jong-playing ladies are wearing qipaos made from fabrics with Art Deco designs, and are seated on Art Deco chairs in a pastel-hued Art Deco house, complete with the classic curve of an Art Deco banister.

One of Shanghai's most beloved skyscrapers is a 21st-century take on Art Deco. The Jin Mao Tower, designed by American firm Skidmore, Owings & Merrill, is inspired by the proportions of a pagoda and the typical angular stepping and massing of Art Deco design.

Nanjing Road is bustling at night.

Dazzling Shanghai cityscape.

Tree-lined avenue in the former French Concession.

The redeveloped longtang (lane) neighbourhood at Xintiandi.

INTRODUCTION

A detailed guide to Shanghai and its surroundings, with the principal sights numbered and clearly cross-referenced to maps.

The limits of this maritime city are defined by its waterways. The Huangpu River separates Shanghai's newest district, Pudong, literally "east of the Huangpu", from the rest of Shanghai, or rather Puxi, "west of the Huangpu". The Suzhou Creek divides the thriving midsection of Puxi from its quieter northern suburbs. New lines have been drawn, but the shape and feel of the old foreign Concessions and Nanshi, the Old Chinese City, are still discernible.

Shanghai Municipality comprises 16 city districts (Chongming became the 16th district in 2016). Streets run north to south and east to west in a grid-like fashion, except for oval-shaped Nanshi and People's Square, the latter defined by the old racetracks. The major streets run the length of the city and have directional tags: Huaihai (West), Huaihai (Central) or Huaihai (East). Buildings are usually num-

Shanghai Grand Theatre.

bered sequentially, odd numbers on one side of the street and even numbers on the other; the numbering on the residential lanes *(longtang)* that run off the main streets has no relationship to the main street numbering.

The 98km (61-mile) outer ring road, A20, takes a lap outside the city limits, while the inner ring Zhongshan Road loops around the perimeter of Puxi and Pudong, changing its name in Pudong and east Hongkou before turning back into Zhongshan Road. The city is bisected from east to west by the Yan'an Road Elevated Highway and from north to south by the Chongqing Road Elevated Highway. A tram service opened in 2017 runs a 17.5km (11-mile) route directly beneath the Yan'an Highway. Crossing Huangpu River to Pudong from Puxi can be done via ferry, metro, the Nanpu, Yangpu or Lupu bridges, or a host of tunnels.

Street signs are in English and Chinese, but most locals will only know a street by its Chinese name – so a rudimentary understanding of the basic street translations will hold the traveller in good stead (see page 259). Buses are packed during peak hours, and difficult to use if you don't speak Chinese. The metro system is an easy way to get around, especially now that there are 14 lines extending throughout the city; the lines are still being extended and are linked to an elevated light railway system. The world's longest metro system is aiming to hit 20 cross-city lines by 2020. Taxis are inexpensive, but hard to get during rush hour and in bad weather.

Central Shanghai

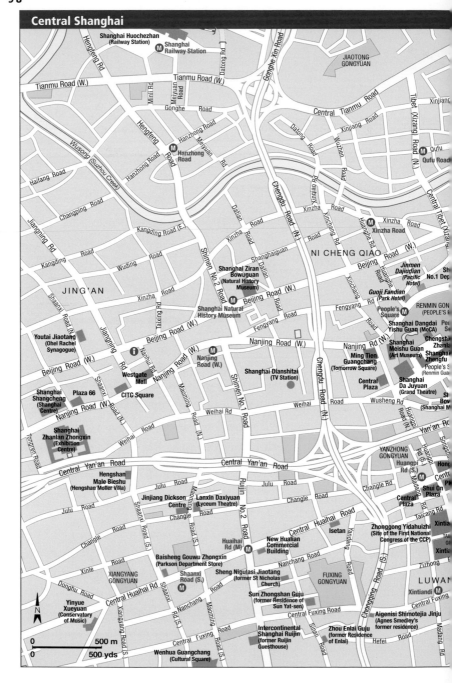

Shanghai Huochezhan (Railway Station)

Ⓜ Shanghai Railway Station

JIAOTONG GONGYUAN

Hengfeng Rd

Tianmu Road (W.)

Gonghe Xin Road

Tibet (Xizang) Road (N.)

Xinjiang

Tianmu Road (W.)

Minli Rd

Meiyuan Road

Gonghe Road

Central Tianmu Road

Xinjiang Road

Wuzhen Road

Ⓜ Qufu

Qufu Road

Hengfeng Road

Hanzhong Road

Meiyuan Rd

Datong Road

Central Tibet (Xizang) Rd

Wusong (Suzhou Creek)

Ⓜ Hanzhong Road

Hanzhong Road

Chengdu Road (N.)

Haifang Road

Changping Road

Kangding Road (E.)

Daitian Road

Xinza Road

Xinchang Rd

Huangjia Rd

Ⓜ Xinzha Road

Xinzha Road

Jiangning Rd

Kangding Road

Wuding Road

Shanghaiguan

Shimen No.2 Road

Daitian Road

NI CHENG QIAO

Beijing Road (W.)

Jinmen Dajiudian (Pacific Hotel)

Sh No.1 Dep

Shanxi Road (N.)

JING'AN

Xinza Road

Taixing Rd

Shanghai Ziran Bowuguan (Natural History Museum)

Beijing Road (W.)

Xinchang

Guoji Fandian (Park Hotel)

RENMIN GON (PEOPLE'S

Jiangning Rd

Beijing Road (W.)

Ⓜ Shanghai Natural History Museum

Fengyang Rd

People's Ⓜ Square

Shanghai Dangdai Yishu Guan (MoCA)

Ped Se

Youtai Jiaotang (Ohel Rachel Synagogue)

Nanjing Road (W.)

Fengyang Road

Shanghai Meishu Guan (Art Museum)

Chengshi Zhanla

Beijing Road (W.)

Nanhui Rd

Ⓜ Nanjing Road (W.)

Ming Tien Guangchang (Tomorrow Square)

Shanghai Zhengfu

Westgate Mall

Nanjing Rd

Nanjing Road (W.)

Shanghai Dianshitai (TV Station)

People's S (Renmin Gua

Maoming Rd

Shimen No.1 Road

Central Plaza

Shanghai Da Juyuan (Grand Theatre)

Shanghai Shangcheng (Shanghai Centre)

Plaza 66

CITC Square

Shanxi Road (N.)

Weihai Rd

Weihai

Chengdu Road (N.)

Wusheng Rd

S Bov (Shanghai M

Shanghai Zhanlan Zhongxin (Exhibition Centre)

Weihai Road

Shimen No.1 Road

Huangpi Road (N.)

Yan'an R

Tongren Road

YANZHONG GONGYUAN

Central Yan'an Road

Central Yan'an Road

Huangpi Rd (S.)

Hong

Songs...

Hengshan Male Bieshu (Hengshan Moller Villa)

Julu Road

Julu Road

Changle Rd

Cent

Ⓜ Shui On Plaza

Ph

Julu Road

Jinjiang Dickson Centre

Lanxin Daxiyuan (Lyceum Theatre)

Shaanxi Road (S.)

Ruijin No.2 Road

Changle Road

Central Plaza

Taicang Rd

Changle Road

Changle Road

Central Huaihai Road

Isetan

Zhonggong Yidahuizhi (Site of the First National Congress of the CCP)

Xintia

Baisheng Gouwu Zhongxin (Parkson Department Store)

Huaihai Rd (M) Ⓜ

New Hualian Commercial Building

Yandang Road

Xintia G

Xinle Road

Shaanxi Road (S.) Ⓜ

Sheng Nigulasi Jiaotang (former St Nicholas Church)

Nanchang Road

Zizhong

Xintia

XIANGYANG GONGYUAN

Maoming Rd (S.)

Sun Zhongshan Guju (former Residence of Sun Yat-sen)

FUXING GONGYUAN

Chongqing Road (S.)

LUWAN

Donghu Road

Central Huaihai Rd

Nanchang Road

Xintiandi Ⓜ

Yinyue Xueyuan (Conservatory of Music)

Xiangyang Road (S.)

Maoming Rd (S.)

Central Fuxing Road

Intercontinental Shanghai Ruijin (former Ruijin Guesthouse)

Zhou Enlai Guju (former Residence of Enlai)

Aigenisi Shimotejia Jinju (Agnes Smedley's former residence)

Central Fuxing Road

Shan Road

Hefei Road

Madang Rd

↑ N

0 ——— 500 m

0 ——— 500 yds

Central Fuxing Road

Wenhua Guangchang (Cultural Square)

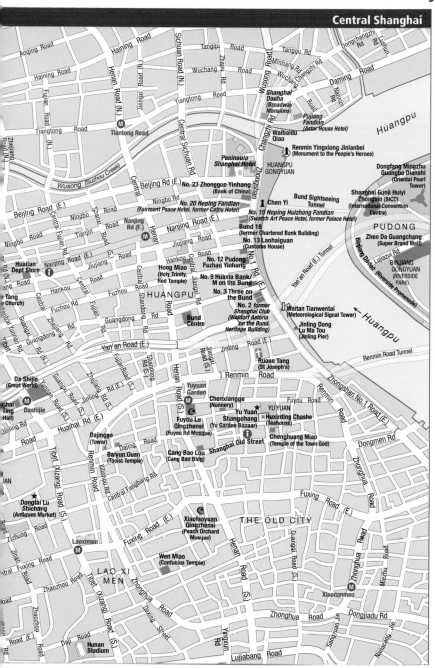

Anqing Road

Haining Road

Haining Road

Fujian Road (N.)

Zhejiang Road (N.)

Tiantong Road

Tiantong Road

Henan Road (N.)

Sichuan Road (N.)

Tanggu Road

Wuchang Road

Tiantong Road

M Tiantong Road

Central Sichuan Rd

Changzhi Road

Wusong Road

Zhongshan

Minhang

Wuchang Changzhi Rd

Tanggu Rd

Daming Road

Haimen Rd

Dongchangzhi Rd

Lishui

Shanghai Dasha (Broadway Mansions)

Pujiang Fandian (Astor House Hotel)

Waibaidu Qiao

Huangpu

Wusong (Suzhou Creek)

Peninsula Shanghai Hotel

HUANGPU GONGYUAN

♠ **Renmin Yingxiong Jinianbei (Monument to the People's Heroes)**

Dongfang Mingzhu Guangbo Dianshi (Oriental Pearl Tower)

Beijing Rd (E.)

No. 23 Zhongguo Yinhang (Bank of China)

Ningbo Rd

Beijing Road (E.)

Ningbo Road

Nanjing Rd (E.)

M Henan

No. 20 Heping Fandian (Fairmont Peace Hotel, former Cathy Hotel)

ℹ **Chen Yi**

Bund Sightseeing Tunnel

Shanghai Guoji Huiyi Zhongxin (SICC) (International Convention Centre)

Shandong Road

Nanjing Road (E.)

Tianjin

Jiujiang Road

No. 19 Heping Huizhong Fandian (Swatch Art Peace Hotel, former Palace Hotel)

PUDONG

Nanjing Road (E.)

Jiujiang Road

Bund 18 (former Chartered Bank Building)

Zhen Da Guangchang (Super Brand Mall)

Hualian Dept Store ℹ

Ningbo Road

Hankou Road

Jiujiang Road

Hankou Road

No. 13 Laohaiguan (Customs House)

Binjiang Dadao (Riverside Promenade)

BINJIANG GONGYUAN (RIVERSIDE PARK)

Central Zhejiang Road

No. 12 Pudong Fazhan Yinhang

Hong Miao (Holy Trinity, Red Temple)

Tang Church

Hankou Road

Fuzhou Rd

Guangxi Road

No. 5 Huaxia Bank/ M on the Bund

No. 3 Three on the Bund

HUANGPU

Fuzhou Road

Guangdong Rd

Bund Centre

No. 2 former Shanghai Club (Waldorf Astoria on the Bund, Heritage Building)

Guangdong Rd

Yan'an Road (E.)

Jiangxi Road (S.)

Jinling Road (E.)

Shandong Rd (S.)

Henan Road (S.)

Waitan Tianwentai (Meteorological Signal Tower)

Jinling Dong Lu Ma Tou (Jinling Pier)

Yan'an Road (E.) Tunnel

Renmin Road Tunnel

Da Shijie (Great World)

Yunnan Road (S.)

Guangxi Road (S.)

Zhejiang Road (S.)

Jinling Rd

Ruose Tang (St Joseph's)

Renmin Road

Yuyuan Garden

Zhongshan No.1 Road (E.)

ghai Ting Hall M

Dashijie

Huaihai Rd (E.)

Fujian Road (S.)

M **Chenxiangge (Nunnery)**

M

Yu Yuan Shangchang (Yu Garden Bazaar) ★

YUYUAN

★ **Huxinting Chashe (Teahouse)**

Renmin Road

Fuyou Road

Jinling Rd

Dajingge (Tower)

Henan Road (S.)

Fuyou Lu Qingzhensi (Fuyou Rd Mosque)

ℹ

Chenghuang Miao (Temple of the Town God)

Dongmen Rd

Road

Renmin Road

Baiyun Guan (Taoist Temple)

Dajing Rd

Cang Bao Lou (Cang Bao Bldg)

Shanghai Old Street

Zhonghua Road

Central Fangbang Rd

JIAN

★ **Dongtai Lu Shichang (Antiques Market)**

Tibet (Xizang) Road (S.)

Fuxing Road (E.)

Fuxing Road (E.)

Henan Road (S.)

THE OLD CITY

Guangqi Road (S.)

Zhonghua Road

Zizhou Road

Laoximen M

Fuxing Road

Xiaotaoyuan Qingzhensi (Peach Orchard Mosque) ☪

Henan Road (S.)

Zhonghua Road

Miezhu Road

LAO XI MEN

Thibet (Xizang) Road (S.)

Wen Miao (Confucius Temple)

Zhaozhou Road

Zhonghua Road

Zhaozhou Road

Daji Road

Hunan Stadium

Tibet (Xizang) Road (S.)

Da3hua Street

Yingxun Rd

Lujiabang Road

Xiaonanmen M

Dongjiadu Rd

Sanguan Jie

Nanxiang Jie

Dongjiadu Rd

The Bund at dusk.

THE BUND AND BEYOND

For the visitor, the Bund is the perfect
introduction to Shanghai's glorious past
– and its even more glittering present.

On this small oblong plot of
land, about the size of Manhattan Island from the Battery
to 58th Street, are jammed all but
a handful of the foreign banks and
all of the important native ones, all
the office buildings, the hotels, the
important shops and big department
stores, most of the clubs... The industry, the finance, the amusements of
the fifth biggest city in the world."
So wrote *Fortune* magazine in 1934.
Shanghai in the 21st century may be
a city defined by a spectacular warp-
speed journey into the future, but the
Bund (Waitan) remains one of its
signature sights. The 2km (1.25-mile)
sweep of historic buildings west of
the Huangpu River is a Concession-
era time capsule, a sepia portrait in a
Kodachrome world.

The sight of so many magnificent
buildings all at once – each more
beautiful, more stately, more glamorous than the last – is nothing short
of breathtaking, particularly when
the Bund is illuminated in soft gold
light at night, and glows as if lit from
within. The stretch of European
buildings has long been one of the
city's most well-known sights. For
years the city slowed down its development plans for the Bund, which
helped retain its original character.

Today, the Bund is firmly back in
the limelight – this time as a premier
dining, entertainment and shopping
hub. The renaissance began with
the opening of the ritzy M on the
Bund restaurant at the Huaxia Bank
building, and renovations to the AIG
building and the former Hongkong
and Shanghai Bank in 1999. In
2004, celebrity chef Jean Georges
Vongerichten opened Jean Georges
at Three on the Bund, and later two
other restaurants within the same
building. Today there are fine-dining

Main Attractions

Shanghai Pudong
    Development Bank
Customs House
Bund 18
Fairmont Peace Hotel
Bank of China
Rockbund Art Museum
St Joseph's Church

Map
Page 102

Historic buildings line the Bund's promenade.

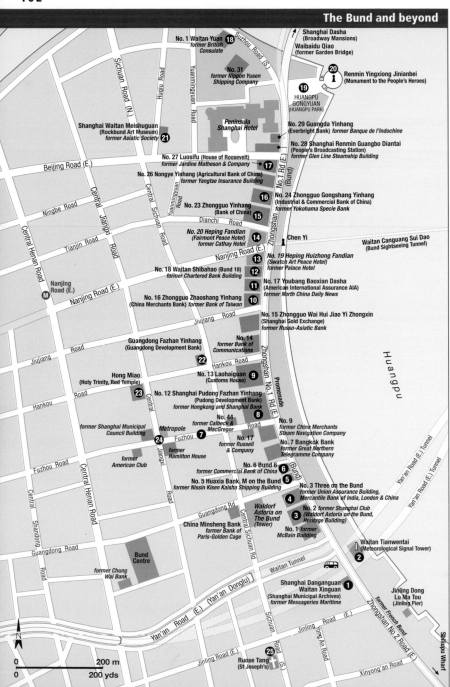

No. 1 Waitan Yuan 18
former British Consulate

No. 31 former Nippon Yusen Shipping Company

Shanghai Dasha (Broadway Mansions)
Waibaidu Qiao (former Garden Bridge)

20 Renmin Yingxiong Jinianbei (Monument to the People's Heroes)

19 HUANGPU GONGYUAN (HUANGPU PARK)

Peninsula Shanghai Hotel

Shanghai Waitan Meishuguan (Rockbund Art Museum) former Asiatic Society 21

No. 29 Guangda Yinhang (Everbright Bank) former Banque de l'Indochine

No. 28 Shanghai Renmin Guangbo Diantai (People's Broadcasting Station) former Glen Line Steamship Building

Beijing Road (E.)

No. 27 Luosifu (House of Roosevelt) former Jardine Matheson & Company 17

No. 26 Nongye Yinhang (Agricultural Bank of China) former Yangtse Insurance Building

No. 24 Zhongguo Gongshang Yinhang (Industrial & Commercial Bank of China) former Yokohama Specie Bank

16

Ningbo Road (E.)

No. 23 Zhongguo Yinhang (Bank of China) 15

Dianchi Road

Tianjin Road

Chen Yi

Waitan Canguang Sui Dao (Bund Sightseeing Tunnel)

No. 20 Heping Fandian (Fairmont Peace Hotel) former Cathay Hotel 14

Nanjing Road (E.)

No. 19 Heping Huizhong Fandian (Swatch Art Peace Hotel) former Palace Hotel

13

No. 18 Waitan Shibahao (Bund 18) former Chartered Bank Building 12

No. 17 Youbang Baoxian Dasha (American International Assurance AIA) former North China Daily News

Nanjing Road (E.)

M

11

No. 16 Zhongguo Zhaoshang Yinhang (China Merchants Bank) former Bank of Taiwan 10

No. 15 Zhongguo Wai Hui Jiao Yi Zhongxin (Shanghai Gold Exchange) former Russo-Asiatic Bank

Jiujiang Road

Guangdong Fazhan Yinhang (Guangdong Development Bank)

No. 14 former Bank of Communications

22

Jiujiang Road

Hong Miao (Holy Trinity, Red Temple)

Hankou Road

No. 13 Laohaiguan (Customs House) 9

Hankou Road

23 No. 12 Shanghai Pudong Fazhan Yinhang (Pudong Development Bank) former Hongkong and Shanghai Bank

former Shanghai Municipal Council Building

Metropole

No. 44 former Calbeck & MacGregor

8

No. 9 former China Merchants Steam Navigation Company

24 7

No. 17 former Russell & Company

former Hamilton House

No. 7 Bangkok Bank former Great Northern Telegramme Company

Fuzhou Road

former American Club

No. 6 Bund 6 former Commercial Bank of China 6

No. 5 Huaxia Bank, M on the Bund former Nissin Kisen Kaisha Shipping Building 5

No. 3 Three on the Bund former Union Assurance Building, Mercantile Bank of India, London & China

4

Guangdong Rd

Waldorf Astoria on The Bund (Tower)

3 No. 2 former Shanghai Club (Waldorf Astoria on the Bund, Heritage Building)

China Minsheng Bank former Bank of Paris–Golden Cage

No. 1 former McBain Building

Guangdong Road

Bund Centre

former Chung Wai Bank

Waitan Tianwentai (Meteorological Signal Tower) 2

Waitan Tunnel

Shanghai Danganguan Waitan Xinguan (Shanghai Municipal Archives) former Messageries Maritime 1

Jinling Dong Lu Ma Tou (Jinling Pier)

Shiliupu Wharf

Jinling Road (E.)

25 Ruose Tang (St Joseph's)

HUANGPU

Doing tai chi.

establishments, beautiful nightclubs and luxury brand boutiques along the entire stretch, while spiffy refurbishments have brought the glamour back to the Fairmont Peace and Waldorf Astoria hotels.

ALONG THE BUND

The banks and financial institutions of Old Shanghai's Wall Street were anchored along the **Bund** and also just behind it in the International Settlement area. This is where visitors will find a treasure trove of architectural imprints made by long-forgotten giants.

Like the buildings that line it, the word "bund" is itself a legacy of the colonial era. The British signatories to the 1842 Treaty of Nanjing, which ended the First Opium War and opened Shanghai to foreign trade (separate treaties were signed by the US and France in 1844), brought with them a new vocabulary, some of it borrowed. Bund comes from the Hindi word *band*, meaning artificial embankment, a word that the British applied to the embanked quay along the shores of the settlements in their Chinese treaty ports and in British colonies from Ceylon to Malacca.

Old Shanghai's maritime soul determined the strategic location of the Bund – on the shore of the Huangpu River where great trading ships sailed in from the Yangtze. Originally a muddy mess with sewage and refuse strewn on its banks, the strip was filled and "bunded"

The Bund promenade with the Customs House in the background.

TIP

Boats departing on cruises (ranging from 1–3.5 hours) of the Huangpu River can be booked at the Tourist Centre of Shiliupu Wharf on Zhongshan East No.2 Road near Hotel Indigo. Note: there are several booths (and some of the signage is in Chinese), so it can be quite confusing. Look out for the Shanghai Huangpu River Cruise Company. Evening cruises run nightly between 6.30 and 9.30pm, departing at 30-minute intervals and taking approximately 45 minutes. Tickets can be bought at the terminal. It's recommended to purchase them before 5pm during high season.

Night view of the Huangpu River and the Bund.

in the late 1880s. Only then did the classic Bund, lined by jetties, with trading houses and financial institutions just behind them, begin to take shape. Waitan, the Chinese name for the area, means "outside beach".

A four-lane highway now runs where once the great mass of labourers hauled crates into the trading houses and rickshaw pullers ran. Remodelled in 2010, the raised promenade has replaced the old jetties, and it's a sign of the times that most of the tourists who pack the promenade want to be photographed against the Pudong skyline (see page 215) – not the Bund.

River cruises

In the pre-aeroplane age, the first sight that greeted vessels approaching Shanghai on the Huangpu River was the Bund. Visitors today can replicate that vision on river cruises from the Shiliupu Wharf (see tip). The cruise boats slide past an eye-popping array of freighters, ships and barges – a sign of the vibrant activity in China's largest port – and give you panoramic riverside views of the Bund and Pudong.

Shanghai Municipal Archives ❶

Shànghǎi Dàngànguǎn Wàitān Xìnguǎn 上海档案馆外滩新馆
Address: 9 Zhongshan No. 2 Road (E); www.archives.sh.cn
Tel: 6333 6633
Opening Hrs: Mon–Sat 9am–5pm
Entrance Fee: free
Transport: Nanjing Road East + taxi

Across the street and about a 10-minute walk away from Shiliupu Wharf is the **Shanghai Municipal Archives**. This was the **former French Messageries Maritime Building**, an Art Deco high-rise and one of the few original buildings left south of Yan'an Road, on the former Quai de France, (the part of the Bund within the French Concession). Inside are photo exhibits chronicling Shanghai's history.

Meteorological Signal Tower ❷

Wàitān Tiānwéntái 外滩天文台
Address: 1 Zhongshan No. 2 Road (E)
Tel: 6321 6542
Opening Hrs: Bund Museum, first floor: daily 9am–5pm
Entrance Fee: free

Meteorological Signal Tower.

Transport: Nanjing Road East + taxi

The boats that ply the river once received periodic typhoon warnings from the 31-metre (102ft) tall redbrick signal tower, north of Shiliupu Wharf. Jesuit priests at Xujiahui Observatory would telephone in weather information to what was then known as the Gutzlaff Signal Tower. One of Shanghai's few Art Nouveau structures, the tower was built in 1908. It now houses a ground-floor photographic exhibition of the Bund buildings, a bar and an outdoor terrace café with excellent perspectives of the length of the Bund (open periodically).

THE MAIN BUND BUILDINGS

Continue north and cross Yan'an Road (E) to the beginning of the Bund proper at **Zhongshan No. 1 Road (E)**. Only highlights along this stretch – which faces the Bund promenade along the Huangpu River – are described in the following pages (for a list of all the Bund buildings, see page 114).

For orientation purposes, the first building you will see is at **No. 1**, the **former McBain Building**, dating back to 1915, which now lies empty.

Waldorf Astoria Shanghai on the Bund ❸

Shànghǎi Wàitān Huá Er Dào Fū Jiǔdiàn 上海外滩华尔道夫酒店

The old boys' club that controlled Shanghai ran it from the leather-and-whisky-soaked confines of the **former Shanghai Club at No. 2**, now part of the **Waldorf Astoria**, which is spread across two buildings. Built in 1911, membership to this club was restricted to white men of a certain class. The famous Long Bar, whose seating was subject to a strict hierarchy – bank managers and tai-pans at the prime Bund-facing end of the L-shaped bar, with the social scale falling as one moved further away – has been recreated and the colonnaded Grand Hall and the caged lifts remain. The heritage building is now all suites decorated in period style while a new tower rises behind, all glitz and gloss to match the new Shanghai.

The atrium of the restored Three on the Bund Building.

Plush Glam bar.

Three on the Bund ④

Wàitān Sānhào 外滩三号

Next, at **No. 3**, the 1916 **former Union Assurance Building** now goes by the swanky name of **Three on the Bund** – housing the eponymous **Jean Georges** restaurant, owned by the French celebrity chef, along with two newer Jean Georges dining concepts: Mercato (Italian) and CHI-Q (Korean). These are joined by Shanghainese fare at **Whampoa Club**, hip American brasserie **POP** with a spectacular rooftop terrace, and one of the city's hottest supper clubs, the Latin-flavoured **Unico**. Three on the Bund opened in 2004, after a seven-year and US$50-million interior makeover supervised by American architect Michael Graves. This was one of the first Bund buildings to undergo such an extensive refurbishment. The interior was completely gutted and retrofitted with a more contemporary look featuring cool marble and monotones. Detractors sniff and dismiss it as looking too much like a faceless hotel with little indication of its historic

No. 44 Fuzhou Road, the former offices of Calbeck & MacGregor.

past, save for its tiny lobby area and facade. Its fans retort that the restoration reflects the cutting-edge style of modern Shanghai.

Huaxia Bank ⑤

Huáxià Yínháng 华夏银行

At **No. 5**, the **former Nissin Kisen Kaisha Shipping Building**, dating to 1925, is today occupied by **Huaxia Bank**, but its most famous contemporary tenant is the **M on the Bund**, the restaurant credited with sparking the renaissance of the Bund. Australian restaurateur Michelle Garnaut, who also owns chic **Glam bar** on the same floor, has revived Shanghai glamour in 21st-century fashion, enhanced by one of the best views of the Bund. In the same building, **Daimon Bistro** is the first Shanghai outpost of Hong Kong's celeb 'Demon Chef' Alvin Leung, dishing up cocktails and

Canto dishes until 2am. Tucked away behind the bistro is Leung's 26-seat gourmet speakeasy, **Bo Shanghai**, which serves a tasting menu themed on China's eight great culinary styles.

Bund 6 ⑥

Wàitān Liùhào 外滩六号

Shanghai's constant rebuilding missed out the rare Victorian Gothic edifice of the **former Commercial Bank of China** at **No. 6** for many years. Refurbished in 2006 into a slick, if nondescript, shopping and banking emporium now known as **Bund 6**, it is the home of several restaurants including the Japanese **Sun with Aqua**, plus HSBC bank. The US$30-million refurbishment erased all signs of the original structure (save for the facade), so you'll have to use your imagination to remember it as it was: the former Municipal Council Hall, housing the governing body of the International Settlement. This was also where the Shanghai Volunteer Corps billeted Russian troops until 1937. A little further along the Bund, duck into Lane 8 and look for the large red door to find Annabel Lee's elegant showroom

displaying a range of quality, embroidered silk pouches, cushions, shawls, jewellery and leisurewear. Next door, Ruyee Life Gallery sells delightful Mongolian cashmere.

Fuzhou Road ⑦

Fúzhōu Lù 福州路

Venture around the corner into **Fuzhou Road**. Just behind **No. 9** of the Bund is the oldest Bund building, the squat 1850s stone Gothic **former Russell & Company warehouse** at 17 Fuzhou Road, today an apartment building with a unique collection of shops in the street-facing part of the building. These include **Blue Shanghai White**, where owner Haichen designs beautiful ceramics inspired by classic blue and white pottery, and **Suzhou Cobblers**, with its exquisite hand-embroidered silk Chinese slippers and accessories. Also part of the same building is an Italian restaurant called **Choir**.

The quaint Tudor-style building across the street, at **No. 44**, used to house the offices of wine importers **Calbeck & MacGregor**; it is now occupied by Chinese companies.

Close-up of an ornate entrance leading to one of the Bund's most magnificent buildings, the Shanghai Pudong Development Bank.

One of the Bund's must-see sights, the grand Shanghai Pudong Development Bank.

Down the road at **No. 60** is **House of Blues and Jazz**, one of the city's best live jazz venues.

Shanghai Pudong Development Bank

Shànghǎi Pǔdōng Fāzhǎn Yínháng
上海浦东发展银行

Head back up the Bund to see the **former Hongkong and Shanghai Bank** at **No. 12**. "Dominate the Bund" was the instruction given by the bank owners to architects Palmer & Turner. Today, the domed neoclassical building, once hailed as "the grandest building east of the Suez", is still the beauty of the Bund. Now occupied (and renamed), the bank remains guarded by a pair of bronze lions (see box below). Opened in 1923 and restored in 1999, the bank's magnificent 2,000-sq-metre (21,500-sq-ft) banking hall and adjacent office building are open to the public during working hours; at weekends only the entrance lobby is open.

No expense was spared on the building of this edifice, with almost every piece crafted overseas. The four marble columns that support the

The stunning domed ceiling of the Shanghai Pudong Development Bank.

banking hall, each weighing more than 7 tonnes and hewn from a single piece of marble, are among only six solid marble pillars of this size in the world – the other two are found in the Louvre Museum in Paris.

Above the octagonal entrance lobby is the spectacular domed mosaic ceiling: eight panels depicting the eight cities in which the bank had its branches in 1923, along with the eight

The Customs House.

BRONZE LIONS

Mythical dragon-lion creatures flanking Chinese doorways are traditional, but the Western-looking lions that guard the main entrance of the Shanghai Pudong Development Bank are an unusual sight. The four bronzes were cast by sculptor Henry Poole: two for the branch in Hong Kong and two for the Shanghai branch, and the mould was then broken.

The lions disappeared during the Japanese Occupation; it was assumed they had been melted down but in fact they had been stored in the basement of a musty old museum. Today, one of them can be seen at the Shanghai Municipal History Museum (see page 217). The replica lions guarding the bank meanwhile continue to be rubbed and patted till this day for good luck.

words of the bank's motto, "*Within the Four Seas all men are brothers*". The 12 signs of the zodiac ring the dome, and panels on the walls illustrate, in Latin, 16 lofty qualities, including temperance, truth and prudence. After HSBC (the Hongkong and Shanghai Banking Corporation) moved out in 1955, the building was renovated and the mosaic was hidden under layers of thick white paint, where it remained during the half-century that the building served as the seat of the Shanghai Municipal Government. Only when the Shanghai Pudong Development Bank began restoration work was it revealed.

In the left-hand corner, where foreign exchange transactions are now handled, stood a separate bank for Chinese customers; it was once decorated in the bright reds and shiny golds favoured by its clientele. All that remains today are the Chinese designs in the ceiling mouldings, cornices and ventilation covers, and in the Chinese characters for fortune in the trim and on the walls. The bank manager's offices, now VIP meeting rooms, still have their original parquet floors and Bund views.

The fourth floor, under the domed rooftop, once housed the Royal Air Force Club of Shanghai. Restoration work found no signs of the seal of the RAF and the images of World War I aircraft that the Fly Boys were said to have laid in mosaic on the floor.

Customs House ❾

Lǎohǎiguān 老海关

The old **Customs House** at **No. 13** was first located in a Chinese temple that was destroyed in an 1853 Taiping uprising. It is still used as a branch of the Customs House today, and visitors can enter only during office hours; access is restricted to the lobby.

A castle-like Gothic brick building took its place before this neoclassical Palmer & Turner building and its distinctive clock tower was built in 1925.

Fondly referred to as the "Big Ching", the clock tower sounded every 15 minutes until the 1960s. The clock chimes were restored in 1986 and both clock and chimes were overhauled later. The Communist People's Peace Preservation Corps once holed up in the Customs House to fight for the liberation of Shanghai, and a carving in the entrance lobby commemorates its contribution. Inside, strips of jarring neon outline the low ceiling, while an interior dome mimics the grander one in the Pudong Development Bank next door. The mosaic here depicts the different types of Yangtze junks.

China Merchants Bank ❿

Zhōngguó Zhāoshāng Yínháng 中国招商银行

At **No. 16** is the **China Merchants Bank**. Like the other banks along the bund, it can be visited during working hours. Built as the Bank of Taiwan in 1924 during the Japanese occupation of Taiwan, the bank's main gallery features blossoms on the tops of the columns, original alabaster lamps and a second-floor gallery

Step into the lobby of the Customs House to see the mosaic depiction of Chinese junks on the ceiling.

The China Merchants Bank (left) and the AIA Building.

Across the road from the Peace Hotel stands the statue of Marshal Chen Yi. One of China's legendary 10 marshals, Chen Yi liberated Shanghai on 25 May 1949. He later became the city's first mayor and China's foreign minister.

Looking towards the Peace Hotel along the newly developed walkway on the west side of the Bund.

from which bank managers still carry out their supervisory duties.

AIA Building ⓫

Yŏubāng Băoxiăn Dàshà
友邦保险大厦

The **American International Assurance** or **AIA Building** (**No. 17**) was the Bund's tallest when it was completed in 1923 as the North China Daily News Building – the "Old Lady of the Bund". The oldest and most important newspaper in the city at the time, the *North China Daily News* operated here from 1864 to 1951. At some point during the 1930s, the building also rented space to the American Asiatic Underwriters, founded in Shanghai in 1919. The firm went on to become the insurance giant AIA, and leased its old premises back after extensive renovations. The lobby is open during office hours so be sure to have a look at its interior. Look up as you climb the staircase before the entrance to see the original cast-iron lamps hanging beneath the gold mosaicked ceiling.

Bund 18 ⓬

Wàitān Shíbāhào 外滩十八号

Cleaning the entrance to Bund 18.

The 2006 Unesco Asia Pacific Heritage Award of Distinction was given to **Bund 18**, at what else but **No. 18**, easily the best example of historic preservation on the Bund. The **former Chartered Bank of India, Australia and China** is home to the **Mr & Mrs Bund** eatery, as well as mod-Cantonese at **Hakkasan**, Michelin-starred **L'Atelier de Joël Robuchon** and late-night hot spot **Bar Rouge**.

Venice-based Kokai Studio's chief architect Filippo Gabbiani and his team took pains to do a proper

restoration rather than gutting and rebuilding the 1923-built structure – it took them two years and US$15 million (compared to the less successful Three on the Bund which cost a whopping US$50 million). Based on a thorough and detailed analysis, the original structure was impeccably restored: the 70-year-old marble was cleaned, the wood was treated and many of the original details (such as the staircase banisters and windows) were retained.

Swatch Art Peace Hotel

Hépíng Huìzhōng Fàndiàn
和平汇中饭店
At **No. 19** is the **Swatch Art Peace Hotel** (an annexe of the Peace Hotel). The hotel is a joint venture between China's Jin Jiang hotel group and the Swatch company of Switzerland. This stately Edwardian red-brick structure, with an ornate wood-panelled and gilt Edwardian lobby, was originally built in 1906 as the **Palace Hotel** and now houses luxury watch boutiques, a swanky hotel and rooftop bar and restaurant. Just outside the original Art Nouveau revolving doors, a panel commemorates the 1909 meeting of the International Opium

Entrance to the Swatch Art Peace Hotel.

Commission. Ironically, it was in this city – whose foundations rested on the right to trade in opium – that the world's first steps towards narcotics controls were taken.

Fairmont Peace Hotel

Hépíng Fàndiàn 和平饭店
The star of the Bund is the fabulous Art Deco **Fairmont Peace Hotel** at **No. 20**, reopened in 2010 after a much-needed renovation. Built in 1929 as the luxurious **Cathay Hotel**, and originally located on the fourth to seventh floors of Sassoon House, the hotel was considered Shanghai's finest – and tycoon Victor Sassoon's (see box) showpiece. Scion of the great opium-trading firm E.D. Sassoon, Victor Sassoon's domination of the city's property market defined the skyline at the time. In addition to his taste for the high life and fast women, Sassoon was apparently also enamoured of greyhound racing – then a popular Shanghai pastime. Two greyhounds dominate the carvings below the hotel's roof and on the exterior.

The first of three buildings designed by the British architectural firm Palmer & Turner on this stretch of the Bund, the Cathay Hotel was a legend in a city of legends. Pure spring water from the so-called

A trio of Venetian glass chandeliers greet visitors at the entrance lobby of the Bund 18 building.

Bubbling Well (see page 173) flowed from silver taps into its imported marble tubs, and every luminary who came to town stayed here: Charlie Chaplin, George Bernard Shaw and Noel Coward; the last wrote *Private Lives* in his Cathay suite. It was renamed the Peace Hotel in 1956.

The renovation has retained many of the interior details of the public areas: the stunning Chinese Art Deco ceilings of the Dragon-Phoenix restaurant, the classic Art Deco detailing of the Grill Room (now a private room), and the magnificent ballroom, where Sassoon held his fabled fancy-dress parties. The tycoon's penthouse suite is now a dining room. The roof garden offers gorgeous views of the Bund, and of the modern Pudong skyline. The ground-floor jazz bar still features the Old Jazz Band – a group of elderly (average age: 82) jazz musicians playing vintage tunes.

Bank of China

Zhōngguó Yínháng 中国银行

Next door to the Peace Hotel at **No. 23** is another Palmer & Turner building. Its harmonious blend of Chinese,

The elongated domed glass ceiling at the Industrial and Commercial Bank of China.

classical and Art Deco themes conspire to make the **Bank of China** a fusion jewel (open during working hours). Reminiscent of an ancient drum tower and built in 1935, the building was commissioned by H.H. Kung two years before the Japanese occupied Shanghai. Kung was the Kuomintang finance chief, Bank of China director and the husband of Ai Ling, one of the famous Soong sisters. Acquired by the Kuomintang government after World War II, the building is best remembered as the institution responsible for the ruinous hyperinflation of post-war China.

The building features traditional Chinese elements like a blue-tiled Chinese roof, ancient dragon designs on the bronze entrance gates, cloud motifs on the columns and latticework panels on the facade. The steps leading into the main banking hall are in three groups of nine – like Beijing's Temple of Heaven. The Chinese theme continues in the beamed ceilings of the marbled lobby and the square pillars. The Bank of China asked Palmer & Turner to make its building taller than Sassoon House next door, and so it was – until an indignant Victor Sassoon countered by adding a green cupola on his roof.

The Bank of China's banking hall.

Industrial and Commercial Bank of China ⑯

Zhōngguó Gōngshāng Yínháng 中国工商银行

The final building in the Palmer & Turner trilogy along this stretch, at **No. 24**, is the classical Greek-themed **Industrial and Commercial Bank of China**, or the **former Yokohama Specie Bank**, built in 1924. Enter during office hours to see its capacious banking hall with its elongated domed glass ceiling, marble columns topped by gold fretwork and giant alabaster pendant lamps.

House of Roosevelt ⑰

Luosifu 罗斯福

The next highlight is at **No. 27**, now the House of Roosevelt, located in what was one of the main hives of commerce in Old Shanghai, the **former Jardine Matheson & Co. Building**. Completed in 1922, it was known as Joyful and Harmonious Trading House, or *"yihe yanghang"* in Chinese. One of the great old *hong* or trading houses of Concession-era Shanghai, the granite-clad seven-storey building, with its once resplendent marble and terrazzo floors and high-ceilinged offices, was located across from Jardine's own jetty. House of Roosevelt is a collection of bars, restaurants and shops with Shanghai's largest wine cellars, and fabulous rooftop views.

Former British Consulate ⑱

Wàitānyuán Yī Hào 英国驻上海总领事馆

The oldest buildings on the Bund proper are the very last ones: that of the **former British Consulate**. The British Consulate oversaw the development of Shanghai from its perch at the end of the Bund, and the buildings included the consulate, consul's residence, former Union Church, and its minister's residence. Built in 1873 on a site acquired by Shanghai's first British Consul, Sir

Rutherford Alcock, the buildings have a simple dignity. The estate is now known as No.1 Waitanyuan and is a popular venue for state banquets and luxury events. The tiny Union Church is also a favoured backdrop for wedding photo shoots. Although the front gates are guarded, the park is actually open to the public if there isn't an event being held. Wander in and enjoy the exquisite heritage gardens, including a trio of 200-year-old magnolia trees.

Next to the consulate is the landmark **Peninsula Shanghai Hotel**. Owned by another well-known Jewish family, the Kadoories, and opened in 2009, it is the Kadoories' first foray back to the city where they made their fortune after they fled their spectacular Marble Hall (see page 178) in 1949. The new hotel has quickly become Shanghai's "it" place to stay and features the excellent Michelin-starred restaurants **Yi Long Court** (two stars) and **Sir Elly's** (one star).

Huangpu Park ⑲

Huángpǔ Gōngyuán 黄浦公园
Address: 500 Zhongshan No. 1 Road (E)

The three pillars of the Monument to the People's Heroes are a tribute to Shanghai's war heroes.

Mural at the base of the Monument to the People's Heroes.

An A–Z of the Bund

Everyone knows of the Peace Hotel, but what about the other Bund treasures? This is a complete listing of all the buildings along the Bund.

This walking tour covers every single building along the Bund. It begins with the first building on the southern end, at Zhongshan No. 1 Road (E), and ends with the former British Consulate at Nos 33–53. (There is the occasional gap where a building was demolished, or, in the case of No. 4, an unlucky number in China, simply glossed over.)

No. 1 Former McBain Building. Dates back to 1915, now used as offices.

No. 2 Former Shanghai Club, now the Waldorf Astoria Shanghai. Dates from 1911.

No. 3 Former Union Assurance Building (later Mercantile Bank of India, London and China), now a restaurant and shopping complex called Three on the Bund. Built by Palmer & Turner in 1916.

No. 5 Former Nissin Kisen Kaisha Shipping Building, now the Huaxia Bank, with M on the Bund restaurant as co-tenant.

Night-time panorama of the magnificent Bund buildings.

No. 6 Former Commercial Bank of China, and headquarters of the original Municipal Council, which ran Shanghai. Now Bund 6, housing designer shops and restaurants.

No. 7 Former Great Northern Telegraph Company, now Bangkok Bank Building.

No. 9 Former China Merchants Steam Navigation Company, now home to Taiwanese designer boutique Shiatzy Chen.

No. 12 Shanghai Pudong Development Bank, formerly Hongkong and Shanghai Bank. Built in 1923 by Palmer & Turner.

No. 13 Customs House. A neoclassical Palmer & Turner building with a clock tower, built in 1925. Now a branch of the main Customs House.

No. 14 Former Bank of Communications, now used by Shanghai Trade Union Bank of Shanghai.

No. 15 Former Russo-Asiatic Bank, now Shanghai Foreign Exchange.

No. 16 Former Bank of Taiwan, now China Merchants Bank.

No. 17 Former North China Daily News Building, now the American International Assurance Building. The tallest on the Bund when it was completed in 1923.

No. 18 Formerly the Chartered Bank of India, Australia and China. This 1923 building was restored and is now known as Bund 18, housing ritzy restaurants and designer boutiques.

No. 19 Former Palace Hotel; now Swatch Art Peace Hotel.

No. 20 Former Cathay Hotel; now Fairmont Peace Hotel.

No. 23 Bank of China. The only Chinese-style building on the Bund. Still retains its original function.

No. 24 Former Yokohama Specie Bank, now Industrial and Commercial Bank of China.

No. 26 Former Yangtse Insurance Building, now the Agricultural Bank of China. The building once housed the Italian Chamber of Commerce and the Danish Consulate.

No. 27 Former Jardine Matheson & Co. Building, now House of Roosevelt.

No. 29 Former Banque de l'Indochine, now Everbright Bank.

No. 31 Former Nippon Yusen Shipping Company, demolished in 2005.

Nos 33–53 Former British Consulate, now a state guesthouse and public gardens.

Tel: 5308 2636
Opening Hrs: daily 6am–6pm
Entrance Fee: free
Transport: East Nanjing Road + taxi

Across the street is **Huangpu Park**, the former Public Gardens. It was laid out in 1868 by a Scottish gardener brought to Shanghai specifically for the job. Today, a Socialist-Realist statue stands at the site of the old British bandstand, and in the mornings many Chinese gather in front of it to practise tai chi.

Along the waterfront facing the park is the **Monument to the People's Heroes ⓴** (Renmin Yingxiong Jinianbei), its three towering pillars commemorating those who died fighting the Opium Wars, the May 4th Movement and Liberation.

WEST OF THE BUND

The area west of the Bund, part of the old International Settlement, is dotted with an impressive collection of old buildings. The grid of narrow streets, occasionally interrupted by landmark new high-rises such as the 50-storey **Bund Centre** on Guangdong Road and the 66-storey **Le Royal Meridien** on Nanjing Road (E), still manages to create a retro aura. The work of the International Settlement surveyors is still evident in the logical grid behind the Bund; streets running north to south bear the names of Chinese provinces while those going east to west are named after China's cities.

Just behind the British Consulate is known as the Rockbund, an emerging cultural and entertainment hub. The grand edifices – many of which can rival their more famous neighbours along the Bund – were once home to Old Shanghai's social institutions, such as the YWCA, the Royal Asiatic Society and the Rotary Club.

Rockbund Art Museum ⓴

Shànghǎi Wàitān Měishù Guǎn 上海外滩美术馆

Address: 20 Huqiu Road (near Yuanmingyan Road and East Beijing Road)
Tel: 3310 9985
Opening Hrs: Tue–Sun 10am–6pm
Entrance Fee: RMB 15
Transport: Nanjing Road East

The Rockbund Museum is set in the former Royal Asiatic Society Building, which was completed in 1932 and designed by British architect George L. Wilson with an Art Deco exterior combining elements of Western and Chinese architecture. British architect David Chipperfield's 2007 renovation has created a pleasant juxtaposition between the historical architecture and the superbly curated current exhibits of modern art, spread across the four floors. Don't miss the rooftop terrace.

Guangdong Development Bank ⓴

Guǎngdōng Fāzhǎn Yínháng 广东发展银行

One block west along **Hankou Road**, the old street of publishers, at the corner of Sichuan Road, stands

The soaring 66-storey Le Royal Meridien at Nanjing Road (E) is a striking landmark just west of the Bund area.

Vegetable vendor at Yong An Road Market.

the **former Joint Savings Society Building**, today the **Guangdong Development Bank**. It was designed by Ladislau Hudec (1893–1958), the Czech architect who fled to Shanghai (and stayed there) after he escaped while en route to a POW camp in Siberia. Hudec's other architectural jewels include the Moore Church (see page 125) and the Park Hotel (see page 123).

Holy Trinity Church

Hóng Miào 红庙

Running parallel to Hankou Road is **Jiujiang Road**, the old banker's street, lined with stately banks in styles ranging from Victorian to Art Deco. At the junction with Jiangxi Road stands the 1866 **Holy Trinity Church**, a classic 19th-century Gothic church in eye-catching red brick – hence its Chinese name Hóng Miào, or Red Temple. The church – tucked behind trees and other adjoining buildings and hardly visible from the road – underwent a long renovation and there are vague plans to reconsecrate it as a church in the future.

The stained-glass rose window of Christ at St Joseph's Church.

Other significant buildings

Two blocks west of the Bund at the intersection with **Fuzhou Road** and **Central Jiangxi Road** are a quartet of buildings – three Art Deco skyscrapers and a low-rise building. On the northeast corner is the **former Metropole Hotel** (reopened as the Metropolo Hotel Classiq Bund Circle) and on the southeast corner its almost identical twin, the **former**

The modern Wanda Reign hotel opened in 2016.

Hamilton House (now apartments). Both were built by Victor Sassoon in the 1930s and designed by Palmer & Turner. On the northwest corner is the squat **former Shanghai Municipal Council Building**, now government offices; a manhole cover nearby reads "SMC PWD" (Shanghai Municipal Council Public Works Department). A short walk east of Fuzhou Road at **No. 209** is the lovely red-brick Georgian-style **former American Club**, built in 1924 and now standing empty.

Located three blocks west of the Bund is the stately 1923 neoclassical former Cotton Goods Exchange at 260 Yan'an Rd. Across the street is the red-brick Art Deco tower of the **former Chung Wai Bank**, now an office building. Next door is the **Bund Centre**, designed by John Portman Associates. The complex includes the **Westin** hotel, apartments and offices.

SOUTH BUND

Following the makeover of the iconic British-built Bund in 2010, attention has shifted to redeveloping the area south of Yan'an Road. Now known as South Bund, the riverfront is the focus of a massive "urban revitalisation project" designed to "grow the Bund" by 2.6 sq km (1 sq mile) and add 35 new skyscrapers by 2020.

A classy new international financial-service centre has sprung up, along with high-rise luxury offices and residences, shopping malls and art centres connected by landscaped public plazas, designed by global heavyweights like Foster + Partners and Heatherwick Studios. Hip hotels in the area include **Wanda Reign on the Bund**, opened in 2016, with towering views of the Bund and Pudong from its ultra-luxe, Deco-styled rooms and suites.

The new development extends westwards into the Old City area, with more than 100 historic buildings earmarked for conversion into offices,

shops and luxury apartments. In its wake, atmospheric old neighbourhoods have been demolished.

St Joseph's Church ㉕

Ruòsè Táng 若瑟堂
Address: 36 Sichuan Road (S)
Tel: 6328 0293
Opening Hrs: open to visitors Sat–Sun 1–4pm
Entrance Fee: free
Transport: East Nanjing Road

To the west are the lovely Gothic spires of the Catholic **St Joseph's Church**, rising like a fairytale castle next to the school it adjoins. Dating back to 1861, a large stained-glass rose window of Christ dominates the French-built church. Also of interest are the four niches holding statues on the building facade. The church underwent a facelift in 2007 and was given a fresh lick of paint. On Sunday mornings a church service is held in Chinese at 9.30am.

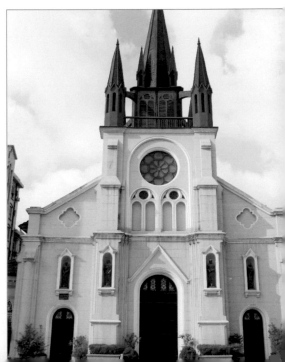

St Joseph's Church.

Relief from the sweltering summer heat in People's Square.

PEOPLE'S SQUARE

The main city-square area contains the best of modern Shanghai, including a world-class museum of Chinese artefacts, another devoted to contemporary art, and a magnificent theatre. But there's also the crush of Nanjing Road, with its remarkable concentration of shops.

The People's Square area is Shanghai's centre, its exact geographical midpoint in fact, according to the city's mapping and surveying department. Several of Shanghai's main metro lines converge at this town square, transporting people from all over the city to its cultural and political hub.

WITHIN PEOPLE'S SQUARE

The core of People's Square today is Showcase Shanghai: world-class museums, a theatre, five-star hotels, and the imposing Shanghai City Hall in the middle of it all. The buildings, all raised during the late 1990s and each one a significant architectural statement, seem to have been lifted from a futuristic urban planner's utopia. They also symbolise Shanghai's arrival as a city that can compete on its own merit on the world stage. With these buildings, no longer does the city government have to take pride in the historic Bund buildings, long a symbol of foreign oppression.

People's Square ❶

Rénmín Guǎngchǎng 人民广场
Opening Hrs: daily 24 hours
Entrance Fee: free
Transport: People's Square

Communal exercises at People's Park.

The perimeter of People's Square, bounded by Nanjing Road (W), Huangpi Road (N), Central Xizang Road and Wusheng Road, once defined pre-Liberation Shanghai's race-course, where millionaires would ride their steeds, and their wives would wager fans and sunbonnets because betting money was too, too vulgar. The wartime Japanese command used the racetrack as a holding camp and the post-war Kuomintang government turned it into a sports arena. By 1952, the

Main Attractions
Museum of Contemporary Art (MoCA)
Shanghai Grand Theatre
Shanghai Urban Planning Centre
Shanghai Museum
Moore Church

Map
Page 120

Enjoying a light moment at People's Park.

government had paved over part of the racetrack into a parade ground and turned the rest into a park for recreation.

People's Park (Renmin Gongyuan), just behind People's Square, is much smaller today than it was during the Concession days. Still, the park has pretty tree-lined paths, a small lake, rock gardens and the night-time haunt called **Barbarossa Lounge**, with its exotic *Arabian Nights*-inspired decor and sweet-smelling sheesha smoke.

Museum of Contemporary Art (MoCA) ❷

Shànghǎi Dāngdài Yìshù Guǎn 上海当代艺术馆

Address: 231 Nanjing Road (W), in People's Park; www.mocashanghai.org
Tel: 6327 9900
Opening Hrs: daily 10am–9.30pm
Entrance Fee: RMB 20
Transport: People's Square

In one corner of People's Park is the

Barbarossa Lounge at People's Park.

Museum of Contemporary Art, popularly known as MoCA Shanghai. It was the city's first independent contemporary art museum, funded by a Shanghai-born Hong Kong millionaire and focused on international and Chinese contemporary art. MoCA, though small, is renowned for its fun and thought-provoking modern art exhibitions: controversial French photographers Pierre and Gilles have exhibited here, as has Japanese artist Kusama Yayoi and Guggenheim's Art in America, which was hailed "the most in-depth exhibition of contemporary modern art to be presented in Shanghai". Exhibitions, which change every two months, are on the first two floors of this three-storey glass structure, while a restaurant with an outdoor terrace overlooking the park is on the third.

Former Shanghai Racing Club ❸

Shànghǎi Pao Ma Zong Hui 跑馬廳
Address: 325 Nanjing Road (W)

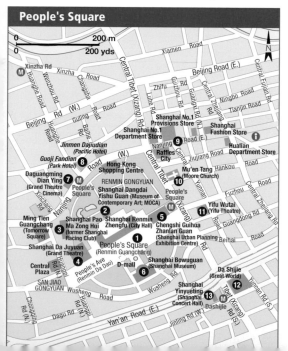

People's Square

0 ___ 200 m
0 ___ 200 yds

The former Shanghai Racing Club.

Transport: People's Square

Virtually the only remnant of People's Square racetrack days is the 1933 **former Shanghai Racing Club** – located just adjacent to MoCA. The letters SRC are still engraved over the granite building entrance, "Big Bertie", the nickname given to the clock tower, still ticks, and the horse heads on the ironwork banisters are still intact, but a renovation in 1999 removed the Turkish baths and bowling lanes. The building was utilised as the Shanghai Art Museum until its collection was transferred to the China Art Museum (see page 223) and its Shanghai Biennale to the larger Power Station of Art in 2013 (see page 144).

Shanghai Grand Theatre ④

Shànghǎi Dà Jùyuàn 上海大剧院
Address: 300 People's Avenue;
www.shgtheatre.com
Tel: 6372 8702 (tickets), 6372 3833
Opening Hrs: tours on Mondays only 9–11am

Entrance Fee: ticket price (for tours): RMB 40
Transport: People's Square

Just opposite is the **Shanghai Grand Theatre**, designed by much-lauded French architect Jean-Marie Charpentier. The futuristic glass confection has flamboyantly upturned eaves – mimicking a traditional Chinese roof – that glow magically at night when the lights come on. Completed in 1998 and dubbed the "Crystal Palace" by locals, the 10-storey theatre has a packed season of ballet, classical music and opera, as well as imported Broadway musicals and revolutionary operas. Tours, which take place only on Mondays, give you access to the high-tech stage; otherwise catch a performance here to appreciate its excellent acoustics.

Shanghai Urban Planning Exhibition Centre ⑤

Shànghǎi Chéngshì Guīhuà Zhǎnlǎn Guǎn 上海城市规划展览馆
Address: 100 People's Avenue; www.supec.org
Tel: 6372 2077

Performance at the Shanghai Grand Theatre.

Martial arts display at the forecourt of the Shanghai Urban Planning Exhibition Centre.

Scale model of Shanghai future at the Shanghai Urban Planning Exhibition Centre.

Opening Hrs: Tue–Thu 9am–5pm, Fri–Sun 9am–6pm
Entrance Fee: RMB 30 (audio guide); RMB 20
Transport: People's Square

To the east, just past the **Shanghai City Hall** (closed to the public), is the **Shanghai Urban Planning Exhibition Centre**. The centre helps to make some sense of the Shanghai building frenzy. Nearly a twin of the Grand Theatre in terms of design, the square building has the same clean lines of the former, though its startling flat roof is an almost kitschy departure.

The mezzanine floor tells the story of Shanghai's development from fishing village to Concession, the second floor houses temporary exhibitions, while the third floor focuses on the government's efforts at providing modern housing, with visitors offered a virtual tour of Shanghai in the "360 Degree Virtual Hall". The 500-sq-metre (5,380-sq-ft) scale model of downtown Shanghai depicts every building over six storeys high, including ones as yet unbuilt. The fourth floor displays the city's plans for the 21st century; visitors can also design their own city, while the top floor offers a cáfe with one of the best views in town. A re-creation of the Sino-Western architecture and *longtang* (lane) houses that dominated the pre-Liberation era is found in the basement.

Shanghai Museum ❻

Shànghǎi Bówùguǎn 上海博物馆
Address: 201 People's Avenue; www.shanghai museum.net
Tel: 6372 3500
Opening Hrs: daily 9am–5pm; closed Mon for renovation works until the construction of new museum in Pudong is complete
Entrance Fee: free; acoustiguide rental RMB 40 (plus RMB 400 or passport for deposit)
Transport: People's Square

A landscaped plaza fronts **Shanghai Museum** across the street. The neatly manicured gardens and flowerbeds are dominated by a soaring musical fountain, whose jets cool children during the steamy summer months. Allow a full morning, at least, to tour the museum. Designed by Chinese architect Xing Tonghe, the massive granite structure was officially opened in 1996. It also has an excellent museum boutique for Shanghai gifts and souvenirs.

Shaped like a *ding*, an ancient round bronze tripod cooking vessel, the museum focuses on the arts and crafts of China in its 11 permanent galleries, arranged thematically across four floors. Beautifully laid out and lit, with informative introductory panels in each gallery, the museum houses one of the largest collections of Chinese art in the world and is easily the best in the country.

Museum highlights include the **Ancient Chinese Bronze Gallery**, which features one of the world's finest and most comprehensive collections of bronzes; and the **Ancient Chinese Ceramic Gallery**, which traces this born-in-China craft from

the Neolithic Yellow River cultures to the Qing dynasty. Other must-sees include the nation's largest and most extensive collection of Chinese paintings in the **Chinese Painting Gallery**, the **Ancient Chinese Jade Gallery** and the colourful **Chinese Minorities Nationalities Gallery**.

AROUND PEOPLE'S SQUARE

One of People's Square's great attractions was that all around the sparkling core – like an antique frame – is a historic ring of the legends that defined the Shanghai of yore: the tallest hotel, the best theatre and the wildest entertainment. These wonders of Old Shanghai now stand in the shadows of several modern high-rise structures, creating a rich and contrasting texture. Today, it's the plush **JW Marriot** hotel (contained within the skyscraping and pincer-edged **Tomorrow Square** building) that looms over the old-world **Park Hotel** and glitzy malls overshadow Shanghai's original "Big Four Department Stores" along busy Nanjing Road (E), the city's main shopping thoroughfare.

Grand Theatre Cinema ➐

Dàguāngmíng Diànyǐngyuàn 大光明电影院
Address: 216 Nanjing Road (W); www.jinjianghotels.com
Tel: 6327 5225
Transport: People's Square

Follow Nanjing Road (W) northeast for a look at the gracious old buildings that once defined progressive Shanghai. Originally opened in 1933 and named the Grand Theatre, the 2,000-seat cinema built by Czech architect Ladislau Hudec was the finest of its time in China. Step inside to see its lively Art Deco lobby. For a more in-depth glimpse of its past, the History Walk (entrance at 248 Nanjing Road West; no charge) tells the Grand's storied, and often controversial, history through photos, newspaper ads and movie clips.

Park Hotel ➑

Guójì Fàndiàn 国际饭店
Address: 170 Nanjing Road (W); www.jinjianghotels.com
Tel: 6327 5225
Transport: People's Square

Park Hotel is another important historical landmark here. In his

TIP

The Acoustiguide is a great resource for more in-depth overviews of and insights into Shanghai Museum's galleries. The guides at the entrance of each gallery can also provide more detailed information if required.

The Shanghai Museum is shaped like a ding vessel.

For those who can't be bothered to walk, hop on one of the trams that ply up and down the length of pedestrianised Nanjing Road (E). Bear in mind, however, that the trams are incredibly slow, so it might actually be quicker on foot.

Nanjing Road East.

memoirs, Shanghai-born architect I.M. Pei recalls seeing the just-completed 24-storey hotel, another Hudec masterpiece. Immediately Pei took out his pencil and began drawing the Park Hotel's Art Deco outline, citing this moment as the inspiration for his career. The hotel's interior has been renovated and its status as Asia's tallest building long since surpassed, but the Park's brown-tiled tower still dominates this section of Nanjing Road (W).

Built in 1934 for the Joint Savings Society, the Park Hotel also served as the first hotel school for Chinese students. Step into the lobby to see the marker for the geographical centre of Shanghai.

Next door is the **Shanghai Sports Association**, formerly the Foreign YMCA Building, with its beautiful beige brick exterior and third-storey rooftop garden.

Continue east along Nanjing Road (W). When the eight-storey **Pacific Hotel** (Jinmen Dajiudian) was built in 1924 at 108 Nanjing Road (W) as the Union Insurance Building, it was the tallest building in the city and its bell tower was used by ships for navigation.

The Art Deco Park Hotel dates back to 1934.

Nanjing Road (E) shops

Further east along Nanjing Road (W), following the curve of the old racetrack for about five minutes, you are rewarded with a glimpse of where young Shanghai shops and eats – **Raffles City** (268 Central Xizang Road). The shopping mall is filled with brand names like French Connection and Starbucks, and also houses an IMAX Theatre.

From here, it's a short five-minute walk to the **pedestrian section** of **Nanjing Road** (E), once the city's preeminent shopping street. The street, with its bright, flashy neon lights and carnival-like atmosphere, is now overshadowed by swankier malls elsewhere in the city, but it's still packed with Chinese tourists, particularly the pedestrian strip from **Tibet Road** (Xizang Lu) eastwards to as far as **Central Henan Road**. A giant screen shows commercials, couples snuggle at street corners and a tourist tram plies the pedestrian street. Most of the older shops have now acquired a glossy look, including Shanghai's famous "Big Four" department stores, staples of Old Shanghai which have

all been refurbished and updated for a new generation: **No. 1 Department Store** (formerly Sun) at 800 Nanjing Road (E); **Shanghai No. 1 Provisions Store** (formerly Sun Sun) at 700 Nanjing Road (E); **Hualian Department Store** (formerly Wing On) at 635 Nanjing Road (E), with a roof garden; and **Shanghai Fashion Store** (formerly Sincere) at 660 Nanjing Road (E).

Moore Church ⑩

Mù'ēn Táng 沐恩堂
Address: 316 Xizang Road (M)
Tel: 6322 5069
Opening Hrs: services: Sun 7.30am, 9am, 2pm and 7pm
Entrance Fee: free
Transport: People's Square

South of Nanjing Road (E) is the red-brick **Moore Church**. Originally named the Arthur J. Moore Memorial Church after the Texan who donated funds for its construction in the late 1920s, the Methodist church was rebuilt by the Czech architect Ladislau Hudec in 1931. The structure features Hudec's characteristically innovative design elements, like the concave-and-convex brickwork that is used to encase the structure. Used as a middle school

during the Cultural Revolution, it was the first church in Shanghai to reopen post-Cultural Revolution (in 1979) and the first to consecrate bishops (in 1988).

Subterranean shopping

From Moore Church, descend into the **Hong Kong Shopping Centre** (Xiang Gang Zhongxin; accessible through People's Square metro station exit 1), at the corner of Tibet Road and Fuzhou Road, for a little underground shopping. The subterranean mall leads to **D-mall** (Dimei Gouwu Zhongxin; entrance also north of the People's Square fountain), an underground rabbit warren of hip fashion boutiques.

Yifu Theatre ⑪

Yīfū Wǔtái 逸夫舞台

About a block south, at 701 Fuzhou Road is the **Yifu Theatre**, which hosts regular performances of colourful Beijing opera (1.30pm and 7.15pm; tel: 6322 5294) as well as other forms of traditional Chinese opera.

Great World ⑫

Dà Shìjiè 大世界

Three blocks south is an ornate wedding-cake structure, on the corner of

Shanghai Fashion Store.

Yan'an and Tibet Road. This is **Great World** whose colourful history is part of Shanghai lore. This was where scions of Shanghai's first families lost their fortunes. It also hosted all kinds of performances, including opera, dance and acrobatics.

The building sat empty for more than a decade as the government debated its next incarnation. Its kooky original exterior has been preserved while the interiors were completely refurbished by Xing Tonghe of Shanghai Museum fame. It was finally reopened in November 2016 as the **Shanghai Intangible Cultural Heritage Exhibition Centre**, showcasing stage arts and handicrafts from sword dancing to paper cutting and lantern making. Great World's popular 12 "distorting mirrors" in the lobby have also been incorporated into the new design. Its reopening comes in time for the centennial anniversary of this historic amusement-arcade venue in 2017.

Shanghai Philharmonic Orchestra rehearsing at the Shanghai Concert Hall.

Shanghai Concert Hall ⓭

Shànghǎi Yīnyuètīng 上海音乐厅
One block west along Yan'an Road is the 1930 neoclassical **Shanghai**

Beijing opera performer at the Yifu Theatre.

Concert Hall, ensconced in a lovely park setting. The concert hall, originally the Nanjing Theatre, was uprooted from its original spot in June 2003 and rolled 66.46 metres (218 ft) southeast to make way for an extension of the Yan'an highway. It has been beautifully renovated and is now home to the **Shanghai Philharmonic Orchestra**, the city's second major orchestra (tickets available from www.culture.sh.cn/english).

SHANGHAI MUSEUM

China's finest collection of ancient arts and crafts are housed in this modern museum shaped like a *ding* food vessel.

THE FIRST FLOOR

Ancient Chinese Bronze Gallery

It is hard to match this exquisite curation of Chinese bronzes. Arguably the best and most complete collection found anywhere across the globe, it includes several very rare pieces going back to China's first dynasty, the Xia (21st to 16th century BC). Highlights include a Shang dynasty square *lei*, or wine vessel, with finely-crafted dragons; a Western Zhou dynasty bell embellished with tigers; and an enormous *jian* wine vessel, with four mythical creatures grasping the rim and peeking into it – taken from the tomb of King Fu Chai of the Wu Kingdom.

Ancient Chinese Sculpture Gallery

This gallery features beautifully rendered sculptures from the Warring States period through the Ming dynasty, most of it religious in theme. The Buddha sculptures reflect the artistic styles of the period, from the delicate, ethereal figures of the Northern Qi and Sui periods to the realistic depictions of the Tang dynasty and the classical figures of the Song dynasty.

The finely wrought Buddhist statues in the Ancient Chinese Sculpture Gallery illustrate how the early images of Buddha, depicted with distinctly Indian features, gradually take on a more Chinese appearance as Buddhism becomes more and more entrenched in China.

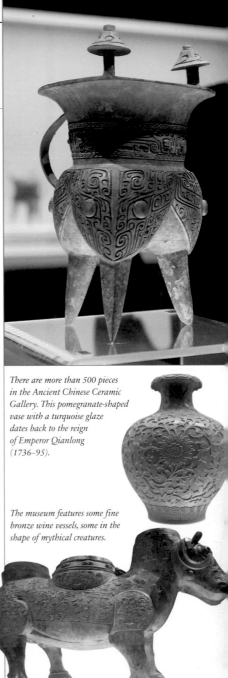

There are more than 500 pieces in the Ancient Chinese Ceramic Gallery. This pomegranate-shaped vase with a turquoise glaze dates back to the reign of Emperor Qianlong (1736–95).

The museum features some fine bronze wine vessels, some in the shape of mythical creatures.

THE SECOND FLOOR

Ancient Chinese Ceramic Gallery

This gallery looks at fascinating Chinese ceramics from their birth along the Yellow River in the Neolithic period to the Qing dynasty, including the development of celadon. Especially beautiful are the delicate Tang dynasty Sancai ceramics with their three-colour glazes, and blue and white Ming and Qing pieces. The Zande Tower Ceramic Gallery, adjacent to the main ceramics exhibit, displays 130 masterpieces from the Jin to the end of the Qing dynasty, many of

which are Qing imperial ware. As you exit, there is also a fascinating potter's workshop, model kilns and, sometimes, pottery-making demonstrations.

The bronze items on display in the Ancient Chinese Bronze Gallery are laid out chronologically, and include exquisitely wrought food vessels called ding.

The Chinese Painting Gallery's 120 masterpieces, dating from the Tang dynasty, are displayed behind glass panels arranged along corridors. Automatic sensors cast light onto the paintings only when the viewer is in front of them.

Seals, or chops – see next page – feature elaborately designed knobs that vary according to the rank of the owner. Royalty and important officials had separate seals for private and official use.

The rare pieces of ancient calligraphy in the Chinese Calligraphy Gallery include early paper rubbings from stone and bronzes.

THE THIRD FLOOR

Chinese Painting Gallery

This is where you'll find a rotating exhibit of the country's largest collection of Chinese paintings, including Tang and Song dynasty album leaves and hand scrolls, and masterpieces such as the *Eight Noble Monks* by Liang Kai and *Misty River and Mountains* by Wang Shen, as well as works by masters of the Yuan, Ming and Qing dynasties.

Chinese Calligraphy Gallery

This is perhaps the most challenging gallery for foreigners who can't read Chinese. It traces the development of this ancient form of brushstroke writing, from early inscriptions on tiny oracle bones to flowing Qing dynasty scripts. The chronological display shows the development of the art, featuring major styles and the works of the masters.

Chinese Seal Gallery

The world's first gallery devoted to the Chinese seal displays 500 intricately carved seals from the museum's stored collection of 10,000. The seals, which cover the period from the Western Zhou to the Qing dynasty, served as signatures in ancient letters and contracts. On display are seals made of ivory, jade, amber and crystal.

The Calligraphy Gallery showcases different writing styles, of which there are four basic types: zhenshu (regular script), caoshu (cursive script), lishu (official script) and zhuan shu (seal character script).

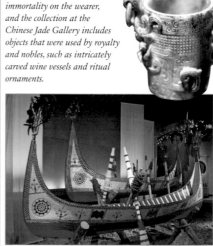

Jade was supposed to bestow immortality on the wearer, and the collection at the Chinese Jade Gallery includes objects that were used by royalty and nobles, such as intricately carved wine vessels and ritual ornaments.

Exhibits at the Chinese Minority Nationalities' Art Gallery include handcrafted fishing boats made without the use of nails.

In the Furniture Gallery, rooms are laid out with antique pieces as they would have been in a traditional Chinese house.

Carved wooden masks used in rituals and dances are displayed in the Chinese Minority Nationalities' Art Gallery.

THE FOURTH FLOOR

Chinese Ming and Qing Furniture Gallery

The furniture gallery showcases the spare, clean lines of Ming dynasty furniture, as well as the more Baroque influence of the Qing era. It offers a look at originals of much-copied pieces, and an insight into the unique Chinese method of joining two pieces of wood, which uses no nails.

Ancient Chinese Jade Gallery

The museum's impressive collection of jade features a display that runs from the Neolithic period to the Qing dynasty, with a range of jade objects used for ritual, burial and as ornamentation.

Chinese Minority Nationalities' Art Gallery

This gallery – always a hit with the children because of its visual appeal – showcases over 600 handicrafts from China's 56 ethnic minorities: costumes, textiles, embroidery, metalware, sculpture, pottery, lacquerware, food and water vessels, and a stunning collection of wooden masks.

Chinese Currency Gallery

This gallery displays currencies through the ages – from the shell money of the Neolithic period to the gold Persian coins from the Silk Road. There is also currency from the Concession-era banks.

At the end of your visit, don't miss the gift boutique on the ground floor, which stocks a smartly curated selection of Shanghai-themed gifts and souvenirs, from children's books to jade jewellery, and jigsaw puzzles to silk robes.

The Chinese Currency Gallery displays ancient copper coins with a square hole in the middle, which allowed a string to be threaded through. Less common are coins in the shape of ingots, spades and knives.

Classical Suzhou-style Yu Garden dates from the 16th century.

THE OLD CITY

Visit the famous Yu Garden and its adjoining bazaar by all means, but to see the real China wander around the Old City's narrow lanes and crowded markets, and experience the sights and sounds of a vanishing way of life.

While parts of Shanghai's original city, **Nanshi** ("Southern City" and better known today as the **Old City**), may be self-consciously Chinese, like a theme-park vision of Ming China, the spirit of the Old City remains very much alive in the tightly packed lanes and crowded old markets along the backstreets, full of the constant din of *renao*, the electric buzz that defines Shanghai.

There is still plenty of life in the lanes. A walk along an old lane may be rewarded by scenes of children playing in the streets, chamber pots being washed out, and women shelling peas outside century-old doors. Shanghai's Chinese population was supposed to live in the Old City during the Concession era, but that stricture quickly broke down.

The Chinese soon lived throughout the Concessions – they paid taxes, but had no voice in the municipal government – leaving the Old City purely, utterly Chinese, with its mysterious maze of lanes.

Some 2,000 years before foreigners arrived, a small fishing town called Hu already existed on the site of today's Old City. Renamed Shanghai in 1280, the original settlement here grew and became

rich, although it never gained any historical importance. In the 1550s, Japanese pirate incursions instigated the building of a 4.8km (3-mile) long and 8-metre (27ft) high wall and a moat enclosing the city. The structure had two watchtowers and six gates that were firmly locked at midnight. The Kuomintang demolished the wall, but its contours still define the 4-sq-km (1.5-sq-mile) area of the Old City. The "walls" today are the high-speed highways of Renmin Road and Zhonghua Road.

Main Attractions

Baiyun Taoist Temple
Chenxiangge Nunnery
Yu Garden Bazaar
Huxinting Teahouse
Yu Garden
Confucius Temple
Dongjiadu Cathedral
Museum of Folk Art

Map

Page 134

Performance at Yu Bazaar.

ALONG RENMIN ROAD

Just along **Renmin Road**, which today defines the western and northern limits of the Old City, as well as just off it, are several historic sights and temples worth seeing.

Dajing Tower ❶

Dàjìnggé 大境阁
Address: 269 Dajing Road (at Renmin Road)
Opening Hrs: daily 9am–4pm
Entrance Fee: RMB 5
Transport: Dashijie

The only remaining section of the city wall makes an ideal entry point to the Old City. **Dajing Tower** is a 1995 recreation of the wall, attached to a refurbished Ming temple – the former War Gods Temple, which was built in 1553. The "Exhibition of the History of Old Shanghai Town", inside the building, is entirely in Chinese, but offers an interesting collection of photographs of life in the old days – its festivals, markets and history, along with a miniature model of the Old City's original layout.

Baiyun Taoist Temple ❷

Báiyún Guàn 白云观
Address: 239 Dajing Road

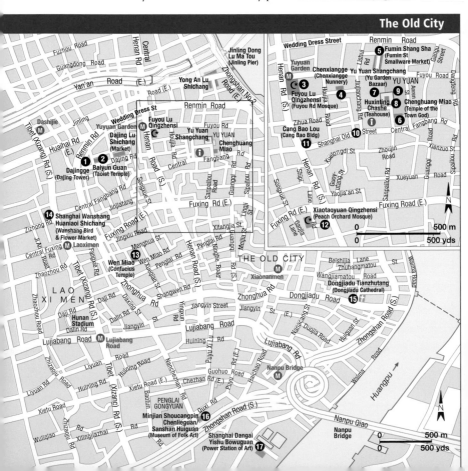
The Old City

(at Renmin Road)
Opening Hrs: daily 8am–4.30pm
Entrance Fee: RMB 5
Transport: Dashijie

Turn left as you exit Dajing Tower for a look at the **Small North Gate**, the only original city gate still standing. Just adjacent, the quietness of **Baiyun Taoist Temple**, which dates back to 1873, belies its historical importance for Shanghai's Taoists. In 1882, Taoist monk Xi Zhicheng extended the temple on this site, called Leizu (Ancestor of Thunder). In 1888, when Xi brought over 8,000 scriptures from Beijing's Baiyun Temple, Leizu was renamed Baiyun Temple.

The temple's three halls were built in 1892, but sustained major damage during the Cultural Revolution, including the destruction of its magnificent collection of paintings and scriptures. The restored Baiyun now proudly displays its seven bronze Taoist gods and is once again a functioning temple. Baiyun also serves as the headquarters for Shanghai's Taoist Association, as well as a research centre for Taoist culture.

FUYOU ROAD TO YU GARDEN

Continue south along **Henan Road (S)** and turn right into **Fuyou Road** where a mosque, a nunnery and some bargain shopping are clustered.

Fuyou Road Mosque ❸

Fúyòu Lù Qīngzhēnsì 福佑路清真寺
Address: Fuyou Road at Henan Road (S)
Opening Hrs: daily 6am–7pm
Entrance Fee: free
Transport: Yuyuan

Right at the junction is **Fuyou Road Mosque**, which comprises three connecting halls. This is a run-down but still intact Qing-era Chinese courtyard building that was the city's first mosque, built in 1853 by Muslim traders and still used today.

Chenxiangge Nunnery ❹

Chénxiānggé 沉香阁
Address: 29 Chenxiangge Road
Opening Hrs: daily 7am–4pm

Statue of a Chinese deity at the Baiyun Taoist Temple.

Part of the Old City wall at Dajing Tower.

Entrance Fee: RMB 5
Transport: Yuyuan

Further down Fuyou Road on the
right, the vibrant mustard walls
of **Chenxiangge Nunnery** indicate Shanghai's largest Buddhist
nunnery (entrance around the
corner, along Chenxiang Road).
Pan Yunduan, who created the Yu
Garden, established this temple in
honour of his mother in 1600. After
a brief interlude as a factory during
the Cultural Revolution, the temple was restored in 1989. Its centrepiece is a gilded Buddha, and there
is a collection of 18 gilded *arhats*
(Buddhist saints).

Charming back lanes

Heading east on **Fuyou Road** leads
to one of the area's prime attractions for shoppers: the **Fuyou Road
Merchandise Mart** (Fuyou Lu Shichang) and the **Fumin Street Smallware Market ❺** (Fumin Shang Sha;
both daily 8am–5pm). These two
warehouse-sized clusters of shops are
stocked with what seems like everything under the sun. China was once
the world's factory, and these markets seem to sell it all – and at heavily
discounted prices too. The range of

Taoist statues at Baiyun Temple.

goods is truly mind-boggling, and
combing the market, plus the shops
outside the buildings, will take a
dedicated shopper hours.

From Fuyou Road, turn right into
Anren Street, a historic lane where
life goes on as it has for centuries, to
Central Fangbang Road.

Turn left here and follow the street
until it becomes a lane lined with
19th-century buildings filled with
old apothecaries, pickle stores with
gigantic jars, and Shaoxing wine
merchants, transporting you into a
medieval time warp.

*Chenxiangge Nunnery
dates back to the 1600s.*

Foodies should take a detour off the street to **Sipailou Road**, lined with some of the city's most delicious street food: from fried noodles, dumplings, kebabs and breads to cotton candy pumped from vintage machines and sugared fruit speared onto sticks.

YU GARDEN AREA

This is the Shanghai of classical gardens and temples, teahouses, bazaars and traditional delicacies. But this is still Shanghai – expect an Old China that is perpetually being reinvented, the bazaars tarted up, the traditional delicacies given creative twists, and the antiques remade.

Temple of the Town God ⑥

Chénghuáng Miào 城隍庙
Address: 249 Central Fangbang Road
Opening Hrs: daily 8.30am–4.30pm
Entrance Fee: RMB 10
Transport: Yuyuan

Return along Central Fangbang Road to the **Temple of the Town God**, dedicated to the gods that protect Shanghai. Each city in Old China had a town god temple that served as its hub, a place where traders gathered and festivals were celebrated; this tradition continues at the adjoining bazaar. Built in 1726, the Temple of the Town God succeeded the 15th-century Jinshan Miao (Golden Hills Temple) and, like the latter, is dedicated to the legendary general Huo Guang. After it was used as a factory during the Cultural Revolution, images of the general and his Taoist deities were restored – look out for the ones sporting British bowler hats.

Yu Garden Bazaar ⑦

Yù Yuán Shāngchéng 豫园商城
Address: 218 Anren Street
Opening Hrs: daily 7am–late night
Transport: Yuyuan

Exit the temple and turn right to enter **Yu Garden Bazaar** – a bold and brash, vehicle-free, reinvented Ming-era Chinese experience centred around speciality shops and delicious local snacks (but there's Starbucks and Häagen-Dazs too).

Among the bazaar's newly minted Ming-style buildings housing restaurants, food stalls and hundreds of small speciality shops are a labyrinth of lanes, made all the more confusing by the pressing crowds. The central plaza is an endless source of entertainment: toy vendors demonstrate their products, street performers awe the crowds, and tourists bounce along in sedan chair rides – just like in the days of the Old City.

There are larger department stores selling overpriced jewellery and antiques, but the individual speciality shops make for more interesting browsing. A sight to behold are the shops specialising in goods like chopsticks, canes, buttons, fans, kites and scissors. The bustling commerce spills onto the streets that ring the bazaar, and these are lined with more shops selling everything from Chinese decorations to kitchen equipment.

Temple bells are rung on special festival days.

Gilded deities at the Temple of the Town God.

The Huixinting Teahouse is supposed to be the subject of the "Blue Willow" pattern plates, first created in 1790 by Josiah Spode during the heyday of the china trade. He based it on an original pattern called the Mandarin.

Famous Shanghai snacks

Yu Garden Bazaar is known for its snacks. Follow the signs to **Nanxiang Mantou Dian**, which is encircled by the most popular food stalls in the bazaar. Domestic tourists line up here for a taste of Shanghai's famous delicacies: the bite-sized, translucent *xiao long bao* (pork dumplings) from Nanxiang, *anchun jiao*zi (sweet glutinous rice pigeon-egg dumplings) and *meimao su*, or eyebrow-shaped shortcakes. The queues for the snacks are almost always worthwhile, but for those who can't be bothered and don't mind paying more, there are the Old City's famous restaurants. Places such as **Shanghai Classic Restaurant**, which has been in business since 1875, and **Green Wave Pavilion** all serve the famous snacks along with a menu of Shanghainese dishes – but unless you're there for breakfast, the atmosphere is too much that of a tour-bus stop.

Huxinting Teahouse ❽

Húxīntíng Cháshè 湖心亭茶社
Address: Yuyuan Bazaar, opposite Yu Garden

Vendor at the Fumin Street Smallware Market.

Tel: 6373 6950
Opening Hrs: daily 8am–9pm
Transport: Yuyuan

Cross the zigzag **Bridge of Nine Turnings** (Jiuquqiao) – which seems to have acquired a few more turns

Rock gardens and pavilions at the Yu Garden.

over the years. The theory is that evil spirits cannot turn corners, thus protecting **Huxinting Teahouse**, found mid-way across the bridge and set in the centre of a man-made lake.

Perhaps because the five-sided teahouse, with its classical pointed roof, has hosted the likes of Queen Elizabeth and Bill Clinton, a cup of tea here costs RMB 50. Still, sipping delicate Chinese tea from a Yixing teacup on the second floor, to views of willows and the tops of the trees in Yu Garden, is a rare experience. If you prefer a caffeine-free version, opt for one of the flower teas (like the fairy jasmine). Most tourists get a thrill when they see the flowers unfurling after hot water is poured into the glass teapot.

Yu Garden ❾

Yù Yuán 豫园
Address: Yuyuan Bazaar, opposite Huxinting Teahouse; entrance also at 218 Anren Street
Opening Hrs: daily 8.30am–5.30pm
Entrance Fee: RMB 40
Transport: Yuyuan

At the centre of the bazaar is Shanghai's most famous garden, the 16th-century **Yu Garden**. Referred to in

Shoppers in Yu Garden Bazaar.

local maps and literature as Yuyuan Garden, it occupies the northern part of the Old City. The garden was built in 1577 by Ming dynasty official Pan Yunduan to please his elderly father – "Yu" means peace and comfort. After years of neglect, the garden was restored in the mid-18th century.

Yu Garden, its walls encircled by an undulating dragon, is a petite 2-hectare (5-acre) classical Suzhou-style garden that has all the ingredients that create a microcosm of the universe – the defining hallmark of the classical Chinese garden. It has 30 pavilions connected by bridges and walkways, interspersed with fishpools, rockeries and ingenious views.

The **Grand Rockery** (Dajiashan), a gigantic sculpture of pale yellow rocks from Zhejiang province, stands 14 metres (46ft) tall as the centrepiece of the garden, with the best views from the aptly named **Hall for Viewing Grand Rockery** (Dajiashan Tang) that stands just opposite the rocks.

On the garden's east side is the enormous **Exquisite Jade Rock** (Yu Ling Long), acquired by the Pan family when the boat carrying the rock to the emperor in Beijing sank off

The Bridge of Nine Turnings that leads to Huxinting Teahouse.

YIXING'S TINY TEAPOTS

At the Huxinting Teahouse, waitresses pour tea from the tiny maroon-brown spout of a Yixing teapot, the vessel that tea connoisseurs say brews the finest tea. Made from the purple clay found only in Jiangsu province's Yixing county, the teapots are unglazed, both inside and out, and this porous quality allows it to become seasoned over time from both the colour and flavour of the tea. Usually, only one type of tea is used in a pot to maintain its purity.

The Yixing teapot was first created during the 10th century, and flourished during the Ming dynasty. The tiny teapots were originally created for personal use. During the Ming dynasty, their owners carried around the pocket-sized teapots, and tea would be drunk directly from the spout.

Tea experts say that a quality teapot should be rough, both on the outside and on the inside, make a clear sound when struck, and the tea should pour out from the spout in a smooth arc.

TIP

Unfortunately, Yu Garden is often invaded by huge tourist groups with loudspeaker-blasting guides, crowding what is meant to be a space for quiet contemplation. To avoid this, visit at 8.30am, when the gardens open.

Shanghai Old Street (Shanghai Laojie).

the coast of Shanghai. Also on this side is the **Hall of Heralding Spring** (Dianchun Tang), which in the early 1850s served as the headquarters of the Small Swords Society, the local branch of the Taiping rebels. A small museum in the hall recounts the Taiping Rebellion, China's first large-scale peasant uprising.

Shanghai Old Street ⑩

Shànghǎi Lǎojiē 上海老街
Address: Central Fangbang Road at Henan Road (S)
Opening Hrs: shops open daily 8am–6pm
Transport: Yuyuan

Exit the bazaar the same way you came, and continue down Central Fangbang Road to **Shanghai Old Street**, which runs for a section along Central Fangbang Road, east of Henan Road, and ends roughly at Anren Street. The street is lined with two-storey buildings that progress architecturally from the Ming

Cheap shoes for sale on Shanghai Old Street.

to the Qing and to the Kuomintang eras. The shops sell traditional Chinese-themed souvenirs: the famous "purple clay" Yixing tea-pots, Chinese lanterns and crafts, tea blends, temple paraphernalia and antiques.

Also on this street is the retro **Old Shanghai Teahouse** (Lao Shanghai Chaguan) at 385 Fangbang Road, where you can capture the soul of Old Shanghai over a leisurely cup of tea, sipped amidst surroundings filled with historical maps, pictures and collectables.

Cang Bao Building ⑪

Cáng Bǎo Lóu 藏宝楼
Address: 459 Fangbang Road
Opening Hrs: daily 5am–5pm
Transport: Yuyuan

Close to the junction of Central Fangbang Road and Henan Road is **Cang Bao Building**. The five-storey building with the Chinese roof, the tallest structure in the area, is fairly quiet on weekdays, but turns into a lively antiques market at weekends. Then, as early as 5am, traders begin laying out their wares on the top floor, and shop owners from all over the city begin jamming the aisles.

The Cang Bao Building is a successor to the former Fuyou Road Sunday market and still has that street market feel to it; most of the "antiques" are obviously scrounged from homes and have more sentimental than antique value. Even if you don't buy anything, just browsing gives an insight into Old Shanghai. This is especially true on the fourth floor, where vendors sell relics from the Concession era, such as monogrammed cutlery from the old clubs, factory cards, photographs from the old studios and rare books.

The third-floor furniture corner has a good supply of Shanghai Art Deco pieces from the 1920s and 1930s, including fixtures such as doorknobs, while the first and second floors have smaller collectables, including vintage clocks, watches and genuine Shanghai advertising posters from the 1930s.

Peach Orchard Mosque ⑫

Xiǎotáoyuán Qīngzhēnsì
小桃园清真寺
Address: 52 Xiaotaoyuan Road
Opening Hrs: daily 8am – 7pm
Entrance Fee: free
Transport: Yuyuan

Turn right as you exit Cang Bao Building, head west across busy Henan Road and then south across Fuxing Road (E) to **Peach Orchard Mosque**, where Shanghai's Chinese Muslim community, the Hui people, worship. The mosque, with its distinctive green spheres on the roof, was built in 1917 and renovated in 1925, but is surprisingly modernist with its restrained fusion of Arabic, Western and Chinese architecture. Look out for the round Art Deco windows more frequently seen in the French Concession area.

Confucius Temple ⑬

Wén Miào 文庙
Address: 215 Wen Miao Road

Settle down with a cup of tea at Old Shanghai Teahouse and enjoy its collection of memorabilia.

Ethnic pottery at Cang Bao Lou.

Confession booth at Dongjiadu Cathedral.

Pretty Dongjiadu Cathedral.

Opening Hrs: daily 9am–4.30pm
Entrance Fee: RMB 10
Transport: Laoximen

Students – and their anxious parents – still pray at the **Confucius Temple**, just south of the Peach Orchard Mosque, especially during "black June", the time of the gruelling three-day college entrance exams. As Confucius is the patron of scholars, the literary theme is strong here.

Of note are the **God of Literature Pavilion** (Kui Xing Ge), with its Chinese arched roof, and the **Respecting Classics Tower** (Zun Jing Ge), a library for Chinese classics that also served as the state library during the Kuomintang period, and a lecture hall. The last served a less than literary purpose during the Taiping Rebellion as the headquarters of the movement's Shanghai branch, the Small Swords Society.

The origins of the temple date back to the 13th century, but what you mostly see is an 1855 reconstruction. Its relatively new sheen comes from more recent renovations. The literary theme continues in an informal Sunday book market, adjacent to the temple in a courtyard surrounded by recreated temple buildings.

BEYOND THE OLD CITY

South of the Old City is an area undergoing change from 1970s housing blocks to modern high-rises. Scattered here and there are unexpected gems well worth seeking out, like a 19th-century Spanish church and a delightful museum devoted to Chinese folk art.

Shanghai Wanshang Bird & Flower Market ⑭

Shànghǎi Wànshāng Huāniǎo

Shìchǎng 上海万商花鸟市场
Address: Dongtai Road
Opening Hrs: daily 8am–5pm
Transport: Renmin Square + taxi

Shanghai's increasing wealth has meant a proportionate increase in luxury items – such as pets. An entire menagerie of animals are sold at the **Shanghai Wanshang Bird & Flower Market**. The covered pet section is stocked with puppies, kittens, rabbits, hamsters and pot-bellied pigs, and a good selection of birds and impressive handmade cages.

During the summer cricket season, an entire segment is devoted to the chirping insects – valued either for their singing prowess or fighting skills. Keeping crickets as pets is a tradition that goes back to the Tang dynasty. These critters are kept in special containers made from ceramic or bamboo. It's not uncommon to see grown men hunched over these creatures, coaxing them to either shrill merrily or to do battle with other crickets.

Dongjiadu Cathedral 15

Dǒngjiādù Tiānzhǔtáng
董家渡天主堂
Address: 185 Dongjiadu Road
Tel: 6378 7214
Opening Hrs: services: Mon–Sat 7am, Sun 6am, 8am
Transport: Laoximen

The Moorish Baroque church, built by the Spanish Jesuits in 1853 and originally called St Xavier Cathedral, was Shanghai's first Catholic church. It is still an active church, holding daily mass in Chinese at 7am, with two services on Sunday at 6 and 8am.

Museum of Folk Art 16

Mínjiān Shōucángpǐn Chénlièguǎn/ Sānshān Huìguǎn 民间收藏品陈列馆/三山会馆
Address: 1551 Zhongshan Road (S)
Tel: 6313 5582

Opening Hrs: Tue–Sun 9am–4pm
Entrance Fee: free
Transport: South Xizang Road

Shanghai has an estimated 100,000 collectors, and many of these exhibit their often arcane collections at the **Museum of Folk Art**. Past exhibitions here have included butterflies, tiny shoes

Songbirds, Wanshang Market.

Crickets for sale at Shanghai Wanshang Market.

Museum of Folk Art.

Altar and sacristy at Dongjiadu Cathedral.

beams and upturned roofs is worth a visit on its own. Built in 1909 as the Sanshan Guild Hall (Sanshan Huiguan) with funds raised by a Shanghai-based Fujian fruit dealer, the hall is the only remaining one of several Chinese-style structures that used to line this area.

Power Station of Art ⑰

Dāngaì Yìshù Bówùguǎn
上海当代艺术博物馆
Address: 200 Huayuangang Road
Opening Hrs: Tue–Sun 11am–7pm
Transport: South Xizang Road

Housed in a former power station, this impressive space is China's first state-run modern art museum, opened in October 2012. Covering 42,000 sq metres (452,100 sq ft), the old Nanshi Power Plant was also the Pavilion of the Future during the 2010 Shanghai World Expo before its current incarnation as the **Power Station of Art**. Important exhibitions include the Shanghai Biennale, which was relocated here from the former Shanghai Art Museum in 2013.

for bound feet, cigarette labels from the 1930s, school badges and ship models. The Chinese-style museum building with its carved

Villa in the former French Concession.

FUXING PARK AND ENVIRONS

The streets of the former French Concession, where revolutionary icons like Sun Yat-sen and Zhou Enlai once lived, still hold vestiges of its elegant past in the form of old churches and mansions. Many have been turned into restaurants and nightspots.

One of the most expensive districts in the city, the Fuxing Park neighbourhood continues to attract high-living sybarites of all nationalities, clustered into an area that boasts concentrations of luxury shopping and stylish dining within an urban landscape of refurbished historic buildings, sleek high-rises and romanticised *longtang* (lane) housing.

AROUND XINTIANDI

Around 12 minutes on foot south from People's Square and just off Central Huaihai Road is **Xintiandi**, the city's first adaptive re-use project – in architecture speak – of an old *longtang* (lane) neighbourhood. After its opening in 2001, Xintiandi quickly became a popular shopping and entertainment hub, and the model has been copied around the country.

Xintiandi ❶

Xīntiāndì 新天地
Address: 2 blocks bounded by Taicang, Zizhong, Madang and Huangpi (S) roads; www.xintiandi.com
Transport: South Huangpi Road, Xintiandi

All taxi drivers in Shanghai will know **Xintiandi** (meaning New Heaven and Earth), a two-block area of refurbished

shikumen houses that is one of the city's popular restaurant-bar-entertainment complexes (see page 161).

Xintiandi's buildings offer a clutch of gourmet restaurants, fashion boutiques and a modern cinema. Brand names fill the old houses, like Shanghai Tang's brightly coloured modern interpretations of traditional Chinese designs, Wolfgang Puck Bar & Grill, and a Paulaner Brauhaus serving up German beers, hearty fare and a live band. Don't expect much authenticity though; some of

Xintiandi at night.

TIP

Taxis are plentiful around Shanghai except when it's raining. The best solution in wet weather is to get in line at a hotel or shopping centre taxi rank. Taxi lines may be long, but at least you're assured of a taxi at the end. Uber was bought by a Chinese company and the app no longer allows linkage to international credit cards in China. For those who can't be bothered to wait, the metro is a very convenient option.

the structures are new and in all the houses the insides have been gutted and only the grey brick facades have been retained. But without a doubt, Xintiandi almost single-handedly made lane houses cool again.

Site of the First National Congress of the Communist Party of China ❷

Zhōnggòng Yīdàhuìzhǐ 中共一大会址
Address: 76 Xingye Road
Tel: 5383 2171
Opening Hrs: Tue–Sun 9am–4pm
Entrance Fee: free; limit of 2,000 visitors per day
Transport: South Huangpi Road, Xintiandi

It is a 19th-century brick lane house that was the home of delegate Li Hanjun. It was here, in 1921, that the Communist Party of China was formed. The table around which the 13 delegates, including a young Mao Zedong, held their first secret Congress, is set with 13 stools, as

Copper statues of the delegates at the Site of the First National Congress of the Communist Party of China in Shanghai in 1921.

if waiting for the return of the delegates. Although that first Congress wasn't completed here – the delegates

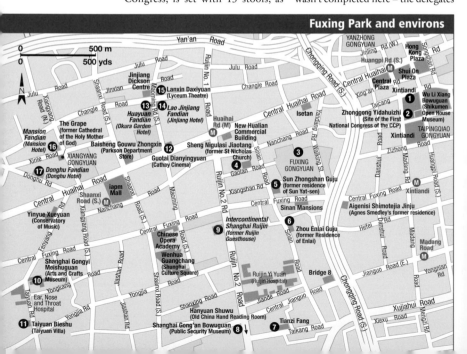

Fuxing Park and environs

evacuated on the eighth day when news of the gathering reached the ears of the French Concession's gendarmes – this remains one of the Party's most sacred sites.

An adjacent exhibition hall recounts the history of the Chinese Communist Party, with grainy pictures of the original delegates, film clips showing the horrors of the capitalist treatment of workers, some of the finest Concession-era artefacts in the city, and a dramatic copper tableau of the first Congress. The gift shop has a selection of postcards, photographs, books, and Mao buttons and pins with the iconic image of the First Party Congress building.

Shikumen Open House Museum

Wū Lǐ Xiāng Bówùguǎn 屋里厢博物馆
Address: Lane 181 Taicang Lu, House 25
Tel: 3307 0337
Opening Hrs: Sun–Thu 10.30am–10.30pm, Fri–Sat 11am–11pm
Entrance Fee: RMB 20
Transport: South Huangpi Road, Xintiandi

Also located in Xintiandi, this small museum recreates the interior of an authentic lane house, also known as *shikumen* (the name refers specifically to its stone-framed entrance). Containing photographs and models, it's a fitting memorial to the hundreds of old houses surrounding Xintiandi that were felled to create the adjacent lake and this sprawling development.

Around Fuxing Park

To the west of Xintiandi past Chongqing Road is **Yandang Road**, a walking street lined with Chinese restaurants, a popular old Shanghainese noodle house and a famous karaoke palace. This is the best way to access the sights around Fuxing Park.

Fuxing Park ❸

Fùxīng Gōngyuán 复兴公园
Address: 2A Gaolan Road; entrances also on Yandang Road and Central Fuxing Road
Opening Hrs: daily 6am–6pm
Entrance Fee: free
Transport: Xintiandi

Laid out by the French in 1909 and originally known as the French Park, **Fuxing Park** – which served briefly

Xintiandi is a favourite photo stop for couples on their wedding day.

A recreated study room at the Shikumen Open House Museum.

as a Japanese parade ground – honours its heritage with European landscaping, albeit interspersed with Communist symbols. Statues of Karl Marx and Friedrich Engels smile benevolently upon the carnival of Chinese martial arts, aerobics, sword play, ballroom dance and tai chi exercises that awaken the park at dawn each day. There's also a quaint children's playground with vintage amusement park rides and an alfresco teahouse popular with local senior citizens.

Former St Nicholas Church ❹

Shèng Nígǔlāsī Jiàotáng 圣尼古拉斯教堂

Exit the park on Gaolan Road and cross Sinan Road to the former Russian Orthodox **St Nicholas Church**. Today it is a business address, but back in its heyday, this elaborate jewel of a church was frequently used for weddings, and served the White Russians who flooded Shanghai after the 1917 Russian Revolution.

The figure of Christ, surrounded by 12 apostles, no longer graces its

Singing practice in session at Fuxing Park.

Former St Nicholas Church.

onion-shaped domes, nor are the four patron saints of Moscow on its four walls.

Former Residence of Sun Yat-sen ❺

Sūn Zhōngshān Gùjū 孙中山故居
Address: 7 Xiangshan Road; www.sh-sunyat-sen.com/e1.htm
Tel: 6437 2954

Opening Hrs: daily 9am–4.30pm; guided tours Mon–Fri 10.30am, 2pm, 3pm
Entrance Fee: RMB 8
Transport: Xintiandi

South along Sinan Road, just one block away, is the **Former Residence of Sun Yat-sen**. The Kuomintang Party that Sun established in 1905 sought to replace the ailing Qing dynasty with democratic leadership, and finally succeeded in 1911. Considered the father of modern China, Sun – who has the distinction of being a political figure revered by Chinese both in Taiwan and the mainland – lived here with his wife Soong Ching Ling from 1918–24.

The taped introduction of the tour reveals a China on the brink of modernity. Among the plush Chinese carpets, artwork and gleaming blackwood furniture – all supposedly originals despite the house having been looted by the Japanese – is a 1924 picture of Sun and Soong in front of the first aeroplane in China.

Sinan Mansions

Sī nán gōng guǎn 思南公馆
A more contemporary lifestyle hub in the Xintiandi mould features a series of restaurants (California Pizza Kitchen, Boxing Cat Brewery) and shops linked by outdoor piazzas, the Hotel Massenet, condominiums and office space, and vintage-style villas (some historic, some exact replicas).

Former Residence of Zhou Enlai ⑥

Zhōu Enlái Gùjū 周恩来故居
Address: 73 Sinan Road
Tel: 6473 0420
Opening Hrs: daily 9.30am–4pm
Entrance Fee: free
Transport: Xintiandi

Tree-shaded Sinan Road, lined with houses that are inspired by a dozen different architectural styles, is also the site of the **former Residence of Zhou Enlai**. This is where Zhou, the first prime minister of the People's Republic of China, lived in 1946 when he was head of the Shanghai branch of the Communist Party.

The house, a Spanish-style villa, is simply furnished, with most of it devoted to the underground revolution. Communist newspapers were produced on the second floor, and the third floor housed a dormitory for comrades who needed a safe house. From the porch, the Kuomintang surveillance house across the road that kept a constant watch on Zhou is visible.

In a separate building, an exhibition hall documents Zhou's life.

SOUTH & WEST OF FUXING PARK

South of Fuxing Park are a number of sights that are fairly dispersed. There is funky art, shopping and dining at Taikang Road and Tianzi Fang but also old-world charm at the former Ruijin Guesthouse and Taiyuan Villa.

Sun Yat-sen statue at his former Shanghai residence. Sun is regarded as the father of modern China.

Sun Yat-sen lived here from 1918 to 1924.

Tianzi Fang was originally popularised by local artists, photographers and designers. Some of their galleries still exist amidst the jumble of souvenir and fashion boutiques. If you're looking to pick-up some red-hot contemporary Chinese art, be sure to also visit the M50 arts enclave at 50 Moganshan Road (see page 212), just north of Suzhou Creek.

Tianzi Fang 🕖

Tiánzǐfāng 田子坊

Sinan Road continues south until it intersects with Taikang Road. This is where a number of shabby-chic old warehouses, factories and surrounding residential lanes have been turned into a popular shopping and dining enclave. Get lost in the labyrinth of grey-brick alleys filled with boutiques and cafés in former *shikumen* (stone-gated) homes. Kommune Café is a pleasant spot for coffee in the sun-dappled courtyard. Casa Pagoda, Platane, Cashmere House, Chou Chou Chic and The Pottery Workshop are other fine finds. Well-known photographer Jin Xuanmin has a gallery close to the entrance of Tianzi Fang. XMJ Space (No. 2 Lane 200, Taikang Road) is a popular spot to pick up books, post cards and iconic photographs of Shanghai.

Shaoxing Road

Shàoxīng Lù 绍兴路

Past **Ruijin Hospital** (Ruijin Yi Yuan) at 197 Ruijin No. 2 Road, one of the city's major hospitals, which is set in the tranquil grounds of the former French Aurora University, is

Trendy XMJ Space.

Potter at work in his studio, located on Taikang Road.

charming **Shaoxing Road**. A short walk along the road leads to the antique-filled atmospheric salon of the photographer Deke Erh, the **Old China Hand Reading Room** (Hanyuan Shuwu) at 27 Shaoxing Road (tel: 6473 2626). This is a good place to browse through architecture books; particularly apt is *Last Look*, which is part of a series on Old

Shanghai architecture photographed by Erh and written by the noted Shanghai architectural historian Tess Johnston. Stock up on trendy fashions and accessories spun from Tibetan yak down, as soft as the finest cashmere, at **Shokay** (35 Shaoxing Road), a Shanghai-based socially responsible label.

A few doors down, at No. 9, the **Shanghai Kunju Opera Troupe** can often be heard rehearsing. There's a small theatre on the second floor with excellent weekend performances.

Shanghai Public Security Museum ⑧

Shànghǎi Gōng'ān Bówùguǎn 上海公安博物馆
Address: 518 Ruijin No. 2 Road
Tel: 6472 0256
Opening Hrs: Mon–Sat 9am–4.30pm
Entrance Fee: RMB 8
Transport: South Shaanxi Road

At the southern end of Ruijin No. 2 Road is the **Shanghai Public Security Museum**, which crime connoisseurs will revel in. See the wax figure of a red-turbaned Sikh guard and a pistol with a gold folding handle that crime boss "Pockmark"

Huang once carried. The exhibits at this three-floor museum can be gruesome but are always fascinating.

Former Ruijin Guesthouse ⑨

Ruijīn Bīnguǎn 瑞金宾馆
Address: 118 Ruijin No. 2 Road
Tel: 6472 5222
Transport: South Shaanxi Road

Further north the busy traffic choking Ruijin No. 2 Road yields to the sprawling lawns and grand manor houses of the former **Ruijin Guesthouse**, once the Morriss estate. H.E. Morriss Jr, son of the founder-owner of the *North China Daily News*, built the estate with its four villas in 1928. An avid horse and greyhound breeder and racer, Morriss would walk his greyhounds through a back door in the estate and out directly to the greyhound race track, the Canidrome (which was demolished in 2006 and replaced with the current Shanghai Culture Square Theatre).

Now the **Intercontinental Shanghai Ruijin**, the hotel occupies a series of red-brick classical buildings within the historic walled garden estate. The first building at the Maoming Road entrance still

Office buildings near Xintiandi.

The old lanes off Taikang Road.

Red Shanghai

Shanghai's Communist legacy is something her citizens are extremely proud of.

After all, this is where Chinese Communism was born, and where the beginnings of the revolution were shaped. Many of Shanghai's Communist luminaries lived and worked here. The government has started a "red tourism" campaign, focused on sites that were key to the birth of New China, identifying some 20 sites of interest across the city.

Visiting these places offers an interesting insight into contemporary Chinese history, and into the importance of Shanghai in the growth and shaping of the Chinese Communist Party.

Red tourism in Shanghai begins with the Site of the First National Congress of the Communist Party of China (see page 148), a must-stop on domestic tours. But there are plenty more – like the Longhua Martyrs Cemetery (see page 187), where hundreds of young Communists were rounded up and executed by the Kuomintang troops. Of interest too are the homes of the men and women who led China's revolutionary struggle: names familiar outside of China, such as Sun Yat-sen, Zhou Enlai, Soong Ching Ling and even a young Chairman Mao, who lived in Shanghai with his wife and two sons before embarking on the Long March. There are also names that are famous today, such as Chen Yun and Cai Yuanpei.

There are charming little finds, such as the offices of the *Bolshevik* newspaper, and the League of Left Wing Writers Museum (see page 207), which celebrates the writers who articulated and agitated the ideas of revolution. There is the memorial hall to Lu Xun (see page 209), whose writing inspired a generation of revolutionaries. There are statues scattered around town: Chen Yi (see page 110), the marshal who liberated Shanghai and later became the city's first mayor after the liberation, on the Bund; and Nie Er, the composer of the national anthem, on Central Huaihai Road. There are sites of famous events, such as Aomen Road, where the May 30th Movement began, as well as more obscure ones. It's a very different side to Shanghai – but one well worth exploring.

The Site of the First National Congress of the Communist Party of China.

features a magnificent piece of stained glass depicting a tiger in a jungle. It is Shanghai's only surviving piece of stained glass from the Siccawei (Xujiahui) Orphanage glass workshop. The Morrisses lived well until the very end; the date on the stained glass is 1949 and the last Morriss spent his final years in the estate's gatehouse. Take a stroll in the beautiful garden that houses a wealth of treasures spanning several centuries, including Shanghai's oldest Dao temple site dating back 600 years and a 14th-century city water well surrounded by ancient cinnamon trees and wisteria vines.

Shanghai Culture Square

Wénhuà Guǎngchǎng 文化广场
Address: 36 Yongjia Road
Tel: 5461 9961
Transport: South Shaanxi Road

On the opposite side of Maoming Road, once the site of the Morriss' Canidrome is the **Shanghai Culture Square**. Opened in 2011, the state-of-the-art performance venue plunges 26 metres (85ft) underground and seats 2,011 for musical theatre, dance and other world-class shows.

Shanghai Arts and Crafts Museum ⑩

Shànghǎi Gōngyì Měishùguǎn
上海工艺美术馆
Address: 79 Fenyang Road
Tel: 6437 0509
Opening Hrs: daily 8.30am–4.30pm
Entrance Fee: RMB 8
Transport: South Shaanxi Road

Set in lush grounds, the **Shanghai Arts and Crafts Museum** is housed in a grand whitewashed mansion, its curved facade reminiscent of the American White House. It was originally designed by Czech architect Ladislau Hudec in 1905 for the

Strolling along Maoming Road.

A crafts demonstration at the Shanghai Arts and Crafts Museum.

Taiyuan Villa has been home to the likes of General George C. Marshall. Today, it has been turned into a guesthouse.

A mall poster along Central Huaihai Road – one of Shanghai's most popular shopping strips.

director of the French Compagnie des Tramways.

Downstairs is the museum's collection of dying traditional crafts – bamboo, jade, ivory, embroidery, costumes, snuff bottles and paper lanterns – while upstairs, visitors can see the artisans at work.

Taiyuan Villa ⓫

Tàiyuán Biéshù 太原别墅
Address: 160 Taiyuan Road
Tel: 6471 6688
Transport: Jiashan Road

A five-minute walk south from the museum, past the Shanghai Ear, Nose and Throat Hospital, is **Taiyuan Villa**. This mansard-roofed mansion looks as if it should be set in the rolling countryside of France.

Built for the Comte du Pac de Marsoulies in the 1920s, it was General George C. Marshall's residence – when it became known as Marshall House – while he was trying to broker a last-minute deal between the Communists and the Kuomintang. It was later turned into a guesthouse and a new wing was added together with a swimming pool. But the interior of the old house was kept intact, including the spiralling wrought-iron staircase, dark

wood panelling and the Comte's coat of arms in the fireplace. The villa now houses **Roosevelt Prime Steakhouse**.

CENTRAL HUAIHAI ROAD AND FURTHER NORTH

Head back north on Shaanxi Road (S) to **Central Huaihai Road**. One of Shanghai's major streets, Huaihai Road cuts an east–west swathe through the city and is one of Shanghai's most popular shopping strips, with stores such as Tiffany, Apple, Uniqlo and the Sony Gallery as well as big department stores like **Parkson** and art mall **k11**.

Also on this strip are a number of wedding boutiques (see box), displaying flamboyant bridal and ball gowns in a range of colours and styles to suit the fickle bride-to-be's every desire.

Cathay Cinema ⓬

Guótài Diànyǐngyuàn 国泰电影院
Address: 870 Central Huaihai Road at Maoming Road (S)
Tel: 5403 2980
Transport: South Shaanxi Road

North of Central Huaihai Road, **Maoming Road (S)** takes on a more rarefied and genteel air, as typified by a clutch of old-world buildings. The first building of note is the Art Deco

Cathay Cinema, at the corner of Central Huaihai Road and Maoming (S) Road. This lovely Art Deco classic opened in 1932. Part of the real-estate mogul Victor Sassoon's empire (which included the nearby Cathay Mansions and Grosvenor House, along with the Peace Hotel on the Bund), the cinema showed Hollywood movies in its heyday; today it screens both Hollywood and Chinese selections.

Okura Garden Hotel ⑬

Huāyuán Fàndiàn 花园饭店
Address: 58 Maoming Road (S); www.gardenhotelshanghai.com
Tel: 6415 1111
Transport: South Shaanxi Road
Further up Maoming Road (S), on the left, is the **Okura Garden Hotel**. With its spreading lawns and cool fountains, it is a welcome oasis after the buzz of Huaihai. The original entrance lobby (on the Maoming Road side) of this **former Cercle Sportif Français**, or French Club, still features the glittering gold mosaic, polished marble columns

and a dramatic stairway, all designed in 1926 by the French Concession's master architect, Paul Veysseyre.

The Cercle Sportif Français – which once had 20 lawn tennis courts, an indoor pool, a rooftop terrace for dancing and a ballroom with a stained-glass ceiling that is still intact – became Mao Zedong's private retreat on his Shanghai trips, before its conversion into a hotel in the 1980s.

Jinjiang Hotel ⑭

Lǎo Jǐnjiāng Fàndiàn 老锦江饭店
Address: 59 Maoming Road (S); www.jinjianghotels.com
Tel: 6258 2582
Transport: South Shaanxi Road
There are several buildings at this site, chief of which is the historical **Jinjiang Hotel** (not to be confused with the newer Jinjiang Towers). The brainchild of Jewish tycoon Victor Sassoon, the Jinjiang – formerly called **Cathay Mansions** – was a risky investment when he commissioned the British firm Arnhold & Company to build it in 1928. It

The famous Grecian nudes on the ballroom columns at the Okura Garden Hotel.

Part of Okura Garden Hotel was the French Club.

SHANGHAI'S BRIDES

As the sepia wedding photos in the antiques markets show, Shanghai's brides have been dressing up in clouds of tulle for over 100 years. The gowns displayed in the ritzy Central Huaihai Road boutiques are not for walking down aisles – they are worn exclusively for the all-important bridal portrait, the most important day in a Shanghai bride's life. Bridal photo packages include dresses, make-up and hairstyles. Brides get to choose from gowns of virginal white, Scarlett O'Hara red, bright blue festooned with flowers, or off-the-shoulder taxicab yellow, and they are photographed against a backdrop of heritage buildings, leafy streets or futuristic Pudong. It's not cheap – wedding-photo packages can run to RMB 100,000 – but as Shanghai brides will tell you, a wedding day lasts 24 hours, but pictures are forever.

The Lyceum Theatre, where Margot Fonteyn once danced.

The Art Deco Jinjiang Hotel was formerly known as the Cathay Mansions.

history as the venue where US President Richard Nixon and Chinese Foreign Minister Zhou Enlai signed the Shanghai Communiqué in 1972, the first step towards normalising US–China relations.

Lyceum Theatre ⑮

Lánxīn Dàxìyuàn 兰心大戏院
Address: 57 Maoming Road (S) at Changle Road
Tel: 6256 5544 (box office)
Transport: South Shaanxi Road

North on Maoming Road, on the corner with Changle Road, is the **Lyceum Theatre**, built in 1930 as the home of the British Shanghai Amateur Dramatic Club – and where the great ballerina Margot Fonteyn performed as a girl (she was known as Margaret Hookham then). Fonteyn's family lived in Shanghai between 1927 and 1933 when her father worked as an executive in the British Tobacco Company. Much later, China's opera legend Mei Lanfang also took command of the Lyceum's stage. Today, the beautifully restored Art Deco theatre hosts dramatic plays and Chinese opera – but Fonteyn is still remembered in a portrait in the lobby.

Thankfully, the 2003 restoration has kept intact the theatre's European-style

was the first high-rise to be built on swampy ground, and there was no guarantee that downtown sophisticates would want to live in what was then the countryside. As it turned out, Cathay Mansions was so successful that Sassoon built two more housing complexes on the premises, the **Grosvenor House** (now luxury apartments and a hotel) and the low-rise **Grosvenor Gardens**, now converted into offices and event spaces.

After the liberation in 1949, Cathay Mansions was turned into a government guesthouse; a year later the hotel's name was changed to the Jinjiang Hotel. The Jinjiang secured its place in contemporary Shanghai

architecture and arched ceilings while introducing unobtrusive modern lighting and sound systems.

Surrounding streets

Cross Maoming Road (S) to **Changle Road** where at No. 400 is the **Jinjiang Dickson Centre**, offering upmarket boutiques like Zegna and Gucci.

Across from JJ Dickson is "*qipao row*", a string of boutiques specialising in the traditional high-necked and form-fitting Chinese silk dresses as well as several small Japanese *yakitori* restaurants. Particularly good is the tiny **Yakitori Fukuchan**, serving delicious barbecued morsels of meat and seafood.

Parallel to the north is **Jinxian Road**, a very traditional Shanghai street where you will find **Chun**, a tiny four-table eatery serving home-style Shanghai cuisine that has won rave reviews from the likes of the *New York Times*.

Heading two blocks west at **Xinle Road** are the sapphire-hued onion domes of the former **Cathedral of the Holy Mother of God**. Stripped of its former glory, part of this 1931 Russian Orthodox church is now home to a Shanghainese restaurant called **The Grape**. Inspired by the

Cathedral of the Saviour in Moscow, the church held more than 2,500 worshippers in its heyday. Locals say its paintings of six cute cherubim and seraphim, now long gone, resembled the faces of the local artist's lovers.

Opposite at No. 82 Xinle Road is the boutique **Mansion Hotel** ⓰ (Mansion Fandian), which occupies a meticulously restored old manor house. The fifth-floor restaurant offers exquisite views of the city from both the dining room and terrace, but the food is just so-so – stick with a drink.

Continue down Xinle Road and take a detour left along **Donghu Road** towards the old wing of the **Donghu Hotel** ⓱ (Donghu Fandian). The main hotel building got a makeover in 2016 and a park on the corner of Donghu and Huaihai was opened to the public – it's a popular spot for couples to dance in the evenings. Donghu Road is a bustling restaurant and nightlife haunt. At No. 20, in a 19th-century villa tucked away from the main road, is hot Spanish restaurant **Elefante**, along with Japanese sensation **Sushi Oyama** on the floor above. **Sichuan Citizen**, **Liquid Laundry** and clubs **Le Baron** and **Craft** are other local favourites in the immediate vicinity.

The Cathedral of the Holy Mother of God is today used as a restaurant.

Shoppers on Xinle Road.

LIFE IN THE LANES

Lane houses and community life are becoming a thing of the past as Shanghai morphs into a modern city of glass and steel.

Over 70 percent of Shanghai residents were born and raised in *longtang* (or lane) neighbourhoods, but these communities are now endangered by progress. The *longtang*, Shanghai's vernacular domestic architecture, is more than just a building style: it's a way of life. These attached dwellings – each with its *shikumen* (stone-gate) entrance – separated by lanes and surrounded by an exterior wall, are thriving hubs of community life.

Because the lane houses are cramped, the internal lanes are treated as extensions of residential living spaces: here, laundry is done and hung up to dry, hair is washed in wooden basins, and peas are shelled. The communities are tightly knit, quarrelling like families and sticking together in times of trouble.

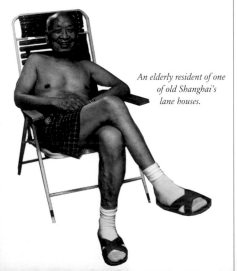

An elderly resident of one of old Shanghai's lane houses.

Hanging up the laundry, a common sight in Shanghai's lanes.

Every available space in the lanes is used up for hanging laundry. There are no secrets here, as any Shanghainese who grew up in a lane neighbourhood will tell you.

The recreated bedroom at the Shikumen Open House Museum in Xintiandi.

XINTIANDI AND THE SHIKUMEN MUSEUM

In 2001, an old lane neighbourhood was gutted and reborn as a modern shopping and entertainment venue called Xintiandi. It's not historic preservation really – some entirely new structures were built and only the grey brick facades were preserved – but defenders of Shanghai's old architecture generally approve of the project for its success in raising awareness of the value of the city's historic buildings.

Xintiandi's Shikumen Open House Museum pays tribute to the lane house, albeit one belonging to a wealthy family. The museum recreates the interior of a 1920s seven-room house, furnished with period furniture and memorabilia, from kitchen stove tops to the jade hair clasp on the dressing table and the scratchy jazz played on the gramophone. There are bedrooms, a kitchen, sitting room, study and the *tingzijian*, the garret above the kitchen, often rented to struggling writers (and from which the term for a genre of literature was coined).

A typical back street in the older neighbourhoods of Shanghai. Cramped living quarters mean that chores are often performed in the street.

More and more old neighbourhoods fall to the wrecker's ball as lane houses are eschewed in favour of modern high-rises.

The Open House Museum's reconstructed courtyard area.

The former home of T. V. Soong, brother of Soong Ching Ling, now Sasha's restaurant.

HUAIHAI AND HENGSHAN

The boundaries of the former French Concession extend to this part of the city. View stately mansions during the day, and hole up in the city's best jazz bars at night.

This section of the upscale Huaihai and Hengshan neighbourhood – part of the elegant former French Concession – has a split personality, drawing sedate, highbrow residents as well as a trendy crowd. Diplomats and Shanghai's new rich are attracted to the area's wide tree-lined boulevards, spacious historic villas with expansive gardens, new luxury apartments, and the rare quality of *anjing* – tranquillity – in a downtown location.

Former missionary-school graduates frequent the parks and markets in this area, some still living in the old apartments and villas built by their families more than half a century ago. Most are just waiting for someone to come along and pay the multimillion-dollar price tags that these properties command today.

CENTRAL HUAIHAI ROAD

Central Huaihai Road is a major artery that cuts across from the east to the west of the city. The eastern section of Central Huaihai Road is – in parts – a brash consumer paradise (see page 156), but here, where it parallels **Hengshan Road** to the south, it is toned down, reflecting the character of its residents.

Yet it's not all well-behaved matrons in this part of the city. A trendy crop of boutiques and restaurants attracts the hipster crowd, while nightfall sees Shanghai's party animals heading for the area's neon-lit strip of bars, clubs and restaurants – and the best jazz in town.

French Consul-General's Residence ❶

Fǎguó Lǐngshìguǎn 法国领事馆
The country manors of the former French Concession were located here

Main Attractions
Normandie Apartments
Soong Ching Ling's Former Residence
Fuxing Road

Map
Page 164

Strolling down Fuxing Road.

TIP

Behind the Normandie building (see page 165) on Wukang Road are manhole covers that read "CMF 1935" – Conseil Municipal Français (French Concession), 1935. There is also a good supply of vintage French fire hydrants in the area.

along Central Huaihai when this was the Avenue Joffre. The size and grandeur of these villas have made them a prime diplomatic enclave today. The corner of Central Huaihai Road and Urumqi Road has a number of consulates, the flags of four nations flying over vintage mansions. Prime among these is the Mediterranean-style **French Consul-General's Residence** (not open to the public) at 1431 Central Huaihai Road. It was built in 1921 for the French Basset family, and later home to colourful characters such as high-living American taipan Frank Raven, who was jailed for fraud.

The residence changed hands several more times over the years, becoming the French Consul's residence in the 1980s. The house, with its original tiled floors, circular sunroom and lush garden, is not open to the public, but curious visitors can see the roof and cheerful sunflower tiles that line the top of the house over high walls.

The French Consul-General's Residence.

US Consulate-General ❷

Měiguó Lǐngshìguǎn 美国领事馆
Across the street at 1469 Central Huaihai Road, straight-backed guards protect the rambling mansion that has served as the **US Consulate-General** (not open to the public) since 1980. The neoclassical Western-style house was built in the early part of the 20th century as the office of the taipan Jardine Matheson.

After stints as the residence of a Japanese businessman and his family and the Swiss Consulate, it was bought by Rong Hongyuan of the Rong family, one of Shanghai's wealthiest industrial dynasties. The gorgeous ground-floor rooms are intact because it was placed under lock and key during the Cultural Revolution.

Shanghai Library ❸

Shànghǎi Túshūguǎn 上海图书馆
Address: 1555 Central Huaihai Road; www.library.sh.cn/english

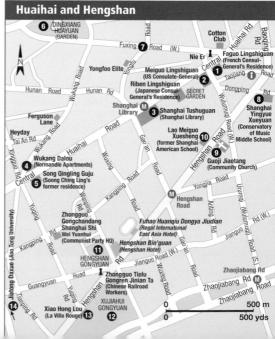

Huaihai and Hengshan

❻ DINGXIANG HUAYUAN (GARDEN)

Cotton Club

Fuxing ❼ Road (W.)

Nie Er ⭐

Faguo Lingshiguan (French Consul-General's Residence) ❶

Yongfoo Elite

Meiguo Lingshiguan (US Consulate-General) ❷

Riben Lingshiguan (Japanese Consul-General's Residence)

SECRET GARDEN

Taojiang Rd

Dongping Rd

Shanghai Library M Shanghai Tushuguan (Shanghai Library) ❸

Shanghai Yingyue Xueyuan ❽ (Conservatory of Music Middle School)

Ferguson Lane

Heyday

Tai An Rd

Lao Meiguo Xuesheng ❿ (former Shanghai American School)

Wukang Dalou ❹ (Normandie Apartments)

Song Qingling Guju ❺ (Soong Ching Ling's former residence)

Guoji Jiaotang (Community Church)

Yongjia Road

M Hengshan Road

Zhongguo Gongchandang Shanghai Shi Wei Yuanhui ⓫ (Communist Party HQ)

HENGSHAN GONGYUAN

Fuhao Huanqiu Dongya Jiudian (Regal International East Asia Hotel)

Hengshan Bin'guan (Hengshan Hotel)

Jianguo Road (W.)

Zhaojiangbang Rd

Zhongguo Tielu Gongren Jinian Ta (Chinese Railroad Workers)

XUJIAHUI GONGYUAN

Zhaojiangbang Rd M

Zhaojiangbang Rd (S.)

Xiao Hong Lou ⓭ (La Villa Rouge) ⓮ ⓬

0   500 m

0   500 yds

Tel: 6445 5555
Opening Hrs: daily 8.30am–8.30pm
Entrance Fee: free
Transport: Shanghai Library

The white-tiled **Shanghai Library**, next to the Japanese Consul's residence, enhances the stately air of the area. This spacious, light-filled facility, which opened in 1996, claims to be Asia's largest library. It has collections of old and rare Chinese books, the Chinese Cultural Celebrities Manuscript Library, and a genealogy section for Chinese throughout the diaspora. Of particular note is a rare 8,000-volume Ming-dynasty edition of the *Taoist Scriptures*. Check out the automated 24-hour return system, a marvel of technology, located just past the entrance of the library, above the driveway.

Normandie Apartments ❹

Wǔkāng Dàlóu 武康大楼
Further west along Central Huaihai Road, at the corner with Wukang

Road, is the unmistakable red-brick **Normandie** apartment block, a local landmark that dominates the north side of the street. Strongly reminiscent of Manhattan's Flatiron building, the Art Deco structure is known locally as the Titanic because of its remarkable resemblance to the great cruise liner.

Built in 1924, the Normandie – then known as the Intersavin Society (ISS) apartments – was constructed with 76 apartments on six floors and 30 servants' quarters. Today, more than 700 people fit into that space and the building is starting to look a bit grimy. But thanks to the Shanghai real-estate boom, several apartments in the building have been bought and renovated – the beginning of gentrification.

Soong Ching Ling's Former Residence ❺

Sòng Qìnglíng Gùjū 宋庆龄故居
Address: 1843 Central Huaihai Road

The Art Deco Normandie apartments are now a much-sought-after residence. Many are being gutted and modernised inside.

Shanghai Library.

The Chinese say of the three Soong sisters: "May Ling loved power, Ai Ling loved money, but Ching Ling loved China." Pictured here is a statue of Soong Ching Ling at her former residence.

Gardens at Soong Ching Ling's Former Residence.

Tel: 6437 6268
Opening Hrs: daily 9am–4.30pm
Entrance Fee: RMB 20
Transport: Shanghai Library

The **Soong Ching Ling Residence**, across from the Normandie, is where Dr Sun Yat-sen's young widow lived from 1948, having donated their Xiangshan Road house (see page 150) as a museum, until she moved to Beijing in 1963.

Today, Soong's house stands as a monument to her. A recent renovation opened up the second floor, allowing visitors to visit Soong's bedroom suite, with furniture given by her parents at the time of her wedding in 1915, and that of her faithful maid, Li Yan E.

Downstairs, the living and dining rooms are lined with photographs of Soong with a host of legends from Mao to Nehru. A modern building in the compound documents the extraordinary Soong clan in letters and artefacts, and in the garage sit two ebony limousines: a 1952 Jin presented by Stalin and Soong's own Chinese Red Flag. The lane behind

Upmarket shopping in Ferguson Lane.

the house makes for a nice, tree-shaded walk.

Ding Xiang Garden ❻

Dīngxiāng Huāyuán 丁香花园

Head back across the street to the Normandie apartments. Turning right down Wukang Road for about five minutes will lead to **Ferguson Lane** complex, a "lifestyle hub" with a collection of stylish eateries and boutiques.

From here, it's a 10-minute walk northwest to the lovely oasis at 849 Huashan Road called **Ding Xiang Garden**. The stucco-and-wood English-style house, with its porches and gingerbread trim, was built in 1900 by an American architect. The Qing dynasty reformer Li Hongzhang acquired the house for his favourite concubine Clove (Ding Xiang), and stored his vast collection of books here. The **Shen Yue Xuan** restaurant in the compound allows both access and delicious views of the garden and its pavilion, all surrounded by walls topped with writhing dragons.

FUXING ROAD ❼

Exit Shen Yue Xuan restaurant and turn left onto **Fuxing Road**, which, with its vintage villas and canopy of

lovely plane trees, is a classic former French Concession street.

Take a short detour right onto **Yongfu Road** and wander down to **The Yongfoo Elite** (tel: 5466 2727) at No. 200. This early 20th-century antique-filled mansion, once the home of a prominent Shanghai family, is now a restaurant. The 2017 *Shanghai Michelin Guide* honoured the restaurant with two Michelin stars for its delicate Shanghai-style cuisine. Its lovely setting – which includes a superb garden, shaded by century-old trees – and opulent Old Shanghai feel make it worth stopping by, at least for a drink in the lounge or on the lawn.

Jazz haunts

Jazz was Old Shanghai's signature tune – 1,200 jazz bands, it is said, performed here in the 1930s – and New Shanghai seems to have embraced it as well. Two of the city's best clubs are located in this area. At the intersection with Central Huaihai Road is the dark and smoky **Cotton Club**, a local legend in Shanghai jazz and blues circles. Its house band plays jazz standards with such verve that even Wynton Marsalis stopped by to jam some years ago when he was in town. At 50 Tai'an Road, **Heyday** is an intimate live music space inspired by Shanghai's Art Deco 1930s heyday. Enjoy nightly performances by Shanghai's hottest jazz musicians washed down with excellent cocktails. Another stalwart of the jazz scene, **JZ Club** has moved from its old home on Fuxing Road to the subterranean nightlife hub of **Found 158** on Julu Road.

From the long-standing Cotton Club, head south down leafy **Hengshan Road**.

The eating and drinking (and shopping) options continue on **Dongping Road** in the next block. There is **Sasha's**, a gracious old-world pub and restaurant in an ochre-painted heritage villa with one of Shanghai's best beer gardens. **Green & Safe** (tel: 5465 1288) at 6 Dongping Road is a chic organic marketplace, café and upstairs restaurant – a great

The former French Concession area is elegant and leafy.

place for a healthy lunch or to grab picnic supplies.

Simply Thai at No. 5C serves piquant Thai cuisine amid elegant minimalist decor, and **Goga** (tel: 6431 9700) at the intersection of Dongping and Yueyang Roads is a hip Cali-Asian bistro with a gourmet pedigree. Next door, **The Camel** (tel: 6437 9446) is a lively Australian sports bar serving hearty pub grub.

Shanghai Conservatory of Music Middle School ❽

Shànghǎi Yīnyuè Xuéyuàn
上海音乐学院

Address: 5 Dongping Road
Opening Hrs: grounds open for events only
Transport: Hengshan Road

The gates in the middle of Dongping Road lead to the grounds of the Shanghai home of the powerful Soong family, who once lived here like dynastic royalty. Some of these Western-style brick villas today house the **Shanghai Conservatory of Music Middle School**, while others play host to chic restaurants.

The bar at Sasha's restaurant.

T. V. Soong lived in the building that now houses Sasha's Restaurant.

The building housing **Sasha's restaurant** (see above) was the home of T.V. Soong, the most prominent of the three Soong sons, who served as the Kuomintang finance minister. The villa next to Sasha's was the home of Kuomintang leader Chiang Kai-shek and Soong May Ling, the sister of Ching Ling and a power-broker in her own right. Adjacent to Chiang's residence was the home of H.H. Kung, financial wizard, Bank of China head, briefly Kuomintang finance minister, and husband of Soong Ai Ling, the oldest sister. Only Ching Ling lived apart from the rest of the Soong clan, and only Ching Ling remained in China's mainland.

Community Church ❾

Guójì Lǐbàitáng 国际礼拜堂
Address: 53 Hengshan Road
Tel: 6437 6576
Opening Hrs: English services on Sun at 2 and 4pm; Chinese services at 4.30am, 10am and 7pm
Transport: Hengshan Road

Back on Hengshan Road, a five-minute walk south leads to the ivy-covered **Community Church**, founded by a group of Americans around 1925. The beautiful red-brick Protestant church, with its rosewood pews and high ceilings, is worth a visit at any time of the day – if the guards let you in – but particularly

during services. Chinese-language services are especially popular, with the congregation often spilling onto the lawns. Foreigners may attend the Chinese services, as celebrities from Jimmy Carter to Desmond Tutu have in the past, listening to the translated service through headphones.

Former Shanghai American School ⑩

Yuàn Shànghǎi Měiguó xuéxiào 原上海美国学校

The stately red-brick building across the street from the Community Church is the **former Shanghai American School**, the first signpost of the American community that once flourished here. The school was set up in 1912 to educate the children of American missionaries and moved to this location in 1923. By 1934, a booming Shanghai saw enrolment at the school pass the 600 mark. Designed by American architect Henry Murphy to resemble the Independence Hall in Philadelphia, the building today houses a naval research facility. The school is closed to the public – but can be admired from the street.

Hengshan Road bar strip

Just before Hengshan Road's well-known bar strip begins, next to the old Shanghai American School, is the Gibson Guitar Store, a gorgeous two-storey palace for guitar-lovers at the throbbing disco-beat **Boiling** (10 Hengshan Road). The bars along Hengshan Road can be a little seedy and they offer none of the glitz and glamour of the Bund. Still, there are plenty of options for late-night party animals, from the Latin-inspired beats at **Zapata's** (9 Dongping Road, House 11) to the fun **Shanghai Brewery** (**15 Dongping** Road) and, further along the road at 237 Hengshan Road, the cosy wine bar **The XO** by local wine delivery app Bottles XO serving well-priced wines and Italian beers.

Hengshan Park ⑪

Héngshān Gōngyuán 衡山公园
Address: corner of Hengshan Road and Wanping Road

TIP

Newly woven reed-wattle fences are an old sight making a comeback in this neighbourhood.

The Hengshan bar strip at night.

La Villa Rouge, another beautiful former French Concession villa.

Xujiahui Park is a fine spot to relax.

the refurbished 1934 **Hengshan Hotel** (Hengshan Bin'guan) at 534 Hengshan Road, takes you to the pocket-handkerchief sized **Hengshan Park**.

Formerly called Pétain Park, it was originally laid out by the French in 1926, and although it has been re-landscaped since, the lush greenery has given the park an almost tropical feel. It is a popular place; beginning at dawn, the park buzzes with tai chi practitioners in one corner, fan dancers in another, and elderly ballroom dancers waltzing to the tunes of yesteryear in the space in between.

Xujiahui Park ⓬

Xújiāhuì Gōngyuán 徐家汇公园
Address: corner of Hengshan Road and Wanping Road
Opening Hrs: daily 6am–6pm
Entrance Fee: free
Transport: Xujiahui

Opening Hrs: daily 6am–6pm
Entrance Fee: free
Transport: Xujiahui

A leisurely 10-minute walk from the Hengshan Road bar strip past the modern **Regal International East Asia Hotel** at 516 Hengshan Road, and

The pristine, manicured grounds of **Xujiahui Park**, which is part of the city's ongoing greening project, is a short walk south. The park

was landscaped as a microcosm of Shanghai – the bridge is the Yanan Road highway; La Villa Rouge, the Concessions; and the old China Rubber Factory smokestack, the industrial zone.

La Villa Rouge ⑬

Xiǎo Hóng Lóu 小红楼
Address: Xujiahui Park, 811 Hengshan Road
Tel: 6431 6639
Transport: Xujiahui

La Villa Rouge is a historic redbrick villa within Xujiahui Park. In its former life as the EMI Studios, this was where some of Shanghai's most famous voices were recorded, including Zhou Xuan, the legendary "golden throat" of the 1930s, and Nie Er, the composer of the Chinese national anthem. The building remained as a recording studio throughout Shanghai's turbulent history, first under the Japanese, then the Kuomintang, and finally as the Shanghai branch of China Records.

Jiao Tong University ⑭

Jiāotōng Dàxué 交通大学
Address: 1954 Huashan Road;
www.sjtu.edu.cn/english
Transport: Xujiahui

From the park's western edge, head northwest – a 15-minute walk along Huashan Road – to Shanghai's prestigious **Jiao Tong University**. This is China's second-oldest university, which counts China's leadership among its graduates. The extensive campus is dotted with stately early 20th-century buildings, now home to the university's renowned science and engineering faculties. The **C.Y. Tung Maritime Museum** (daily 1–5.30pm; free), dedicated to the late Shanghai-born shipping tycoon and housed in a refurbished 19th-century dormitory, has exhibits on the history of Chinese shipping and the legacy of the Tung family's shipping business. (C.Y. Tung's son, Tung Chee Hwa, was the first chief executive of Hong Kong SAR.)

Playing in Xujiahui Park.

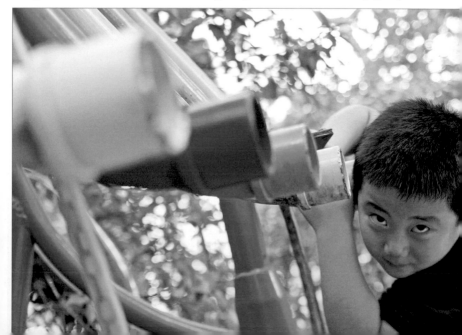

Worshippers gathered around the giant incense burner at Jing'an Temple.

上海静安寺山门重建落成庆典

JING'AN

Expect a mixed bunch of sights in this area, from posh hotels and swanky shopping malls to the Gothic fantasy Moller Villa, the Shanghai Exhibition Centre and the striking new Natural History Museum.

Premium office buildings, showy shopping malls and a constellation of five-star hotels define the prestigious business and commercial area of **Jing'an**, home to some of the city's most expensive real estate. Outside the foreign Concessions until the boundaries expanded in 1899, Jing'an's wide open spaces attracted the Hardoons and the Kadoories, two of the richest Jewish families in Old Shanghai. Each built concrete symbols of their wealth – magnificent mansions just minutes away from each other. Here, too, were the Bubbling Well Cemetery and the Bubbling Well Temple, whose Chinese name – Jing'an, or "Tranquil Repose" – gives the area its name, as well as the legendary Paramount nightclub.

The cemetery has yielded to a park, the actual "Bubbling Well" has long been smothered by a busy highway, and the lavish Hardoon mansion has become the site of a Sino-Soviet symbol of friendship. But not everything is radically different. Prayers are offered still at Jing'an Temple, they're dancing again at the Paramount, and the area's malls and shops are crowded.

A bit further afield, Shanghai's Natural History Museum has been revamped and relocated in a smart new building integrated into the

manicured landscape of Jing'an Sculpture Park. The new site opened to the public in 2015 and hosted more than 10,000 visitors on opening day.

JING'AN'S EASTERN FLANK

Although Jing'an's eastern flank is only steps away from its glittering heart, its mix of run-down buildings, small shops and the occasional high-rise give it the feeling of being much more remote – the downmarket part of an upscale neighbourhood. A walk through the streets of these

Main Attractions
Shanghai Exhibition Centre
Jing'an Temple
Municipal Children's Palace
Chinese Printed Blue Nankeen Exhibition Hall
Shanghai Natural History Museum

Map
Page 174

Posing at Shanghai Exhibition Centre.

TIP

Do note that the rooms at Hengshan Moller Villa are housed in the cheaper and colourless annexe, which was added in 2002. The main villa is utilised as restaurants and event spaces.

neighbourhoods yields both a look into the lives of downtown residents – lively, crowded lanes, snack vendors on every corner – and some interesting historic artefacts from Shanghai's past.

Hengshan Moller Villa ❶

Héngshān Mǎlè Biéshù Fàndiàn 衡山马勒别墅饭店
Address: 30 Shaanxi Road (S); www.mollervilla.com
Tel: 6247 8881
Transport: West Nanjing Road

The fairytale steeples and spires of the **Hengshan Moller Villa** rise like a Gothic fantasy. The sheer grandeur of the place – the rich wood panelling throughout, the elaborate carving, the chandeliers dripping crystal – bring alive the glamour of old Shanghai. After spending the post-Liberation years as the Communist Youth League, the house that British shipping magnate Eric Moller built in 1936 has been restored to its old splendour as a boutique hotel and restaurants owned by the Hengshan group. Moller was a passionate racer of horses, and a statue of his favourite steed stands in the garden; its body is reportedly buried in the grounds. Take in the sight with a cup of tea at the Vie en Rose café in the grounds.

Ohel Rachel Synagogue ❷

Yóutài Jiàotáng 犹太教堂
Address: 500 North Shaanxi Road
Opening Hrs: closed to the public; open to worshippers on Saturdays
Transport: West Nanjing Road

The ivy-covered Greek **Revival Ohel Rachel Synagogue**, to the northwest, was built in 1920 by Jacob Sassoon in memory of his wife Rachel. The synagogue served as the spiritual home for the city's wealthy Sephardic Jewish community until 1952. It was used as a stable by the Japanese during World War II and later as a warehouse and

The fairytale Moller Villa is now a boutique hotel owned by the Hengshan group.

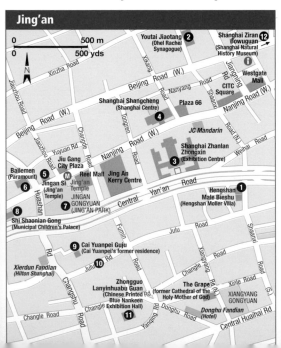

lecture hall during the post-Liberation years.

In 1998 the synagogue was renovated and sanctified for the visit of former US First Lady Hillary Clinton and Secretary of State Madeleine Albright.

Next door is the **former Shanghai Jewish School**, established by Horace Kadoorie in 1932. Both the synagogue and school are part of the Shanghai Education Bureau compound, and are visible from the street, but not open to the public.

NANJING ROAD (W) AT JING'AN

Nanjing Road's westernmost flank, **Nanjing Road (W)**, dominates the Jing'an district. Much has changed on Nanjing Road since the time it was called Bubbling Well Road and a 1930s guidebook claimed it was "one of the seven most interesting streets in the world".

The fashion vibe begins at the **Fenshine Fashion & Gift Market** on the corner of Nanjing and Chengdu roads, a sprawling three-storey building filled with fashion knock-offs, which has been slated for its transformation into a legit luxury mall. Heading west on Nanjing Road (W), grimy 1930s apartment buildings yield to Starbucks cafés, one in every other block. Things get more upscale on the north side of Nanjing Road (W), which is wall-to-wall with designer malls: **818 Mall**, **CITC Square**, **Westgate Mall and Plaza 66**, where Shanghai's yuppies flock to sip lattes, slurp on Häagen-Dazs sundaes and shop at multi-storey luxury brand flagships. In stark contrast, sunburnt fruit pedlars from the countryside stand outside the gleaming malls, balancing shoulder poles carrying baskets full of the season's offerings.

Directly across the street from Westgate Mall is **Meilongzhen** (No. 22 Lane, 1081 Nanjing Road (W); tel: 6253 5353), one of the city's most famous Chinese restaurants. Located in a pink-brick French-style mansion, it serves Shanghainese delicacies in a vintage dining room. Between here and Jing'an Temple are several of the street's most recent developments, including **Jing'an Kerry Centre** and **Reel Mall**, packed with excellent shopping and dining, interspersed with pleasant alfresco courtyards.

Just behind Nanjing on Wujiang Road is a bustling pedestrian street

Celebrating the Jewish festival of Hanukkah at Ohel Rachel Synagogue.

Festivities at the Ohel Rachel Synagogue – the nine candles are lit to celebrate the Jewish festival of Hanukkah.

FACT

Luo Jialing, the wife of Silas Hardoon, a Jewish millionaire who made good in Shanghai, was herself a much-whispered-about Shanghai legend.

packed with fast-food outlets and the occasional local stall like **Yang's Dumplings**.

Shanghai Exhibition Centre

Shànghǎi Zhǎnlǎn Zhōngxīn 上海展览中心

Address: 1000 Central Yan'an Road
Opening Hrs: daily 9am–5pm
Transport: West Nanjing Road, Jing'an Temple

Shanghai Exhibition Centre sits on the sprawling grounds of *Ai Li Yuan*, one of the Concession-era's most sumptuous estates. *Ai Li Yuan* (or "Beloved Li") belonged to Silas Hardoon, a Sephardic Jew who arrived penniless in Shanghai and worked his way up from watchman to Shanghai's richest man. His estate, named after his half-French, half-Chinese wife, Luo Jialing (see margin note), was once dotted with pretty pavilions, arched bridges, lakes and bamboo groves.

The Shanghai Exhibition Centre was one of the many buildings constructed in major Chinese cities during the 1950s as an expression of the common cause of the Soviet Union

A book exhibition at the Shanghai Exhibition Centre in Jing'an.

and the People's Republic of China. Designed by a Russian architect, the 9.3-hectare (23-acre) centre was created on a titan scale, incorporating Communist stars, Christmas wreaths, a Roman central dome and a Socialist-Realist Atlas sculpture – all topped by a 106-metre (348ft) tall gold-plated steeple, inspired by Russian Orthodox church architecture. Famous names like Mao Zedong, Deng Xiaoping and Georges Pompidou have all passed through these portals. A 2001 renovation gave it a new lease of life, and it still remains popular for exhibitions, openings and events, with equally palatial interior features.

Shanghai Centre

Shànghǎi Shāngchéng 上海商城
Address: 1376 Nanjing Road (W); www.shanghaicentre.com
Tel: 6279 8600
Opening Hrs: shops open 9am–9pm
Transport: Jing'an Temple

Across the street, the John Portman-designed **Shanghai Centre** is at 1376 Nanjing Road (W). The city's first international residential, business and hotel complex is ground zero for the expatriate population, who need never leave its comforts. There is an upscale grocery shop, clinic,

The ornate Sino-Soviet-built Shanghai Exhibition Centre.

tennis courts, a pool, the **Portman Ritz-Carlton Hotel** (Boteman Lizi Kaerdun Jiudian) and a large clutch of restaurants. The **Shanghai Centre Theatre** (Shanghai Shangcheng Juyuan) within the complex is the home of the **Shanghai Acrobatic Troupe** (see page 50) which carries on a 2,000-year-old tradition that would dazzle even the most jaded soul.

Jing'an Temple ⑤

Jìngān Sì 静安寺
Address: 1686 Nanjing Road (W)
Tel: 6256 6366
Opening Hrs: daily 7.30am–5pm
Entrance Fee: RMB 50
Transport: Jing'an Temple

Two blocks west is the landmark **Jing'an Temple**, which has stood at this location since 1216, when the lapping waves of the Suzhou Creek eroded the foundations of the original temple, built on its banks in 247. Originally called Hudu Chongyuan Temple, it was renamed Jing'an in 1008, but became more popularly known in pre-1949 Shanghai as the Bubbling Well Temple – named after the natural springs that stood at the intersection of Nanjing Road (W) and Wanhangdu Road.

Dedicated to Sakyamuni Buddha, the temple lost many of its statues and scriptures during the Cultural Revolution, when it served as a factory. The street-facing main halls are now done up in Burmese teak with elaborate gold-capped stupas and the front courtyard is filled with incense. The pavilion housing the copper Hongwu Bell, which dates from the Ming era, has also been recreated in teak, while images of 18 *arhat* (Buddhist saints) and a gold Sakyamuni Buddha sit in the new Grand Hall.

The temple is noted for its rare Mi shrines from a sect that is a branch of Buddhism with its own gods and practices, which originated in India and flourished briefly in China during the Tang dynasty, before spreading to Japan. Mi then disappeared in China, before the monk Zhisong revived it in 1953, when Jing'an's Mi shrines were first built. To the rear of the temple, however, is a massive, gilded Thai-style tower.

Paramount ⑥

Báilèmén 百乐门
Address: 218 Yuyuan Road
Tel: 6249 8866

Praying for good luck and blessings at Jing'an Temple.

Monk standing before a giant urn at Jing'an Temple.

Opening Hrs: daily from 7.15pm onwards
Transport: Jing'an Temple

Just west of Jing'an Temple is the **Paramount**. One of Old Shanghai's great nightclubs, the Paramount reopened again in 2017 after a stylish second renovation.

Jing'an Park ❼

Jìngān Gōngyuán 静安公园
Address: 1649 Nanjing Road (W), entrance also on Huashan Road
Entrance Fee: park is free but entrance to the "Eight Scenes of Jing'an Temple" within the park costs RMB 3
Transport: Jing'an Temple

Directly across the street from Jing'an Temple is where elderly men sit on benches shaded by the plane trees that once lined the entrance to Bubbling Well Cemetery (Yong Quan), **Jing'an Park**'s previous incarnation. The well has long since been paved over, but the park has built a

The Municipal Children's Palace was known as Marble Hall in the Concession days. This was where the wealthy Jewish Kadoorie family lived.

reproduction of the eight famous scenes of ancient Jing'an Temple at one corner. The idyllic **Thai Gallery** restaurant in the park serving Thai cuisine has an outdoor terrace that overlooks a lily pond.

Jing'an Park.

SOUTH OF YAN'AN ROAD

The area south of Yan'an Road, the old dividing line between the International Settlement and the French Concession, is much more residential. Plane trees line the streets, and the shopping and dining options are on a much more boutique scale.

Municipal Children's Palace ❽

Shì Shàonián Gōng 市少年宫
Address: 64 Central Yan'an Road
Tel: 6248 1850
Entrance Fee: free (but call to arrange visit)
Transport: Jing'an Temple

West of Jing'an Park, across Huashan Road, is the **Municipal Children's Palace**, where gifted children are trained in art, music, drama, dance and, more recently, IT. There are several Children's Palaces in the city, but this is the largest and most visited. Originally built as the **Marble Hall** – marble was used throughout the house, particularly in the

gorgeous fireplaces and hallways – for the wealthy Jewish Kadoorie family, the mansion was completed in 1924 after six years of construction. Run by a coterie of 43 servants, this was the first house in the city to have air conditioning. Visitors can come here and watch apple-cheeked children perform under the 5.5-metre (18ft) tall chandeliers in the magnificent ballroom.

Cai Yuanpei's Former Residence ❾

Cài Yuánpéi Gùjū 蔡元培故居
Address: No. 16, Lane 303 Huashan Road
Tel: 6248 4996
Opening Hrs: Tue–Sun 9–11.30am, 1–4.30pm
Entrance Fee: free
Transport: Changshu Road

It's a 10-minute walk south, past the **Hilton Shanghai** (Xierdun Fandian), to **Cai Yuanpei's Former Residence**, a German-style villa where the great education reformer Cai Yuanpei lived in 1937. An exhibition tells the life of the man who was the first Kuomintang minister of education and past president of Jiao Tong University.

Julu/Fumin Road dining and nightlife

The restaurants and bars of **Julu Road ❿** are just across the street. Once one of Shanghai's raunchiest bar strips, Julu Road (Julu Lu) has gone upscale and with its cross street, Fumin Road (Fumin Lu), is home to a host of chic restaurants – including trendy **Lost Heaven Silk Road** and stylishly hip Japanese eatery **Shintori** – galleries and cafés.

A right turn on **Fumin Road** leads to galleries like **Madame Mao's Dowry** (at No. 207), which specialises in early modern Chinese design, beloved Hunan restaurant **Guyi** and drinking hotspots like **Dr Wine** and **Dr Beer**.

Chinese Printed Blue Nankeen Exhibition Hall ⓫

Zhōngguó Lànyìnhuābù Guǎn
中国蓝印花布馆
Address: No. 24 Lane 637, Changle Road
Tel: 5403 7947
Opening Hrs: daily 9am–4.30pm
Entrance Fee: free
Transport: Changshu Road

A right turn from Fumin Road into Changle Road reveals a vista of "Tudor-bethan" houses, leading to the **Chinese Printed Blue Nankeen Exhibition Hall**. Here, in a lovely Concession-era villa, are displays of Shanghai's famous indigo-blue cloth.

Local lore credits the famous weaver called Huang Daopo with bringing this wax-resistant dying technique (much like batik) to the Jiangnan area, where it was applied to *nankeen* cloth, a brownish-yellow fabric woven from the indigenous *gossypium religiosum* cotton. The fabric is named after Nanking, now Nanjing.

The small museum here documents the process of making *nankeen* cloth, in which wax is first

Monument to Cai Yuanpei (1863–1940) – the famous Chinese educator, scholar and politician.

Exhibits at the Chinese Printed Blue Nankeen Exhibition Hall.

TIP

For great city views, take a night ride in the glass elevator to the 39th floor of the Hilton Hotel (Xierdun Fandian) at 250 Huashan Road.

poured onto hand-cut stencils which feature designs linked to folk tales or traditional symbols. The cloth is dunked into a steaming dye bath of indigo leaves – indigo that first came to China from India via the Silk Road – after which the wax is scraped off to reveal the designs. The museum also features a small collection of antique *nankeen*, while the adjoining shop sells clothes, fabrics and accessories, all made of *nankeen* fabric.

Shanghai Natural History Museum ⑫

Shànghǎi Zìrán Bówùguǎn 上海自然博物馆
Address: 510 Beijing W Road, Jingan Qu
Tel: 6862 2000
Opening Hrs: Tue–Sun 9am–5.15pm
Entrance Fee: RMB 30 adults, RMB 12 children more than 1.3 metres (4.3ft), free children under 1.3 metres (4.3ft)
Transport: Shanghai Natural History Museum, West Nanjing Road

Close-up of Chinese blue nankeen cloth.

The **Shanghai Natural History Museum** has been moved, improved, and is now housed in a stunning new building in the Jing'an Sculpture Park. The innovative design, created by Perkins + Will, is inspired by a snail's shell; the spiral roof (topped with grass) rises dynamically out of the sculpture park.

The building is also energy saving – fitting for a museum boasting the tagline "Nature, Humans, Harmony". A branch of the Shanghai Science and Technology Museum (see page 222), the Natural History Museum (opened in 2015) has ten permanent exhibition halls over five floors focussing on evolution, the diversity of ecology and human civilisations. With more than 11,000 models spanning the seven continents, 280,000 exhibits, a 4D theatre, a range of visual displays, and a discovery centre, this titan collection is exceptional, although for many the main highlight is still the building itself.

The new Natural History Museum building, modelled on a snail's shell.

St Ignatius (or Xujiahui) Cathedral.

XUJIAHUI AND LONGHUA

South of downtown Shanghai are shopping malls galore. But scattered in this area are gems such as the French Gothic St Ignatius Cathedral, the city's most authentic Chinese temple at Longhua and the lush Botanical Gardens – perfect for an escape from the city.

A n improbable combination of mass-market shopping and two of the city's most revered holy sites, the Xujiahui and Longhua areas bristle with a chaotic cacophony of mega-malls and skyscrapers, all heightened by the confused flow of traffic at the confluence of eight roads. Crossing over from tranquil Xujiahui Park and the elite Huaihai/Hengshan neighbourhood (see page 163), it is almost as if an invisible line has been crossed – and in a way, it has.

AROUND XUJIAHUI

Xujiahui lies on the western border of the former French Concession. The area still offers the real-estate bargains that attracted the churches, temples, airports and prisons of yesteryear. Today, it houses cathedrals of commerce, and condominiums for yuppies who can't afford the prices downtown.

Meaning "Xu family village", Xujiahui is named after China's first Catholic family. Ming court official Xu Guangqi or Paul Xu was born here in 1562 and was Jesuit missionary Matteo Ricci's first convert as well as his personal assistant. Xu's legacy lived on for centuries afterwards, sometimes in unexpected ways: illustrious Xu descendants include another

Shanghai first family, the Soongs (on their mother's side).

Shanghai Library Bibliotheca Zi-ka-wei ❶

Shànghǎi Túshūguǎn Xújiāhuì Cángshū Lóu
上海图书馆徐家汇藏书楼
Address: 80 Caoxi Road
Tel: 6487 4095 ext 208
Opening Hrs: Mon–Sat 9am–5pm; library tours on Sat 2–4pm but call ahead to reserve
Entrance Fee: free

Main Attractions
Shanghai Library
  Bibliotheca Zi-ka-wei
St Ignatius Cathedral
Longhua Pagoda and
  Temple
Shanghai Botanical
  Gardens

Map
Page 184

Bibliotheca Zi-ka-wei.

Wedding photos outside St Ignatius.

The Gothic interior of St Ignatius.

Transport: Xujiahui

The lovely **Shanghai Library Bibliotheca Zi-ka-wei** is part of that Xu legacy. Built in 1847 on land that had been donated by Xu for the founding of a Jesuit community, this was the first public library in Shanghai. The three-storey building originally served as the priests' residence, while the adjacent two-storey building, then as now, holds the Jesuit library.

The ground floor of the two-storey building is designed in the style of a classic Qing library, while the beautiful upper storey is a fine copy of the Vatican Library. The Bibliotheca holds 80,000 volumes in several languages, and includes collections inherited after their original owners fled Shanghai in the wake of the liberation, including the collection of the Royal Asiatic Society. Look out for the fine wooden carving of St Ignatius of Loyola on his deathbed, and another of St Francis in the public reading room on the second floor.

The ground floor is taken up by an art gallery.

St Ignatius Cathedral ❷

Xújiāhuì Tiānzhǔtáng 徐家汇天主堂
Address: 158 Puxi Road
Tel: 6438 4632
Opening Hrs: Sat–Sun 1–4pm, mass (in Chinese) on weekdays at 7am, Sat at 7am and 6pm, and Sun at 6am, 7.30am, 10am and 6pm
Transport: Xujiahui

The soaring twin towers and flying buttresses of the French Gothic **St Ignatius Cathedral** (also known as **Xujiahui Cathedral**) is another legacy of Xu's Jesuit community. The very first St Ignatius Cathedral was built here in 1846. Named after the founder of the Society of Jesus order, the cathedral has remained essentially unchanged since a 1910 expansion – with the notable exception of the dramatic amputation of the 50-metre (165ft) twin tower and destruction of the stained-glass windows during

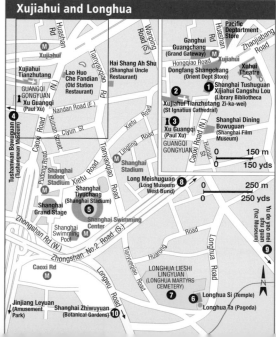

the Cultural Revolution, when the church was forcibly closed.

The towers are now back in place, and new stained-glass windows, designed and created by a glass studio operated by nuns, are installed in the upper windows. The fascinating stained-glass panels take into account their Chinese context, with Chinese symbols and images rendered like traditional paper cut-outs. A large rose window shows a phoenix, surrounded by the Chinese zodiac. The church grounds feature a lovely grotto with a statue of the Virgin Mary with floral offerings at her feet. Services in Chinese are held daily and masses at Christmas and Easter are especially popular.

Guangqi Park ❸

Guāngqǐ Gōngyuán 光启公园
Address: 17 Nandan Road
Opening Hrs: 6am–6pm
Entrance Fee: free
Transport: Xujiahui

The meteorological observatory that Xu established on the grounds of Xujiahui Cathedral is gone now, but its legacy lives on at the **Shanghai Meteorological Bureau**, a five-minute walk south of the cathedral.

Just next to the Bureau on a grassy plot of land is a **Statue of Paul Xu**, the scholar who made all this possible. Turn right just past the statue onto Nandan Road to pay your respects to Xu at his tomb at leafy **Guangqi Park**. Xu was buried here in 1641, and the tomb was last renovated in 1903. The ornamental columns and stone sculptures of goats and horses that lead to the tomb – the traditional "Spirit Way" – were added then.

Tushanwan Museum ❹

Tushanwan Bówùguǎn 土山湾博物馆
Address: 55 Puihuitang Road
Tel: 5424 9688
Opening Hrs: Tue–Sun 9am–6pm
Entrance Fee: free
Transport: Xujiahui

Located in the old Jesuit orphanage that taught Western arts and crafts to its charges – and is considered the cradle of Western art in China – this high-quality museum showcases the exquisite work made at the orphanage. There are paintings, photographs, prints and woodcarvings, but the highlight is a *pailou*, or ceremonial gate, made for the San Francisco World Fair in 1915 and returned to Shanghai in 2010, the year of the Expo.

Shopping and eating

Continue north along **Caoxi Road** to one of the few Jesuit buildings to survive the redevelopment of Xujiahui. After a tasteful restoration, the old Catholic convent, south of the cathedral, is now occupied by the **Old Station Restaurant** (Shanghai Lao Zhan). It serves elegant Shanghainese cuisine in an interior embellished with beautiful floor tiles, carved wood and coloured glass.

Continue along Caoxi Road to the intersection, where there is a different kind of shrine – this one to shopping. Here, the skyscrapers, traffic, giant ads and TV screens make it look like Times Square on speed. Sunlight floods the glass dome of the **Grand Gateway** (Ganghui

The upper level of the Bibliotheca is a copy of the Vatican Library.

Workers put the finishing touches to the ceremonial gate (pailou) on display at the Tushanwan Museum.

Multi-armed Guan Yin image at Longhua Temple.

Guangchang) mall, one of the city's largest, and the escalators that glide up six floors – four levels of shopping and two of restaurants and entertainment centres, plus a street-level food alley. The mall, which opened in 2000, has eclipsed its predecessors, the mid-market **Orient Department Store** (Dongfang Shangsha) at 8 Caoxi Road (N) and the **Pacific Department Store**. Computers and electronics are also a speciality of the area, found in places such as Fei Diao Tower (1065 Zhaojiabang Road).

Shanghai Stadium ❺

Shànghǎi Tǐyùchǎng 上海体育场
Address: 666 Tianyaoqiao Road
Transport: Shanghai Stadium
Continuing south on Tianyaoqiao Road leads to the east gate of the 80,000-capacity **Shanghai Stadium**, built in 1997 to host the China National Games. One of the projects "built to enhance people's lives", the stadium underwent a major spruce-up in 2007 for the Special Olympics Summer Games. This was also the site of preliminary football matches for the 2008 Olympics.

Next door (and part of the same complex), the **Shanghai Grand Stage**

hosts a wide variety of concerts, from the Rolling Stones to Hong Kong pop stars like Sandy Lam. If you'd like to do more than just watch, the stadium has tennis and badminton courts open to the public.

Shanghai Film Museum

Shànghǎi Diànyǐng Bówùguǎn 上海电影博物馆
Address: 595 Caoxi North Road
Tel: 6426 8666
Opening Hrs: Tue–Sun 9am–4.30pm
Entrance Fee: RMB 60 adults; RMB 30 students
Transport: Shanghai Indoor Stadium
About a 10-minute walk from the stadium is the four-storey **Shanghai Film Museum**. Shanghai was the cradle of the Chinese film industry for much of the 20th century. This museum was created by the Shanghai Film Group on the site of the city's original film studio, and features 3,000 artefacts with interactive bilingual information panels, multimedia installations and a 4D cinema. It also comprises working production studios where visitors can get involved in the post-production process, such as creating movie sound effects.

Snooker at Shanghai Grand Stage.

LONGHUA AREA

Heading southeast to **Longhua Road** leads to downtown Shanghai's only pagoda and temple. The site is now easily accessed by metro (get off at Longhua Station, not Longhua Rd Station) and is well worth a visit – it's one of the city's most authentic Chinese places of worship.

Longhua Pagoda and Temple ❻

Lónghuá Tǎ Hé Sì 龙华塔和寺
Address: 2853 Longhua Road
Tel: 6456 6085
Opening Hrs: daily 7am–4.30pm; no entry to tower
Entrance Fee: RMB 10
Transport: Longhua

The maroon wood and brick octagonal **Longhua Pagoda** looks as if it popped straight out of ancient China. The 40-metre (131ft) tower, whose tinkling bells on upturned eaves could once be heard all the way to the Huangpu River, was first built in AD 242 by a nobleman from the Wu Kingdom, although its current shape dates from an AD 922 reconstruction.

Rebuilt several times over the centuries, the pagoda served as a flak tower equipped with anti-aircraft guns during World War II.

Across the street stands the rambling **Longhua Temple complex**. With its incense-filled courtyards, giant joss burners and imposing Buddha images, this atmospheric temple is Shanghai's largest and most active. If there's one temple that you should see in Shanghai, this is it. Originally founded in AD 345, the Chan (Zen) Buddhist temple has been rebuilt several times over the years, and is considered a particularly fine example of Southern Song architecture. The current structure dates back to the 10th century.

Longhua contains some significant Buddha images: Sakyamuni Buddha's Bodhisattva form, in the **Hall of Heavenly Kings**, and in the **Maitreya Hall**, the Maitreya (or Future) Buddha incarnation, known as the "cloth bag monk". The temple's **Grand Hall** features a gilded meditating Sakyamuni Buddha, under a spiralling dome, with a statue of Guanyin (the Goddess of Mercy) in the rear, while the **Three Saints Hall** showcases the three incarnations of the Buddha.

Striking Longhua's **bronze bell**, cast in 1894 and weighing 6,500kg (14,330lbs), exactly 108 times (to erase the 108 worries of Buddhist thought) has become a Shanghai New Year's Eve tradition, as has the reinstituted Chinese New Year temple fair, China's largest, full of folk traditions and dances. The fair's popularity has led to another being held in the spring.

Longhua Pagoda is a key landmark in south Shanghai.

Shanghai Longhua Martyrs Cemetery ❼

Lónghuá Lièshí Língyuán
龙华烈士陵园
Address: 180 Longhua Road
Tel: 6468 5995
Opening Hrs: daily 9am–3.30pm
Entrance Fee: free
Transport: Longhua

Exit the temple and enter this cemetery, which commemorates a tragic moment in Shanghai's

Burning incense at Longhua Temple.

Memorial statue at the Longhua Cemetery of Revolutionary Martyrs.

Dino Beach.

history. Hundreds of idealistic young Communists were killed during what has become known as the White Terror, the ruling Kuomintang's reign of terror against the Communists, carried out in Shanghai by the notorious Green Gang. On 12 April 1927, these revolutionaries were pulled from their homes, rounded up and taken to the execution grounds at what was then the Longhua Garrison. Each April, Longhua's orchard of peach trees blossom in remembrance, looking remarkably like the tissue-paper flowers made for funerals.

The cemetery today is all landscaped gardens and high-tech fountains, with a blue-glass Louvre-esque pyramid and a Memorial Hall dedicated to the Communist martyrs. Outside, an eternal flame burns in front of a Herculean sculpture being swallowed up by the earth, and the marble graves of the martyrs lie in a semicircle.

A corner of the park features the tiny prison cells of the **KMT Songhu Garrison Headquarters**, later the infamous Longhua prison camp – the setting for much of J.G. Ballard's 1984 autobiographical account of the Japanese Occupation of Shanghai, *Empire of the Sun*. But the focus here is the ill-treatment of Communist revolutionaries by Chiang Kai-shek's army, with exhibition rooms featuring re-creations of the prison and photographs of those martyred.

Long Museum West Bund ❽

Lóng Měishùguǎn 龙美术馆
Address: 3398 Longteng Avenue
Tel: 6422 7636
Opening Hrs: Tue–Sun 10am–6pm
Entrance Fee: RMB 50
Transport: Longhua Middle Road

The second **Long Museum** established by Liu Yiqian and his wife Wang Wei, this West Bund branch opened in 2014 and has quickly become an important Shanghai art institution. The sleek building, with curved concrete walls, was designed by Liu Yichun of Atelier Deshaus and enjoys an atmospheric location right on the waterfront.

The couple's collection is extensive, with traditional and contemporary Chinese art spread across four storeys, as well as pieces from wider Asia and Europe. The Long Museum Pudong – see page 224 – is also worth a visit.

Yuz Museum ❾

Yú Déyào Měishùguǎn
余德耀美术馆
Address: 35 Fenggu Road
Tel: 6426 1901
Opening Hrs: Tue–Thu, Sun 10am–9pm, Fri–Sat until midnight
Entrance Fee: RMB 140 Tue–Thu, Sun, RMB 100 Fri–Sat, RMB 70 concessions
Transport: Yunjin Road

This vast contemporary art gallery, opened in 2014, is housed in an old 1950s aircraft hangar and spans 9000 sq metres (96,875 sq ft).

The building has been impressively converted and now boasts a flat glass roof and is flanked by pretty trees. Temporary exhibitions rotate alongside the private art collection of the gallery's director, Budi Tek, a Chinese-Indonesian entrepreneur and philanthropist.

The **Yuz Museum** was set up by the Yuz Foundation, a non-profit organisation aiming to promote contemporary art and artists alongside a commitment to social welfare.

SOUTH SHANGHAI

This area is close enough to commute, but far enough away to provide space for greenery and relaxation. The attractions range from the lush greenery of the Botanical Gardens to two artificial playgrounds for the family.

Shanghai Botanical Gardens ❿

Shànghǎi Zhíwùyuán 上海植物园
Address: 1100 Longwu Road
Tel: 5436 3369
Opening Hrs: summer daily 7am–6pm, winter 8am–5pm
Entrance Fee: RMB 15 garden only, RMB 40 includes Bonsai Garden
Transport: Shanghai South Railway Station

The **Shanghai Botanical Gardens**, located about 2km (1.25 miles) south of Longhua Pagoda, is a rambling green vista of lakes, pine trees and more than 9,000 plants. It is known for its bonsai collection in the Penjing Garden, the Orchid Garden, medicinal plants and a pair of 18th-century pomegranate trees, as well as its spring and autumn flower festivals. Fans of Shanghai's blue and white *nankeen* fabric should pay their respects at the Huang Daopo Memorial Temple in the grounds: Huang is the legendary figure who brought the technique of *nankeen*-dyeing to the Jiangsu region.

Jinjiang Amusement Park

Jīnjiāng Lèyuán 锦江乐园
Address: 201 Hongmei Road
Tel: 5420 4956
Opening Hrs: daily 8.30am–5pm
Entrance Fee: RMB 70
Transport: Jinjiang Park

West of the Botanical Gardens, in Minhang district, is **Jinjiang Amusement Park**, home of the world's second-largest Ferris wheel. Local children universally seem to enjoy the swinging pirate ship and the haunted house attractions.

Dino Beach

Rèdài Fēngbào Shuǐshàng Léyuán 热带风暴水上乐园
Address: 78 Xinzhen Road
Tel: 6478 3333
Opening Hrs: daily 9am–9pm, until later from mid-July to mid-August
Entrance Fee: RMB 150

Also in Minhang is **Dino Beach**, which has the world's biggest wave pool, along with white-water rafting, slides, tubes and a huge man-made beach. It's a good way to cool down in summer, but weekends see huge crowds.

Shanghai Botanical Gardens.

HONGQIAO AND CHANGNING

The suburb of Hongqiao, where expatriates live in high-walled compounds, contains a few scattered sights like the Soong Ching Ling Mausoleum and a zoo. Changning, which is fast catching up, is home to leafy Zhongshan Park and some architectural gems.

There's a much more suburban feel in the western districts of Hongqiao and Changning, with their big houses, schools, large supermarkets and shopping. Lying outside the central downtown core, land is cheaper, something that parks, warehouse shops, office buildings and hotels are taking advantage of.

The same was true when the area lay outside the Concession borders, when tycoons built their country estates here, to allow them to live in the manner of the landed gentry. Remnants of their old lives still linger here – mansions, gardens and churches dot the area, adding to the character.

HONGQIAO

The expatriates on corporate packages and wealthy Chinese who live in Hongqiao's high-walled compounds, each bigger and fancier than the last, are merely the latest to seek the lifestyle of the gentry in Hongqiao. A century ago, this was all rolling land, perfect for large country estates, horseback riding – and the unique Shanghai Paper Hunt. Brought to Shanghai in the late 19th century by military officers who had "hunted" in other parts of the world, paper hunting involved a 16km (10-mile) cross-country ride on

Soong Ching Ling Mausoleum.

horseback, following a twisting, turning trail of paper to the finish line.

Soong Ching Ling Mausoleum ❶

Sòng Qìnglíng Língyuán 宋庆龄陵园
Address: 21 Songyuan Road
Tel: 6275 4034, ext 541
Opening Hrs: daily 8.30am–5pm
Entrance Fee: RMB 5

There is perhaps no more concrete evidence of foreign presence in Shanghai than the "**Foreigners Tomb Area**" in the **Soong Ching**

Main Attractions
Soong Ching Ling Mausoleum
Antiques shops and warehouses at Hongqiao Road and Wuzhong Road
Changning District Children's Palace
Zhongshan Park
Changfeng Ocean World

Maps
Pages 192, 196

Antique bedside table at one of the Hongqiao Road antiques shops.

Ling Mausoleum. Built in 1909 as the International Cemetery, the tomb stones here bear identical stone markers and strange spellings ("Feliks, Nanooer, Eoolc, Marly Jone"), indicating that the original graves were moved and new markers recreated. Some of Shanghai's famous names lie here: Sir Elly Kadoorie, whose magnificent Marble Hall still stands as the Municipal Children's Palace (see page 178), and Lady Laura Kadoorie, who died trying to rescue her children's nanny when an earlier home went up in flames. Joseph Sassoon Gubbay and Aaron Sassoon Gubbay, a branch of the family who built the Peace Hotel, also rest here, having died within three days of each other in August 1946.

There are more luminaries in the adjacent "celebrity cemetery", where the tombstones are carved in the likeness of the dead. Here rest patriots, war heroes and martyrs. The centrepiece of course is Soong Ching Ling's gravesite, with a white marble statue in her likeness set above the grave. The grave itself is marked by a simple stone slab and surrounded by pine trees.

One of the three Soong sisters and wife of Sun Yat-sen, Ching Ling is the only one of the influential Soongs who remained in China's mainland. Children come here to pay homage to the childless Soong, who was instrumental in setting up the Shanghai Children's Palaces – an after-school programme offering children training in art, music, dance and drama, and now also IT.

The **Soong Ching Ling Exhibition Hall**, located near the main entrance, recounts Soong's life as an exemplary Communist and is filled with all sorts of interesting memorabilia and artefacts documenting her life.

ANTIQUES ROW

Head west along Hongqiao Road to the so-called **Antiques Row ❷**. Cavernous shops here such as **Alex's Antiques**

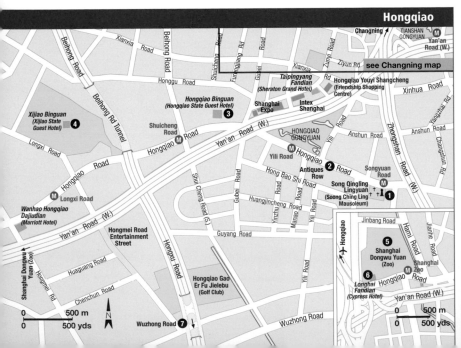

Hongqiao Road antiques shop.

(No. 1970; tel: 6242 8734) are an antiques-lover's dream, offering a window into a China when bridal dowries arrived in wedding baskets, ginger was preserved in porcelain jars, and washbasins and chamber pots were commonplace. Some of the cabinets, chairs, altar tables and beds have already been refinished; watching the craftsmen at work is a real treat. Be aware that with Qing-era antiques dwindling, reproductions are common these days.

Hongqiao State Guest Hotel ❸

Hóngqiáo Yingbīnguǎn 虹桥迎宾馆

Continuing west along Hongqiao Road, there is some exceptional accommodation, starting with the **Hongqiao State Guest Hotel** at 1591 Hongqiao Road. Set within some 40 hectares (100 acres) of lush gardens is a collection of vintage villas in architectural styles ranging from Art Deco to Spanish Colonial. The sprawling lawns and shady trees assure the privacy of its long-term residents and VIP guests.

Xijiao State Guest Hotel ❹

Xījiāo Bīnguǎn 西郊宾馆

The well-guarded **Xijiao State Guest Hotel** at 1921 Hongqiao Road, about a 10-minute walk west, is where notables like the Queen of England have stayed in the past. The complex includes a stunning Frank Lloyd Wright-inspired house, now Building No. 4, built for a Chinese entrepreneur in 1949. Set on a sloping hill, its sliding roof, use of glass walls and an indoor garden with a Japanese bridge create a link between the interior and exterior. A stream runs through the peaceful compound, whose vast lawns include a lake and pavilions.

Shanghai Zoo ❺

Shànghǎi Dòngwù Yuán 上海动物园
Address: 2831 Hongqiao Road
Tel: 6268 7775 ext 8000
Opening Hrs: daily 7.30am–5pm
Entrance Fee: RMB 40 (children up to 1.4 metres/4.6ft free)
Transport: Shanghai Zoo

Continuing west on Hongqiao Road leads to the rolling grounds of the former Hungjao Golf Club, which became the **Shanghai Zoo** in 1954.

The sprawling grounds of Xijiao State Guesthouse.

TIP

All the prime buildings in Shanghai have guards, many of whom will deny entrance at first. Smile, be polite, conceal cameras, and tell them you'd like to "*kan yi kan*", or look around, and they may let you in.

The grounds are dotted with pavilions, and the streams are stocked with swans, pelicans and Mandarin ducks, but the zoo, like most zoos in China, is hardly idyllic. The lethargic giant pandas, a symbol of China, are on most tourist agendas, but equally popular are the chimp habitats, funded by the local branch of Jane Goodall's environmental organisation, Roots & Shoots. Kids will enjoy feeding the ducks and stroking the goats at the petting zoo.

Cypress Hotel ❻

Lóngbǎi Fàndiàn 龙柏饭店

Further west is another unique lodging, the **Cypress Hotel**, at 2419 Hongqiao Road. It is set in the verdant country estate of Jewish millionaire Victor Sassoon, who built the Peace Hotel (see page 111). His half-timber faux-Tudor mansion, formerly called **Sassoon Villa**, and scene of many a wild party given by the avid horse-racer and man about town in the 1930s, still stands next door.

Sassoon Villa on the grounds of the Cypress Hotel – where many a wild party was thrown in its heyday.

Giant panda at the Shanghai Zoo.

South of Hongqiao Road

Head south, across Yan'an Road, to the **Hongmei Entertainment Street**, a lively food street which is popular with expatriates who live nearby. Packed with branches of favourite downtown restaurants and bars (like Simply Thai, Blue Frog, Big Bamboo) as well as local eateries, it's a nice place for a leisurely dinner or a night out at the pub.

The 18-hole **Hongqiao Golf Club** (Hongqiao Gaoerfu Julebu) – another reason why expats favour this area – is a little further south, with the entrance at 567 Hongxu Road.

Continue south along **Hongxu Road** to **Wuzhong Road** ❼; a clutch of good antiques shops and warehouses are found along both roads. On Hongxu Road is the well-respected **Shanxi Antique Furniture** (No. 731; tel: 6401 0056). Wuzhong Road is equally good for antiques and furniture. One of the best (and most honest) stores, **Hu & Hu** used to be here until it moved further south to No. 8 Caobao Road (tel: 3431 1212; www.hu-hu.com). The friendly owner, Marybelle Hu, is a veteran of Sotheby's, and her shop offers both antiques and reproductions as well as custom-made pieces.

CHANGNING

Up-and-coming **Changning** district, which borders Hongqiao to the north, is in the process of revamping itself. New luxury apartments, offices and hotels are fast coming up in an area that was formerly in the "B" list realm.

Xingguo Guesthouse ⑧

Xīngguó Bīnguǎn 兴国宾馆

At the edge of this one-time renegade neighbourhood, in the old French Concession area, is a touch of old-world gentility at the **Xingguo Guesthouse** (78 Xingguo Road). Commissioned in 1934 by the Butterfield and Swire company, British architect Clough Williams-Ellis created an English country estate complete with playing fields on the serpentine curve of Avenue Haig, now Huashan Road. Today, the vast lawns and spreading camphor trees meander around an architectural mélange of French, Italian and neoclassical whitewashed mansions, which still evoke a gracious

weekend-in-the-country air. Butterfield and Swire left China in 1950. Whenever he was in Shanghai, Chairman Mao Zedong enjoyed staying at **Building Number One**, with its dramatic, sweeping staircase, stately Ionic columns and wide outdoor terrace.

Today, the guesthouse is a preferred government official accommodation. Now under the management of the **Radisson Plaza Xingguo Hotel**, Number One is renovated and still a guesthouse (but only open to long-term guests when it is not occupied by state visitors). The other old houses on the estate serve as offices and restaurants. More recent 1990s prefab houses occupied by expatriates sit on the old playing fields, while the Radisson Plaza Xingguo's modern high-rise hotel lies on the cusp of the estate.

No. 3 Middle School for Girls ⑨

Dìsān Nǚzhōng or Shìsān Nǚzhōng
第三女中 **or** 市三女中

Changning is full of lovely old houses like this one.

Chinese furniture on sale at a Wuzhong Road shop.

No. 3 Middle School for Girls was formerly known as the McTyeire School. This was where the famous Soong sisters were educated.

Jiangsu Road, north of the hotel, is a bustling thoroughfare lined with shabby office buildings, shops and the occasional ostentatious former residence of a Kuomintang official. On the corner with Wuding Road, a vestige of the street's old incarnation as Edinburgh Road surfaces. The Gothic turrets and stained-glass windows of the **No. 3 Middle School for Girls** (ask for permission to enter) indicate the building's origins as the McTyeire School for Girls, founded in 1890 by the Southern Methodist Mission and named after Bishop Holland McTyeire, the Mission's head in China and then chancellor of Tennessee's Vanderbilt University.

McTyeire was once the city's most exclusive school for the daughters of Shanghai's elite. When the precocious Soong Ai Ling entered its gates at the age of five, her enchanted older classmates made her the school mascot, dubbing her "Soong tai-tai" (Madam Soong). Three decades later, the world would come to know the Soong sisters – Ai Ling, Ching Ling and May Ling, McTyeire girls all – as the wives of wealthy banker H.H. Kung, Republic of China founder Sun Yat-sen and Chiang Kai-shek, respectively.

After a brief respite as a co-educational school during the Cultural Revolution, the city's girls are back at the renamed top-ranked girls' school. Dressed in egalitarian uniforms, they line up in the shadow of the dove-grey Gothic buildings for classes. Every spring, the girls still play baseball, a McTyeire American tradition that has been retained.

Shanghai Philharmonic Orchestra office

Shànghǎi Jiāoxiǎng Yuètuán 上海交响乐团

Two blocks north and around the corner on Wuding Road (W) at No. 1498 is the **office building** of the

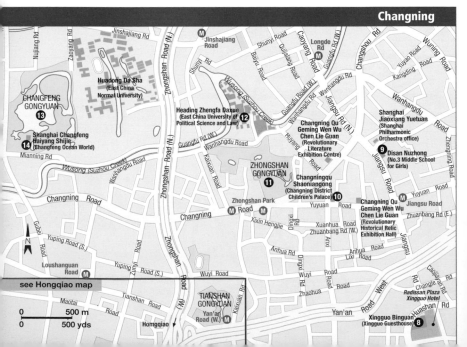

Shanghai Philharmonic Orchestra (ask for permission to enter), its black ironwork gates embellished with treble clefs and the orchestra logo. The orchestra inherited the mansion from the Shanghai Opera School, which had claimed it after the liberation. A stone fountain, its edges carved with grimacing masks, is found in the garden, while inside, sensitive restoration has returned the mansion to something of its former glory.

Changning District Children's Palace ⑩

Chángníngqū Shàoniángōng 长宁区少年宫

Address: No. 31, Lane 1136, Yuyuan Road
Tel: 6252 4154 to arrange for a visit
Transport: Jiangsu Road

Just a few houses west, the florid Teutonic castle-like exterior of the **Changning District Children's Palace** hints at its colourful

history. The dream house of the Kuomintang minister of transportation, Wang Boqun, created a stir when it was built in 1930 as a gift for his second wife – the house was overly ostentatious and Wang's new wife, Bao Zhining, was almost 30 years his junior. The sprawling 5,000-sq-metre (53,820-sq-ft) garden once had small bridges with flowing water and pavilions nestled among the flowers and trees. The main building's marble columns, Gothic arches, 32 rooms and fireplaces are still intact.

During the Japanese occupation years (1937–45), it became the home of the head of the Japanese-endorsed Kuomintang puppet government, the traitor Wang Jing-wei. After the war, Kuomintang spies took over the house and it became a prison and execution ground for Communist revolutionaries. Pressed into use as government offices after 1949, the building has served

Girls at the Changning District Children's Palace practising the pipa.

Students at the No. 3 Middle School for Girls.

Changning District Children's Palace was built in 1930.

Marine life at Changfeng Ocean World, in Changfeng Park.

peaceably as the local Children's Palace since 1960, its after-school activities programme offering gifted children training in art, music, dance and drama, and IT.

Zhongshan Park ⓫

Zhōngshān Gōngyuán 中山公园
Address: 780 Changning Road
Opening Hrs: daily 6am–6pm
Entrance Fee: free
Transport: Zhongshan Park

A futuristic-looking glass pyramid two blocks west encases the metro stop at **Zhongshan Park** and serves as a design accessory to the slick, landscaped plaza that fronts it.

Inside the park, the contours of the Concession-era Jessfield Park remain. Anchored by a lotus-filled lake, the grounds are a favourite weekend destination for children who love the carnival atmosphere with its games, rides and proximity to McDonald's, just outside the park gate.

Mornings and evenings see tai chi practitioners and ballroom dancers doing their thing in this leafy park.

East China University of Political Science and Law ⓬

Huádōng Zhèngfǎ Daxue 华东政法大学

The back entrance of the park on Wanhangdu Road leads to the leafy green campus and syncretic Sino-Anglo buildings of the **East China University of Political Science and Law** (1575 Wanhangdu Road). It was founded in 1878 by the American Episcopal Mission as St John's University. St John's alumni once occupied the highest echelons of Shanghai and overseas Chinese society. Originally part of the Jessfield estate, the campus, with its century-old trees, makes for a nice stroll. The headmaster's house fuses 19th-century gingerbread design with classical Chinese eaves and roof.

Changfeng Park ⓭

Chángfēng Gōngyuán 长风公园
Address: 25 Daduhe Road
Opening Hrs: daily 6am–6pm
Entrance Fee: free
Transport: Daduhe Road

Northwest and across Suzhou Creek, sprawling **Changfeng Park** is a breath of fresh air in a gritty neighbourhood, particularly during the spring flower festival when vibrant tulips, daffodils and peonies bloom, and sculptures are fashioned from flowers.

Changfeng Ocean World ⑭

Shànghǎi Chángfēng Hǎiyáng Shìjiè
上海长风海洋世界
Address: Gate 4, Changfeng Park, 451 Daduhe Road
Tel: 6223 5501
Opening Hrs: daily 8.30am–5pm
Entrance Fee: RMB 180 adults, RMB 120 children 1–1.4 metres (3.2–4.6ft)
Transport: Daduhe Road

Within Changfeng Park is **Changfeng Ocean World**, Shanghai's first modern aquarium. Designed with a South American jungle theme, the lush greenery enhances the aquatic exhibits, which include re-creations of rivers, rainforests and oceans. At its popular shark tunnel, oversized toothy sharks and giant rays swim overhead as you walk beneath; certified divers can arrange for a swim with the sharks. Children especially love the "touch pool", which allows a hands-on experience with sealife such as starfish, shrimps and crabs. There is also an adjoining 2,000-seat stadium for shows with dolphins and whales.

Flying a kite at Zhongshan Park.

Tai chi session at Zhongshan Park – a familiar sight at most parks in Shanghai.

HONGKOU

This unassuming area north of Suzhou Creek took major roles on the historical stage: it was the base for Japanese occupying forces, the home of the acerbic Chinese writer Lu Xun and the largest Far East refuge for Jews fleeing Nazism in Europe.

U ntil recently, **Hongkou** district, the area north of Suzhou Creek, was largely spared the redevelopment of its old neighbourhoods witnessed elsewhere in the city. Apart from the memorial hall to Chinese writer Lu Xun as its major tourist attraction, this is a very local area, without the mass-market appeal of Shanghai's big-name draws. Still, Hongkou has a rich history of its own. But a renaissance is beginning: the old warehouses on Moganshan Road have been transformed into the city's best-known art district; a Cultural Street commemorates the great literary movements of the early 20th century; and the newly instated 'North Bund' area is emerging as a fresh tourist hub home to the Shanghai International Cruise Terminal, five-star hotels and restaurants.

Hongkou was little more than vegetable farms and swamps when Bishop William Boone – the first Anglican bishop in China – established the American Episcopal Church Mission here in 1848. It wasn't until six years later, in 1854, that the American Settlement was established, which subsequently merged with the British Settlement

to form the International Settlement in 1863. By 1900, the Japanese had established their presence here too. It made perfect sense, therefore, for the International Settlement to locate its support systems, like post offices, prisons, warehouses and waterworks, in Hongkou, given its combination of space and easy proximity to the financial district.

Hongkou also played a major war role as the home of both the Japanese occupying forces and stateless Jewish refugees fleeing Hitler's Germany

Main Attractions
Shanghai Post Museum
Ohel Moishe Synagogue
Gongqing Forest Park
Duolun Road area
Lu Xun Park
M50 art galleries
Jade Buddha Temple

Map
Page 202

Waibadu Bridge, which was built in 1907, spans Suzhou Creek.

Broadway Mansions and Waibadu Bridge.

Suzhou Creek – and much of the history of Hongkou. Until 1856, the only way to cross Suzhou Creek into Hongkou was by ferry, but when the International Settlement found that inconvenient, a British entrepreneur decided to build a wooden bridge, naming it Wills Bridge after himself. His system of making the Chinese pay one copper coin for crossing the bridge while allowing foreigners to cross on credit didn't go down well, and the bridge was eventually dismantled and replaced by a floating bridge. In 1907, it was replaced by the steel Waibaidu Bridge (known in English then as Garden Bridge).

During the Japanese occupation, the bridge served as the demarcation line between occupied Hongkou and Zhabei, and the International Settlement; it was guarded by turbaned Sikh policemen from the British forces on the Bund side and Japanese soldiers on the occupied side. Today, the bridge is an excellent

to one of the few places that would accept them.

NORTH OF SUZHOU CREEK

Cross into Hongkou the old-fashioned way, across **Waibaidu Bridge** (Waibaidu Qiao) which spans the

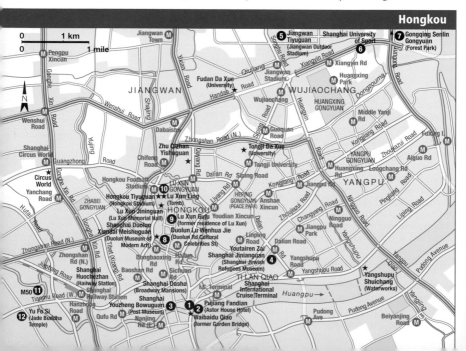

vantage point for views of Pudong to the east and the Suzhou Creek to the west.

Broadway Mansions ❶

Shànghǎi Dàshà 上海大厦
Address: 20 Suzhou Road (N);
www.broadwaymansions.com
Tel: 6324 6260
Transport: Tiantong Road

Across Waibaidu Bridge, on the western side, is the 22-storey Art Deco facade of the **Broadway Mansions**, one of Asia's first high-rises, built in 1934 as a hotel. The building is best remembered as the wartime Foreign Correspondents Club, which occupied the top six floors. From this perspective, some members recorded Shanghai's most memorable events: the 1937 Japanese bombing, and, in 1949, watching Marshal Chen Yi march in to liberate Shanghai.

A 2006 renovation has retained the high ceilings and spacious rooms, but not all the original details. The 18th-floor terrace offers stunning views of Suzhou Creek, the Bund and Pudong.

Astor House Hotel ❷

Pǔjiāng Fàndiàn 浦江饭店
Address: 15 Huangpu Road;
www.pujianghotel.com
Tel: 6324 6388
Transport: International Cruise Terminal Station

The Victorian building on the eastern side of Waibaidu Bridge is the **Astor House Hotel** – once one of Shanghai's most elegant hotels. Today, it has been downgraded to a modest three-star hotel. Built in 1910, the Astor attracted luminaries such as Charlie Chaplin and Albert Einstein in its heyday. The hotel was also famous for a number of Shanghai firsts: the first electric light, telephone, talkies, dance ball – even the taxi. Local lore has it that an Astor House bellboy, handsomely rewarded for recovering a Russian guest's wallet with its contents, spent

a third of it on a car. That car became Shanghai's first taxi and spawned the Johnson fleet, now known as Qiangsheng taxi. The interior architecture remains, its sweeping staircases and grand galleries recalling its past splendour.

Shanghai Post Museum ❸

Shànghǎi Yóuzhèng Bówùguǎn 上海邮政博物馆
Address: 250 Suzhou (N) Road
Tel: 6362 9898
Opening Hrs: Wed, Thu, Sat, Sun 9am–5pm
Entrance Fee: free
Transport: Tiantong Road

The **Shanghai Post Office**, a short walk west, still dominates the area, much as it did when it was built in 1924 to serve both foreigners and Chinese. Today, it is still the city's main post office. The **Shanghai Post Museum** is tucked at the back of the second floor and offers a good perspective on the history of the Chinese postal service – plus astounding views of Shanghai from its roof-terrace (open periodically).

The Astor House Hotel.

A re-creation of bygone postal days at the Shanghai Post Museum.

Jewish sanctuary

Shanghai was a safe haven for many Jewish people fleeing Nazi Europe. Hongkou, where they mostly lived, became a Jewish ghetto of sorts.

Shanghai has always had a Jewish presence, beginning with the Sephardic Jewish families such as the Sassoons, Hardoons and Kadoories who built their vast fortunes in the city. They were followed by the Russian Jews, who fled the anti-Jewish pogroms and upheavals of early 19th-century Russia. During the 1930s, the new wave of Jews arriving in Shanghai comprised those fleeing the Holocaust in Europe.

For many European Jews, the smashing of the synagogues by rampaging anti-

Ho Fengshan, the Chinese Schindler.

Jewish mobs in 1938 was the final push they needed to be convinced to leave their homeland, but the doors throughout the world were closed: Shanghai was the only place that did not require a visa or family connections. As a result, between 1938 and 1940, some 20,000 European Jews arrived in Shanghai.

In Austria, Jewish persecution reached a frenzy after it was annexed by Nazi Germany in March 1938. Although Shanghai did not require visas for entry, Jews who wanted to flee Austria were not allowed to leave unless they had visas to prove to the Nazis that another country had accepted them.

In order to help them, the Chinese Consul-General to Austria, a dapper young man named Ho Fengshan, quietly granted several thousand visas to Austrian Jews – with Shanghai as the end destination. Ho knew the visas were only a means of escape for Austrian Jews; in reality many of the visa recipients went on to other parts of the world. Under his watch, the Chinese Consulate in Vienna issued an average of 500 visas a month over the two-year period of his term from 1938–40. Ho is regarded today as China's Schindler and has been honoured for his work by Israel.

The Japanese, who occupied Shanghai then, herded the Jewish refugees into a "designated area for stateless persons" in a section of Hongkou.

Times were difficult and food was scarce, but the refugees made the best of what they had, creating a "Little Europe" with cafés, delis and even a theatre – with financial help from longer-established Jewish families. Leaving the ghetto, for those who went to school or work outside, required a pass. They also had to bow low to the Japanese sentries when crossing Waibadu Bridge; failure to do so invited abuse.

As hard as life was under the Japanese in Shanghai, many refugees look back fondly on their time in the city. It was a time when people pulled together. And it was a time that saved many from almost certain death.

Just west of the post office, along Suzhou Creek, is the startlingly modern **Embankment House**. Built by the Sassoons (see page 111) in 1932, this was Shanghai's largest apartment house at the time, with 194 rooms.

EAST HONGKOU

Heading east along the Huangpu River is the historic **dock area**, the cradle of Shanghai industry, once lined with the factories that fuelled Shanghai's growth. Now transformed into the **Shanghai International Terminal** with a host of high-rises surrounding it, the area still retains some of its historic warehouses – notably the castle-like **Yangshupu Waterworks** (Yangshupu Shuichang). Located by the waterfront at Yangshupu Road, it was built by the British in 1881. The waterworks has buildings for each step of the water-filtration process and Victorian equipment that is still used today. From the Yangshupu Waterworks building, there are beautiful views of the majestic Yangpu Bridge.

Shanghai Jewish Refugees Museum ④

Yóutàirén Zài Shànghǎi Jìniànguǎn
犹太人在上海纪念馆
Address: 62 Changyang Road
Tel: 6512 6669
Opening Hrs: daily 9am – 5pm
Entrance Fee: RMB 50
Transport: Dalian Road

The Hongkou redevelopment zone, bordered by Zhoujiazui Road in the north, Wusong Road in the west and Dalian Road in the east, has destroyed what was left of "Little Vienna", Hongkou's old Jewish neighbourhood that provided a safe haven for some 23,000 refugees between 1933 and 1941.

A few old buildings are left, at the heart of them the **Ohel Moishe Synagogue**, founded by the Russian Ashkenazi Jews in 1927. Today, the synagogue is the **Shanghai Jewish Refugees Museum**. It commemorates the exodus of Jewish people who fled from Europe to Shanghai during World War II, and who settled mostly in this area. The museum features exhibitions of historic pictures.

North of Yangshupu Waterworks, a plaque in **Huoshan Park** (Huoshan Gongyuan; daily 6am–6pm; free), on Huoshan Road, commemorates the area as the "designated area for stateless refugees" between 1937 and 1941. Back in the day, Huoshan Road and Zhoushan Road were homes to the Broadway Theatre and the original Vienna Café. Former US Treasury Secretary Michael Blumenthal and pop artist Peter Max were some of the more famous Jewish migrants who lived in Hongkou as World War II refugees.

The castle-like turrets at Yangshupu Waterworks – built by the British in 1881.

View of Yangpu Bridge from Hongkou.

Shanghai University of Sport; its architecture fuses Western Art Deco with Ming-dynasty design.

Lush Gongqing Forest Park.

Today, this area has reverted to being almost entirely Chinese.

YANGPU DISTRICT

Head northeast from Hongkou along Siping Road to one of the city's best-kept secrets. Chiang Kai-shek built his "new city" centre here in Yangpu district.

The first "new city" building on the wide boulevard is **Jiangwan Outdoor Stadium** ❺ (Jiangwan Tiyuguan; daily 5.30am–1pm) at 346 Guohe Road, with its plain white, almost Grecian exterior decorated with Chinese designs in ornamental plaster. The jewel in the crown, though, is the **Shanghai University of Sport** ❻, housed in the former City Hall at 650 Qiu Yuan Huan Road. A stunning two-storey building with more than a touch of Forbidden City architecture, the interior is now being used as office space for university staff. From the steps of the old City Hall, two other Chinese-style buildings are visible, both of which are now being used as classrooms.

Gongqing Forest Park ❼

Gòngqīng Sēnlín Gōngyuán
共青森林公园
Address: 2000 Jungong Road; www.shgqsl.com
Opening Hrs: daily 6am–5pm
Entrance Fee: RMB 15
Transport: Hailun Road + taxi

A 15-minute drive from here leads to the very picturesque **Gongqing Forest Park**, where visitors can ride on horseback, boat on the lake, fish in the pond, have a barbecue, or simply enjoy lying on the grass – a luxury in Shanghai, where this harmless activity is forbidden in most parks. This vast expanse of forested parkland offers a nice getaway from the buzz of the city.

DUOLUN ROAD AREA

Considered the father of modern Chinese literature, Lu Xun was part of a circle of literati who lived around **Duolun Road**. His literary railing against social injustice earned him a place in the pantheon of modern China's most celebrated personalities.

Duolun Road.

Hongkou takes great pride in the fact that Lu Xun chose to live in this area from 1927 until his death in 1936.

Duolun Road Cultural Celebrities Street ❽

Duōlún Lù Wénhuà Jiē 多伦路文化街
Address: Duolun Road & Sichuan Road (N)
Transport: Baoshan Road

The pedestrian street is lined with teahouses, art galleries, antiques shops and cafés. In addition, several of the old houses, in styles ranging from Shanghainese *shikumen* (stone-gate) houses to Swiss villas, have been restored as museums. The 550-metre (1,804ft) L-shaped stretch of Duolun Road is also dotted with life-size bronze figures of the celebrities who lived here, posing here and there along the street.

League of Left Wing Writers Museum

Zhōngguó Zuǒlián Jìniànguǎn 中国 左联纪念馆
Address: No. 2, Lane 201, Duolun Road
Tel: 6540 8126
Opening Hrs: daily 9.30am–4pm
Entry Fee: free
Transport: Baoshan Road

Lu Xun, together with other progressive writers, was instrumental in founding the League of Left Wing Writers. One of the writer's houses has been turned into the **League of Left Wing Writers Museum**. The former Chinese Arts University, where the league was founded in 1930 to "struggle for proletarian liberation" through writing, has preserved its interior. Collections of the league's works are showcased, along with an exhibition on the lives of the five martyred writers who were executed by a Kuomintang firing squad at the Longhua garrison during the "White Terror" in 1927 (see page 188).

Shanghai Duolun Museum of Modern Art

Shànghǎi Duōlún Xiàndài Měishùguǎn 上海多伦现代美术馆
Address: 27 Duolun Road; www.duolunart.com
Tel: 6587 2530
Opening Hrs: Tue–Sun 10am–6pm
Entrance Fee: RMB 10
Transport: Baoshan Road

Located at the southeast end of Duolun Road, this box-like, almost windowless seven-storey facility was China's first modern museum of

TIP

Shanghai's summer plum rain season is a constant downpour that lasts for two to three weeks from mid-June to early July. The rains are named after the plum fruit that are harvested during this period.

Tribute to Lu Xun (left) in bronze at Duolun Road Cultural Celebrities Street.

contemporary art, featuring experimental works by both international and Chinese artists as well as art-related workshops and events. The publicly funded museum adheres to the principle of originality.

Duolun Road's other sights

From the museum's upper floor, the distinctive Chinese tiled roof of neighbouring **Hongde Church** (Hongde Tang), built in 1928, can easily be seen among other low-rise red roofs.

Stop by for coffee at the **Old Film Café** (No. 123) with its film memorabilia and screenings of old Chinese movies. Further down the road are several mini-museums featuring Mao buttons, chopsticks and clocks.

Lu Xun's Former Residence ❾

Lǔ Xùn Gùjú 鲁迅故居
Address: No. 9, Lane 132, Shanyin Road
Opening Hrs: daily 9am–4pm
Entrance Fee: RMB 8
Transport: Hongkou Football Stadium
A short walk northeast leads to this

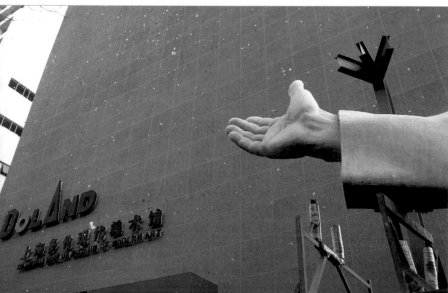

Body-art exhibition at the Shanghai Duolun Museum of Modern Art.

plain red-brick Japanese Concession house where Lu Xun lived from 1933 until he died from tuberculosis in 1936. Smaller than the homes in the European Concessions, the simply furnished house, in keeping with Lu Xun's character, is left just as it was when he lived here. Among the

Entrance to the Shanghai Duolun Museum of Modern Art.

items on display is a clock showing the exact time Lu Xun died: 19 Oct 1936 at 5.25am.

Lu Xun Park ⑩

Lǔ Xùn Gōngyuán 鲁迅公园
Address: 146 Jiangwan Road (E)
Opening Hrs: daily 6am–6pm
Entrance Fee: free
Transport: Hongkou Football Stadium

This lovely park contains both the writer's tomb and a memorial hall. The park's peanut-shaped pond area, which attracts early morning ballroom dancers and tai chi practitioners, is a refreshing spot of greenery after Hongkou's gritty streets, and is very popular with the locals.

A bronze seated figure of Lu Xun welcomes visitors to the **Tomb of Lu Xun** (Lu Xun Ling) within the park. The inscription on the tomb is by Mao, and the trees on either side of the grave were planted by Zhou Enlai and Lu Xun's widow.

The **Lu Xun Memorial Hall** (Lu Xun Jinianguan; daily 9am–4pm; tel: 6540 2288; free), at the eastern end of the park, has recreations of his study, newspaper articles and photos from

Visitor at the Lu Xun Memorial Hall.

the period, as well as translations of works by and about him.

Zhu Qizhan Art Museum

Zhū Qīzhān Yìshùguǎn 朱屺瞻艺术馆
Address: 580 Ouyang Road;
www.zmuseum.org
Tel: 5671 0741
Opening Hrs: Tue–Sun 10am–4.30pm
Entrance Fee: free
Transport: Hongkou Football Stadium

This contemporary art museum (a 10-minute walk northeast of Lu Xun Park) opened in 1995 in honour of the famous Chinese painter and

Calligraphy demonstration at Lu Xun Park.

THE LEGACY OF LU XUN

Modern China's most revered literary figure was a product of the May 4th Movement in 1919. The movement affected the politics, economics, language and literature of the time, and is regarded as a cultural watershed. For young Chinese idealists like Lu Xun (1881–1936), it was about social justice for the downtrodden.

Lu Xun's legacy was a radical new style of writing called *bai hua*, or plain language, that turned its back on the flowery classical style understood only by scholars. The very first *bai hua* short story, *Diary of a Madman*, was a brutal satire of the fuedal society he wanted to eradicate. His most famous work, however, is *The True Story of Ah Q*, another jab at the fuedal system. Lu Xun railed against the social ills of his time.

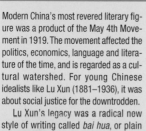

Aficionados of modern art should not miss the cutting-edge art galleries at M50.

The ShanghART Warehouse.

calligrapher Zhu Qizhan, whose works are prominently displayed. Although the museum later introduced contemporary art by other artists, the focus of its displays is narrow, usually only exhibiting paintings and photography.

SOUTH OF SUZHOU CREEK

Towards the converted art warehouses of M50 is all new high-rises and new roads, dotted with occasional old houses. To the southwest is the Jade Buddha Temple tucked behind big, mustard-coloured walls.

M50 ⓫

Address: 50 Moganshan Road
Opening Hrs: most galleries open daily 10am–6pm
Transport: Jiangning Road

For a look at the heart of Shanghai's exciting contemporary art scene, head southwest to the Suzhou Creek area and the art galleries at **M50** on **Moganshan Road** (see page 212). The warehouses in this once-seedy neighbourhood that formed the backbone of Shanghai's industry are now experiencing an artistic renaissance.

Well-known galleries, which represent some of the hottest young talent in China, include **ShanghART Warehouse** (Bldg 16; daily 10am–7pm; tel: 6359 3923; www.shanghartgallery.com) and **Eastlink Gallery** (5/F, Bldg 6; daily 10am–7pm; tel: 6276 9932; www.eastlinkgallery.cn) and **Shine Art Space** (Blk 9; Tue–Sun 10am–6pm; 6266 0605; www.shineartspace.com). There are also interesting, smaller galleries and artists' workshops.

Jade Buddha Temple ⓬

Yù Fó Sì 玉佛寺
Address: 170 Anyuan Road; www.yufotemple.com
Tel: 6266 3668
Opening Hrs: daily 8am–4.30pm
Entrance Fee: RMB 20
Transport: Changshou Road + taxi

South of Suzhou Creek is one of Shanghai's major religious attractions, the **Jade Buddha Temple** – almost hidden among the surrounding area's sprawl of factories and government housing. The temple's Song-style architecture belies the fact that it is relatively new, dating only

from 1918. This is one of Shanghai's most popular temples, mainly thanks to the presence of a pair of exquisite jade Buddhas from Burma.

In 1882, the monk Hui Gen of nearby Putuoshan Island returned from his pilgrimage to Burma with five Sakyamuni Buddha images, each one carved from a single piece of jade. Transporting all the heavy statues back to the island by ferry – particularly the largest, which weighed 1,000kg (2,200lbs) – proved impossible, so two were left behind in Shanghai, and a temple was built that same year to house them. The original temple burnt down in 1918 and was replaced with the Jade Buddha Temple on the same site. Hui Gen took the other three jade statues back with him to his monastery on Putuoshan, but these have since disappeared.

The walled temple is entered through the *san men* ("three gate") entrance, referring to the "three extrications" that every Buddhist must make in this material world in order to enter into a spiritual state of emptiness. The temple's five halls include the **Hall of Heavenly Kings**, which has an enormous gilded image of the laughing Maitreya Buddha, and the **Grand Hall**, with the image of the Sakyamuni Buddha meditating on a lotus, flanked by the 20 warrior-like heavenly kings.

The temple's main draw are the two legendary jade Buddhas, housed in separate halls. On the second floor of the **Jade Buddha Hall** is the seated Sakyamuni Buddha, all of 1.92 metres (6.5ft) tall and resting in a glass case. The creamy white, almost luminous statue of the beatifically smiling jade Buddha, draped with a gem-encrusted robe and seated in the lotus position, shows Buddha at the moment of enlightenment.

On the ground floor of the **Hall of the Reclining Buddha** is the other smaller but much more exquisite reclining jade Buddha at 96cm (37in), depicting a tranquil Sakyamuni, with the same beatific smile, at the moment of death. Don't confuse this with a larger polished stone version of the reclining Buddha, just opposite in the same hall.

Hall of the Reclining Buddha, Jade Buddha Temple.

CUTTING-EDGE ART AT M50

Forget about stuffy museums – the best of Chinese contemporary art is found at M50, a collection of funky warehouse art galleries.

A hub of the Chinese contemporary-art boom in Shanghai is M50, a funky catch-all name given to this collection of galleries in old warehouses at 50 Moganshan Road, near Suzhou Creek. These Concession-era warehouses were previously dilapidated spaces inhabited by galleries looking for low-cost storage. Today, the space has been reinvented and many of the galleries – and the artists – have taken on a sophisticated veneer that can only come from selling expensive – very expensive – art. A stroll through the galleries, which carry everything from well-known artists to newbies, photography to installation, is a free tour of Chinese contemporary art. And no wonder, as most important contemporary Chinese art galleries in Shanghai are represented at M50, along with artist studios.

M50's art galleries are light and spacious. They are housed in the old British warehouses and factories that fuelled Shanghai industrialisation during the Concession days.

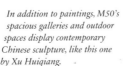

In addition to paintings, M50's spacious galleries and outdoor spaces display contemporary Chinese sculpture, like this one by Xu Huiqiang.

The range of artwork on view at M50 ranges from naïve to realist to avant-garde, sometimes all in one studio. Here, artist Xu Huiqiang ponders his work.

In addition to galleries, M50 is also home to artist studios such as this one, where well-known contemporary painter Pu Jie works on his canvases.

Island 6, an old flour mill, once owned by the Shanghai industrialist Rong Yiren, is located just behind M50. It is a non-profit, artist-run arts centre, the first of its kind in Shanghai.

Painter Ding Yi became famous for both his canvases covered with tiny squares of colour, and his funky Moganshan Road studio – Ding Yi was one of the pioneer artists to begin working here.

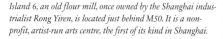

PUDONG

Once empty marshland, Pudong's futuristic facade has taken on several impressive superlatives – China's highest hotels and tallest buildings are all here. Shanghai Disney Resort is the newest addition to the sparkling Pudong landscape.

P udong is Future Shanghai. Anchored by the rocket-like Oriental Pearl Tower, this zone east of the Huangpu River with its forest of glittering skyscrapers (not one was built before 1990) looks like the set of a space-age film. Much of Shanghai's fast-forward progress since 1990, when plans to develop Pudong as a special economic area were first announced, has been telescoped into this 350-sq-km (135-sq-mile) area. Large tracts have been carved out as development zones under the preferential policies of the Shanghai Free Trade Zone (FTZ), including Waigaoqiao container port, Jinqiao Economic and Technological Development Zone and Zhangjiang High-Tech Park. And there's Disneyland!

As the face of 21st-century Shanghai, Pudong is the showcase for the best, the brightest and the most advanced. This is the site of China's tallest building, New China's first stock exchange on the mainland, an impressive cable bridge, a showcase airport, technologically sophisticated exhibition centres and state-of-the-art museums and theatres. Pudong is an urban planner's utopia: high-rises interspersed with large sweeps of greenery and straight boulevards – man and nature coexisting with industry and commerce.

Looking out from Jin Mao Tower.

Most of modern Pudong is quite a contrast to its pre-1990 self – when it was a country village.

LUJIAZUI

Economic incentives have lured the world's financial giants as well as the Shanghai Stock Exchange, the Futures Exchange and the Diamond Exchange to the **Lujiazui financial zone** (Shanghai's own Wall Street). This is the city's ultra-modern business and museum district, with a trio of the tallest buildings in China,

Main Attractions
Oriental Pearl Tower
Shanghai Municipal History
  Museum
Riverside Promenade
Jin Mao Tower
Shanghai Tower
Shanghai Science and
  Technology Museum
Shanghai Oriental Arts
  Centre
China Art Museum
Shanghai Disney Resort

Map
Page 216

Getting to Pudong the surreal way, through the Bund Sightseeing Tunnel.

and, indeed, the world: the Shanghai Tower (632 metres/2,073ft); Shanghai World Financial Center (492 metres/1,614ft); and the Jin Mao Tower (420 metres/1,380ft).

Getting to Pudong

Pudong, meaning "east of the Huangpu", was so insignificant to Shanghai that the namesake river was not spanned until the 1990s. Until then, the only way to get across to Pudong was a 5-minute ride on a ferry from **Jinling Pier** at the southern end of the Bund. The ferry (daily 6am–10pm) still makes for an atmospheric ride, with boats and barges sliding past. On landing at Dongchang Road, it is but a short walk to the main Lujiazui sights.

In contrast, the **Bund Sightseeing Tunnel** (Waitan Guanguang Suidao) on Zhongshan No. 1 Road (near the Chen Yi statue and opposite the Fairmont Peace Hotel; RMB 70 round trip, RMB 50 one way) is the surreal 21st-century way to travel: train cars – accompanied by flashing lights, waving "people" on the tracks and scenes projected onto the tunnel walls – whisk visitors to Pudong. Beyond the sheer kookiness, few travellers find this attraction worth the ticket price.

It takes a little longer to cross by road, via either the **Yangpu Bridge** (Yangpu Daqiao) or **Nanpu Bridge** (Nanpu Daqiao), the world's

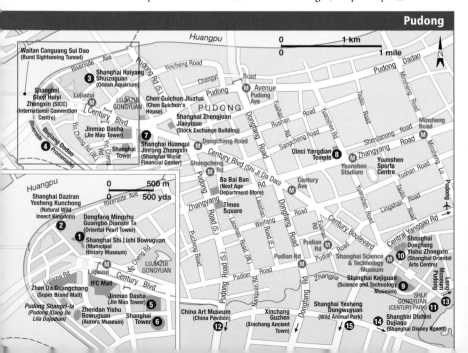

longest and fourth-longest cable bridges, respectively, but the dramatic spider-webbed bridges and the travel on elevated highways make the experience worthwhile. The most popular – and least interesting – crossing is via the **Yan'an Road (E) Tunnel** or **Fuxing Road Tunnel**, which can suffer from horrible jams at peak hours. The government has announced plans for six additional tunnels and bridges by 2020; until then, the fastest way to cross to Lujiazui is by metro.

Oriental Pearl Tower ❶

Dōngfāng Míngzhū Guǎngbō Diànshì Tǎ 东方明珠广播电视塔
Address: 2 Lujiazui Road
Tel: 5879 1888
Opening Hrs: daily 8am – 9.30pm
Entrance Fee: RMB 85 – 135, depending on type of ticket
Transport: Lujiazui

However you choose to arrive in Lujiazui, begin your visit at the iconic **Oriental Pearl Tower**. This symbol of modern Shanghai, which looks like a Jetsons-era rocket ready for take-off, elicits great passion in locals and mock horror in overseas tourists. The 468-metre (1,535ft)-tall television tower, one of the world's tallest, has a series of silver and cranberry-coloured "pearls" along its length, three of which are opened to visitors.

Tickets are priced according to which parts of the tower you visit, but what's recommended is buying the RMB 85 ticket (which also gives you access to the Shanghai Municipal History Museum). This ticket will zip you vertically in the high-speed lift – travelling at an ear-popping 7 metres (23ft) per second – to the observation deck on the second accessible bauble, perched at 263 metres (862ft). Here, compass points and landmarks are displayed prominently on the windows. The 360-degree view of the city is one of the best ways to orientate yourself, provided it's a clear day. A revolving Chinese restaurant is located at 267 metres (876ft), and above that, the third sphere (called the Space Capsule) at 351 metres (1,092ft).

Shanghai Municipal History Museum

Shànghǎi Shì Lìshǐ Bówùguǎn 上海市历史博物馆
Address: basement of the Oriental

Shanghai's iconic Oriental Pearl Tower.

The Pudong skyline at night.

Pearl Tower
Tel: 5879 3003
Opening Hrs: daily 9am–9pm
Entrance Fee: RMB 35 (museum only; combination tickets with Oriental Pearl Tower also available)
Transport: Lujiazui

Not to be missed is the **Shanghai Municipal History Museum** in the basement of the Pearl Tower. The two-storey museum takes you through Shanghai's history, with a Chinese spin on the imperialist invaders. The museum's excellent audiovisual exhibits and dioramas include re-creations of an early stock exchange, traders and artisans at work, 19th-century cobblestone streets and an arrogant taipan's office (complete with voice recording). There is also the original bronze lion from the Hongkong and Shanghai Bank (see page 108) and a gun from the Opium War's Wusong battles, in addition to models of Old Shanghai architecture. This is one museum both adults and kids will enjoy.

Shanghai Natural Wild Insect Kingdom ❷

Shànghǎi Dàzìrán Yěshēng Kūnchóng Guǎn 上海大自然野生昆虫馆

Old Shanghai is realistically created at the Shanghai Municipal History Museum.

Address: 1 Fenghe Road
Tel: 5840 6950
Opening Hrs: daily 9am–5pm
Entrance Fee: RMB 60 adults, RMB 40 under-18s
Transport: Lujiazui

A short walk west of the Oriental Pearl Tower is the **Shanghai Natural Wild Insect Kingdom** – a sure hit with the kids. There are exhibits of scorpions, spiders and all manner of creepy crawlies in several galleries, all given a tropical, somewhat tacky, jungle setting. In addition, there are interactive insect shows (weekends only) that allow the audience to touch and feel the creatures, as well as an indoor lake; kids can catch (and keep) the fish with nets supplied.

Shanghai Ocean Aquarium ❸

Shànghǎi Hǎiyáng Shuǐzúguǎn
上海海洋水族馆
Address: 158 Yin Cheng Road (N); www.sh-soa.com
Tel: 5877 9988
Opening Hrs: daily 9am–6pm
Entrance Fee: RMB 160 adults, RMB 110 children under 1.4 metres (4.6ft)
Transport: Lujiazui

East of the Oriental Pearl Tower is **Shanghai Ocean Aquarium**, an impressive facility with a focus on Chinese sea creatures, including the endangered Yangtze alligator. With a high percentage of exotic creatures, such as the alien-looking Japanese spider crab and dramatic displays, it has a high "ooh" factor. The marine tunnel, in which sharp-toothed sharks and giant rays swim lazily overhead, is the world's longest at 155 metres (509ft) and never ceases to amaze the kids (and adults too).

Riverside Promenade ❹

Bīnjiāng Dàdào 滨江大道

Continuing north, you'll pass the **Shanghai International Convention Centre** (Shanghai Guoji Huiyi Zhongxin), flanked by double globes;

it has been the venue for the Fortune and APEC conferences in the past. Hugging the eastern banks of the Huangpu River is the **Riverside Promenade**, a 2.5km (1.5-mile) long walkway that offers spectacular views over the water to the Bund, especially at night. Enjoy the view from the river, or sit at one of the restaurants and cafés that line the promenade.

Strolling south along the promenade leads to **Super Brand Mall** (Zhen Da Guangchang), Pudong's largest, at 168 Lujiazui Road, which is filled with a lively mix of bars, restaurants, shops and a cinema.

Just south of Super Brand Mall is a cluster of Shanghai's fanciest hotels, including the **Ritz-Carlton**, **Park Hyatt**, **Four Seasons**, **Mandarin Oriental** and **Grand Kempinski**, along with older stalwarts, the **Shangri-La** and the **Grand Hyatt**.

Jin Mao Tower ⑤

Jīnmào Dàshà 金茂大厦
Address: 88 Century Boulevard
Tel: 5047 5101
Opening Hrs: observation deck daily

The Super Brand Mall.

8.30am–9.30pm
Entrance Fee: RMB 120
Transport: Lujiazui

The **Jin Mao Tower** stands out against the Pudong skyline, and not just because it is one of the world's tallest buildings at 420 metres (1,378ft). "I wanted to evoke the subtle memory of a pagoda, the ancient Chinese high-rise and marker for the landscape," explained the building's American architect, Adrian Smith. Designed around the factor of eight, like the pagoda, the 88-storey

Shanghai Ocean Aquarium.

The Shanghai World Financial Center.

The Grand Hyatt's spiralling atrium at the Jin Mao Tower.

building was built in 1999 and was China's tallest for almost a decade (the Shanghai World Financial Center next door eclipsed it in 2008, followed by others since). The Jin Mao's stunning Art Deco design elements makes it an architectural summation of the city. Interestingly, the 88th-floor observatory offers city views from an almost identical perspective to the Oriental Pearl Tower. The **Grand Hyatt Shanghai** (Jinmao Kaiyue Dajiudian) occupies the 53rd–87th floors; the 56th-floor atrium affords a breathtaking view of the building's core, rising in a dizzying concentric spin to the 88th floor.

Shanghai Tower ❻

Shànghǎi Zhōngxīn Dàshà 上海中心大厦
Address: 479 Lujiazui Circle Rd
Opening Hrs: daily 9am–9pm
Entrance Fee: RMB 160 adults, RMB 90 children under 1.4 metres (4.6ft)
Transport: Lujiazui

The 632-metre (2,073ft) **Shanghai Tower** opened in 2016, completing the triptych of supertowers that dominate the east-bank skyline. Shaped like a twisting dragon's tail, the skyscraper is the world's second-tallest building, but its observation deck is the planet's highest (as of 2017), topping Burj Khalifa's (Dubai) by 11 metres (36ft). Ascend to the 118th floor (119th floor open weekends only) to survey Shanghai from 561 metres (1840ft) in the sky. In addition to staggering views, you'll experience one of the smartest "vertical cities" ever built.

Shanghai World Financial Center ❼

Shànghǎi Huánqiú Jīnróng Zhōngxīn 上海环球金融中心

The **Shanghai World Financial Center** is the world's seventh-tallest building at 492 metres (1,614ft). Designed by the American architectural firm Kohn Pedersen Fox, its distinctive design feature is a trapezoidal opening at the building's apex, which locals call "the bottle-opener". The sleek and soaring wide-shouldered building contains offices, restaurants and a luxury **Park Hyatt** hotel. Across the road, the stylish ifc mall features an Apple store, gourmet supermarket, excellent restaurants and multiple levels of fashion boutiques.

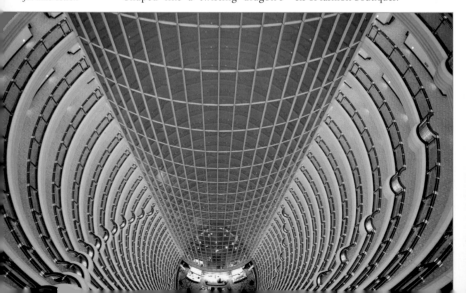

Shanghai Stock Exchange Building

Aurora Art Museum

Zhèndàn Yìshù Bówùguǎn 震旦藝術博物館
Address: G/F, Aurora Building, 99 Fucheng Road
Tel: 5840 8899
Opening Hrs: Tue–Sun 10am–5pm
Entrance Fee: RMB 60
Transport: Lujiazui

Tucked away in the Aurora Building, best known for its giant "I Love Shanghai" facade projection by night, is the excellent private collection of Taiwan's Aurora Group. The museum showcases thousands of ancient Chinese cultural relics, including jade artefacts, Buddhist sculptures and porcelain. It's housed in an "Oriental curio box" building on the riverfront designed by Japanese architect Tadao Ando which glows sapphire by night and has impressive views across the river to the Bund.

Chen Guichun's House

Chén Guìchūn Jiùzhái 陆家嘴开发陈列馆 (陈桂春旧宅)

Across Century Boulevard is the only building here that looks as if it might be more than a decade old, a 1917 wood and brick courtyard house that was once the home of wealthy shipping merchant Chen Guichun. The spacious house was once part of a sprawling estate that

housed several families and served as the headquarters of the Japanese army and the Kuomintang government. A museum until 2007 (rather uninspiringly known as the Lujiazui Development Showroom), the house is now used as a memorial to famous painter Wu Changshuo (free).

AROUND CENTURY BOULEVARD

Century Boulevard (Shi Ji Da Dao) cuts dramatically through Pudong. The magnificent 5km (3-mile)-long street, which runs from the World Financial Center to Century Park, has a generous 100-metre (320ft)-wide avenue with 10 hectares (25 acres) of greenery on either side. Designed by French architect Jean-Marie Charpentier (who also designed the Shanghai Grand Theatre), it makes for one of the city's most pleasant drives. Pudong's landmarks are well spread out on either side of the boulevard, with run-down 1970s government-built housing poking up from between shiny skyscrapers, reminders that despite the movie-set look of Pudong, a local population still lives here.

Jin Mao Tower as seen from one of the courtyards at Chen Guichun's House.

You could take a boring taxi ride into the city from Pudong International Airport, or you could experience a heart-stopping ride on the Maglev train – which uses electromagnetic technology to glide above the guard rails at a top speed of over 430km (267 miles) an hour! The downside? The train only goes to as far as Longyang Road metro station in Pudong, where you have to lug your bags one floor down the escalator and get a taxi or the metro into town. See Transport for details on the Maglev (see page 258).

The Shanghai Science and Technology Museum building is bright and airy.

At the top end of Century Boulevard, keep an eye out for the distinctive shape of the **Shanghai Stock Exchange Building** (Shanghai Zhengquan Jiaoyisuo), designed to resemble an ancient Chinese coin with a square space in its centre. Visitors are not allowed on the trading floor. At 3,600 sq metres (38,750 sq ft), the Shanghai exchange is the largest in Asia and operates an advanced electronic trading system.

A 10-minute taxi ride from riverside Lujiazui via Century Boulevard will take you to Pudong's shopping nexus, where you'll find the 10-storey **Next Age Department Store** (Ba Bai Ban), and, across the street, **Times Square** with its large collection of designer boutiques.

Qinci Yangdian Temple ❽

Qīncì Yǎngdiàn Dàoguàn 钦赐仰殿道观
Address: 476 Yuanshen Road
Opening Hrs: daily 8am–4pm
Entrance Fee: RMB 5
Transport: Dongchang Road + taxi

Pudong's most important temple, with its curved, tiled roof and ochre-coloured walls, looks out of place in the forest of concrete and glass that make up Pudong. The temple was first built during the Three Kingdoms period (AD 220–280), and has been

Exhibit at the Shanghai Science and Technology Museum.

rebuilt several times over the years. The latest rebuilding, in 2007, saw the Taoist temple's Qing-era buildings demolished and replaced with brand-new buildings and gods – taking away its authenticity. The temple's most powerful deity, Yan Wang, is also known as the god of hell; Qinci Yangdian has a collection of city gods too and a "treaty" god.

Shanghai Science and Technology Museum ❾

Shànghǎi Kējìguǎn 上海科技馆
Address: 2000 Century Boulevard; www.sstm.org.cn
Tel: 6862 2000
Opening Hrs: Tue–Sun 9am–5pm
Entrance Fee: RMB 60 adults, RMB 20 children
Transport: Science and Technology Museum

Back on Century Boulevard, veer right at the "Oriental Light" sculpture, a contemporary sundial, to the **Science and Technology Museum**. The theme of the museum, taking up 68,000 sq metres (731,950 sq ft) of space, is "man, nature, science and technology". The popular IMAX theatre screens daily shows (separate fee), and the five interactive science halls hold everything from an exploding volcano to a recreated rainforest with more than 300 types of plants. In addition there is a simulated laboratory where experiments can be conducted, and an interactive children's area. The swanky new Shanghai Natural History Museum in Jing'an (see page 180) is a branch of the Science and Technology Museum.

Shanghai Oriental Arts Centre ⑩

Shànghǎi Dōngfāng Yìshù Zhōngxīn 上海东方艺术中心
Address: 425 Dingxiang Road; www.shoac.com.cn
Tel: 3842 4800
Transport: Science and Technology Museum

On the opposite side of Century Boulevard is the stunning **Shanghai Oriental Arts Centre**, home of the Shanghai Symphony Orchestra. Designed by Pudong Airport designer Paul Andreu in the shape of a butterfly orchid when viewed from the top, the SOAC is Pudong's answer to the Shanghai Grand Theatre.

The facility for performing arts is encircled by a lush garden and has three performance theatres and an exhibition hall. Andreu carried his theme of nature inside as well: the black granite floor symbolises the forest floor, steel girders are the trees, and the clear, round lights, suspended at different levels, are dewdrops.

Century Park ⑪

Shìjì Gōngyuán 世纪公园
Address: 1001 Jinxiu Road
Tel: 3876 0588
Opening Hrs: daily 6am–6pm
Entrance Fee: free
Transport: Century Park

Continue down Century Boulevard to **Century Park**. French architect Jean-Marie Charpentier also designed this beautifully landscaped 140-hectare (346-acre) eco-park, its forest and park area anchored by a huge lake. The park is the site of sporting events such as the annual Terry Fox run and other large celebrations.

China Art Museum ⑫

Zhōnghuá Yìshù Gōng 中华艺术宫
Address: 161 Shangnan Road
Tel: 6222 8822
Opening Hrs: Tue–Sun 10am–6pm (last entry 5pm)
Entrance Fee: free
Transport: China Art Museum

A short metro-ride away at the 2010 Shanghai World Expo site, the iconic **China Pavilion** from the Expo, dubbed the 'Crown of the East', now showcases the world's biggest collection of modern Chinese art. Covering 166,800 sq metres across five levels, works by iconic 20th-century painters hang alongside Chinese calligraphy and ink-brush paintings, propaganda art and socialist-realist sculptures, charting the development of modern art in China since the late Qing Dynasty.

Long Museum Pudong ⑬

Lóng Měishùguǎn 龙美术馆
Address: 2255 Luoshan Road
Tel: 6877 8787
Opening Hrs: Tue–Sun 10am–5.30pm
Entrance Fee: RMB 50
Transport: Huamu Road

Billionaire husband and wife team Liu Yiqian and Wang Wei own the largest private art collection in China,

The striking interior of the Shanghai Oriental Arts Centre takes its design cue from nature.

The Shanghai Oriental Arts Centre resembles a butterfly orchid when viewed from above.

split across two branches of the Long Museum in Shanghai. The **Long Museum Pudong** was the first to open in 2012; the second, opened in 2014, is the West Bund branch – see page 188.

The striking cuboid building in Pudong, designed by Chinese architect Zhong Song, houses a range of traditional Chinese art, revolutionary "red classics" and contemporary pieces across four floors. Traditional works include exquisite examples of calligraphy and painting, as well as ancient Chinese artefacts and items of furniture. The building also houses a reading room, an academic auditorium, an art shop, and a café.

Shanghai Disney Resort ⑭

Shànghǎi Díshìní Dùjiàqū 上海迪士尼度假区
Address: 360 Shendi West Road, Chuansha
Tel: 2099 8002
Opening Hrs: 9am–7pm (Shanghai Disneyland)
Entrance Fee: RMB 370 adults (weekdays) 499 (weekends), 280 children under 1.4 metres/4.6ft (weekdays) 375 (weekends)
Transport: Shanghai Disney Resort

The Enchanted Storybook Castle is the centrepiece of the Shanghai Disney Resort.

Just over a 20-minute drive from Century Park, "the most magical place on earth" opened in far-flung Pudong in June 2016. Crowned by the tallest and most interactive Enchanted Storybook Castle ever created, **Shanghai Disney Resort** comprises Shanghai Disneyland theme park, Wishing Star Park, Disneytown shopping and dining district, plus an Art Nouveau-styled Disneyland hotel and Toy Story hotel. Disney's first-ever high-speed TRON Lightcycle Power Run rollercoaster is worth the queue.

NANHUI AND OUTSKIRTS

Rural Nanhui district merged with Pudong in 2009. The area, in the south of Pudong, retains a character distinct from much of the district's business-like sterility. Nanhui is most famous for its peach orchards, which transform into a sea of pink blossoms towards the end of March and

Children enjoying a show at the Shanghai Wild Animal Park.

The Wild Animal Park's sea lions play ball.

the start of April. Apart from this, Nanhui hosts an animal park for children and Shanghai's only authentic water village.

Shanghai Wild Animal Park ⑮

Shànghǎi Yěshēng Dòngwùyuán 上海野生动物园
Address: 178 Nan Liu Gong Lu, Pudong
Tel: 5803 6000
Opening Hrs: daily 8am–5pm
Entrance Fee: RMB 130 adults, RMB 65 children

A 45-minute drive from central Pudong takes you to this safari park. It is divided into bus and walking zones by animal type: wilder animals such as hunting leopards and South China tigers are safely viewed from buses, while the walking zones allow gentler species such as kangaroos, deer and lemurs to roam freely. There are also animal shows throughout the day. Unfortunately, keepers ignore the fact that visitors feed the animals, some of which are unnecessarily tethered, sometimes harshly, during the photo sessions and performances.

Xinchang Ancient Town

Xīnchāng Gǔzhèn 新场古镇
This atmospheric canal town in the Nanhui area – about an hour's drive from the centre of Pudong – dating back to the Song Dynasty (AD 960–1279) is perhaps Shanghai's best and most authentic water village, sensitively restored by one of the city's leading preservationists and as yet undiscovered by the tourist hordes.

Xinchang has been largely overshadowed by better-known touristy old towns like **Zhujiajiao**, offered as standard fare on most bus tours to Shanghai's outskirts. But this is a good thing and long may it remain so. Unlike the city's other water villages, Xinchang's residents still live in the houses that their ancestors built.

Xinchang's Ming-era main street has been preserved along with over 20 of the town's original mansions as well as courtyard houses. Highlights include the beautiful **Zhang Mansion** (Zhang Ting) at 176 Xinchang Street, with its Dutch floor tiles and European touches. Another must-see sight is the century-old **No. 1 Teahouse** (Lao Cha Guan), an atmospheric three-storey building.

Idyllic Xinchang canal town.

Dragon Meeting Pond Park. Jiading.

WESTERN SUBURBS AND CHONGMING ISLAND

Shanghai city slickers escape here for the slower pace and taste of country living. Jiading, Songjiang and Qingpu districts all have their own appeal and are now connected to the Shanghai metro network. Further west is Chongming Island, China's third-largest island and a birdwatchers' haven.

Amusement parks, Ming-dynasty canal towns, ancient pagodas and nature spots run riot through the countryside that borders the city's western flank, a curious mixture of tradition, kitsch and industrialisation. Shanghai's western suburbs and Chongming Island are part of the greater Shanghai municipality, yet are still too rural to be really considered part of the city of Shanghai.

The western suburbs – which were carved out of neighbouring provinces and provided the burgeoning city with food and room for expansion – offer a taste of Old China, with scenes of lonely pagodas brooding on silent hillsides and crumbling Ming houses in forgotten lanes. The rural quiet belies what was a thriving area during the Song and the Tang dynasties, and, in the case of Songjiang county's Songze village, a history that goes as far back as Neolithic times – before the land mass of Shanghai even existed.

Today, Shanghai's long shadow still defines the character of the area. Elements of antiquity, so lacking in the city, are tarted up and gift-wrapped for Shanghai tourists. Acres of ripening fields are yielding to the city's relentless progress as they are taken over by mega-sized factories and, increasingly these days, luxury housing.

JIADING DISTRICT

Jiading district typifies the western suburbs with its dual character, part Old China, part ultra-modern China. Once the seat of the imperial examinations, the district is dotted with classical gardens and temples. But it is also the home of the Formula One race in China, and is a leading auto-manufacturing centre.

Nanxiang ❶

Nánxiáng 南翔

Jiading's most famous export is *xiao*

Main Attractions
Jiading Town
Shanghai International
  Circuit at Anting
Sheshan Observatory
Sheshan Cathedral
Chongming Island

Map
Page 228

A countryside toddler.

Soup dumpling.

Pavilion at the Garden of Ancient Splendour at Jiading.

long bao, from **Nanxiang**, some 17km (10.5 miles) northwest of Shanghai. The bite-sized pleated dumplings, stuffed with pork and enough boiling liquid to do serious damage if popped into the mouth whole, are available in seemingly every restaurant in this small town. The quality of these dumplings can vary quite dramatically, though, from one restaurant to the next.

Garden of Ancient Splendour

Gǔyīyuán 古漪园
Address: 218 Huyi Road, Nanxiang
Tel: 5912 2225
Opening Hrs: daily 7am–6pm
Entrance Fee: RMB 12
Transport: Nanxiang

Designed by bamboo sculptor (and native son) Zhun Sansong, this Suzhou-style garden, which dates back to 1566, retains its Ming contours despite a 1746 reconstruction and 1949 expansion. A Song stone pagoda

and a Tang stele with Buddhist scriptures stand in the garden. A pavilion built during the Japanese occupation has a corner left incomplete, held up by a defiant fist, to signify a broken China under the occupation.

At the Chinese pavilion on the edge of the garden is **Guyi Garden Nanxiang Xiao Long Bao** restaurant, where you can partake of this delicate Nanxiang speciality.

Jiading Town ❷

Jiādìngzhèn 嘉定镇
Some 10km (6 miles) northwest of Nanxiang is **Jiading Town**, a quiet canal-fringed little town that is the largest in the Jiading district.

Dragon Meeting Pond Park

Huìlóngtán Gōngyuán 汇龙潭公园
Address: 299 Tacheng Road
Opening Hrs: daily 8am–5pm
Entrance Fee: RMB 5
Transport: Jiading Xincheng

The town's Ming-era park, named

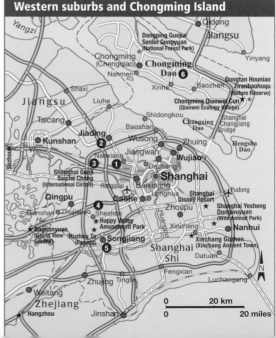

Western suburbs and Chongming Island

after the five streams that converge here, may be contemplated in relative solitude. (And yes, there is a dragon sculpture in one of the ponds.) The lovely garden is dotted with bamboo trees, pagodas and pavilions – including one with a ceiling featuring a dizzying series of concentric whorls and a mirror at its interior apex.

Confucius Temple

Kŏngmiào 孔庙
Address: 183 Nan Da Street, Jiading Town
Opening Hrs: daily 8am–4.30pm
Entrance Fee: free
Transport: Jiading Xincheng

At one time, Jiading Town was important enough to be the seat of the imperial examinations, held at the Southern Song-style **Confucius Temple**, first built in 1281. Located west of Dragon Meeting Pond Park, a massive statue of Confucius, the patron saint of scholars, dominates the main hall of the temple, with

statues of his favourite students lining one wall.

Examination candidates would offer prayers to Confucius, and in return, the Yuan dynasty sculpture of a fish and dragon over the temple's main gate would bless the scholars with good luck. The sculpture is a visual representation of the saying "a carp leaping over the dragon gate", a metaphor for achieving success. There is more symbolism along the stone fence that fronts the temple, with its 72 stone lions representing the 72 disciples of Confucius.

The temple grounds are also home to the beautifully designed **Imperial Examination Museum** (Zhongguo Keju Bowuguan; daily 8am–4.30pm), which documents the rigorous examination system that dominated China's civil service from the Han dynasty until its abolishment in 1904. Among the exhibits are books, original lists of triumphant scholars, dioramas featuring the examination

A prayer tied to a tree next to the main prayer hall at the Confucius Temple.

The main prayer hall.

The Formula One race track at the Shanghai International Circuit in Anting, designed by the German-born Hermann Tilke, is reputedly one of the most challenging on the circuit.

Sheshan Cathedral was built by Jesuit Catholic missionaries.

cells, and profiles of successful candidates who later became famous.

Fahua Pagoda

Fǎhuátǎ 法华塔

Exit the temple at Nan Da Street and head north towards the graceful Southern Song-era **Fahua Pagoda**, rebuilt in 1919. Legend has it that Jiading's examination candidates uniformly failed the imperial examinations until the pagoda was built; today, visitors can climb the seven-storey pagoda to the top via a wooden staircase for views over the city.

Garden of Autumn Clouds

Qiūxiápǔ 秋霞圃
Address: 314 Dong Da Street
Opening Hrs: daily 8am–4.30pm
Entrance Fee: RMB 10

A stroll north along Lianqiu River leads to Shanghai's oldest garden and certainly one of its loveliest, with scenic spots aplenty. Laid out in 1502 as the private garden of a Ming official called Gong Hong, the garden has been renovated several times.

Shanghai International Circuit ❸

Shànghǎi Guójì Sàichē Chǎng 上海国际赛车场
These days, Jiading is best known as

the home of the **Formula One** race, which takes place in the **Shanghai International Circuit** in Anting every September. The site includes a world-class Hermann Tilke-designed track (see box) and is also the home of VW China.

Nearby is a German-themed residential town, designed by Albert Speer, son of Hitler's favourite architect, called "Anting New Town", one of a series of themed residential developments that have been built throughout suburban Shanghai.

SONGJIANG

Songjiang, 30km (19 miles) southwest of Shanghai and the site of Neolithic remains at Songze village, is known as the cradle of Shanghai civilisation. Today, its most famous site is the French Jesuit-built cathedral in **Sheshan ❹**. The district is also taking advantage of its lush, natural setting to reinvent itself as a weekend getaway, complete with outlet shopping and complementary bicycles.

Sheshan Observatory

Shéshān Tiānwéntái 佘山天文台
Address: Sheshan Hill
Tel: 5765 3423
Opening Hrs: daily 7.30am–5pm
Entrance Fee: RMB 30 for both

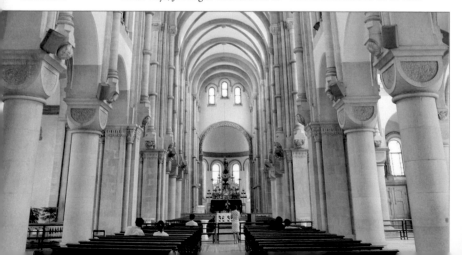

observatory and cathedral; cable car costs an additional RMB 10
Transport: Sheshan

Once regarded as one of the most important in Asia, the 1898 observatory stands on the highest point in Shanghai municipality. Visitors can either walk up the 100-metre (328ft) high hill, or take the cable car up for a bird's-eye view of the surroundings. The century-old telescope is still intact, and the observatory is now a small museum dedicated to the history of Chinese stargazing. A new telescope was installed just below the crest of the hill, but as recently as 1986, the old machine was used to track and take photos of Halley's Comet for scientific use – just as the Jesuits who built the observatory did when the comet visited in 1910.

Sheshan Cathedral

Shéshān Tiānzhǔjiàotáng 余山天主教堂
Address: Sheshan Hill
Tel: 5765 1521
Opening Hrs: daily 8am–4pm; mass Mon–Sat 7am (6.30am in summer), Sun 8am (7.30am in summer)

The Jesuits also built the sturdy

The Sheshan Observatory in Songjiang district.

hillside church next door, first named the Holy Mother Cathedral in 1866 and, subsequently, in 1935, the Basilica of Notre Dame. A subtle "M" (for Mary) and "SJ" (Society of Jesus, ie the Jesuits) are inscribed in the old iron gate in the southwestern corner of the churchyard. Pilgrims usually walk up the south gate, lined with grottoes and shrines, stopping to say prayers or the rosary along the way. Local Catholics make a pilgrimage here each May.

Happy Valley Amusement Park

Huān lè gǔ 欢乐谷
Address: Linyin Lu, Sheshan, Songjiang
Tel: 3355 2222
Opening Hrs: daily 9am–6pm; July–Aug until 10pm
Entrance Fee: RMB 200, children under 1.2 metres (4ft) RMB 100, includes all rides
Transport: Sheshan + shuttle bus

Billed as one of China's largest theme parks, **Happy Valley** has rides in six different themed areas, along with China's only wooden rollercoaster and some truly scary rides. Try Space Shot, Turbo Drop and the Diving Coaster (two nearly vertical drops!) if you dare, but there are also plenty of tamer rides, making it ideal for a family outing.

The Garden of Autumn Clouds in Jiading is Shanghai's oldest public garden.

ANTING

Every spring, Shanghai goes car crazy: that's when the city hosts the Chinese Grand Prix, the Formula One race in Anting, Jiading district. Drivers say that the Hermann Tilke-designed track may well be the best on the circuit – fast, technical and consisting of seven left and seven right turns, including a series of double-snail bends and hairpin turns cleverly designed in the shape of the character *shang*, which means "above" (from "Shanghai", meaning "above the sea"). In addition, the 1.2km (0.75-mile) straightaway allows drivers to get up to speeds of 326kmh (203mph). Thanks to F1, Anting has gone from being a backwater to Shanghai's "automobile city". Volkswagen has a manufacturing base here, and there is also an automobile college, exhibition centre and hotels. Anting "New Town", styled after a German town, is one of 11 planned satellite towns built in Shanghai's far-flung suburbs as part of a 2001 urbanisation programme. Each new town was to be themed on a different European country, including British-style Thames Town, Holland Town and Italian Town, the latter complete with Venetian-esque canals.

Square Pagoda

Fāngtǎyuán 方塔园
Address: 235 Zhongshan Rd (E)
Tel: 5782 2157
Opening Hrs: daily 8.30am–4.30pm
Entrance Fee: RMB 12

Continue on to **Songjiang Town ⑤** and its pride, the **Square Pagoda**. Built in 1077, the 50-metre (160ft) structure will reward climbers with views of the countryside. The 14th-century brick screen wall that fronts the pagoda depicts the legendary monster *tan*, with deer antlers, a lion's tail and ox's hooves, which tried to devour the sun but ended up drowning instead – the moral being that greed is not good.

Other sights

The Garden of Drunken Poet Bai (Zuibai Chi; daily 9am–4.30pm), a 5-minute walk west of Square Pagoda, dates back to the 17th century. It was commissioned by a Qing official who was a fan of the Tang poet Li Bai, who fell into a pond while drunkenly trying to capture the moon's reflection in the water.

Zuibai Chi garden.

Songjiang district's Muslims flock to the lovely **Songjiang Mosque** (Songjiang Qingzhen Si; daily 8am–7pm) every Friday for prayers. The 14th-century Chinese-style mosque is one of the oldest in China.

QINGPU DISTRICT

Rural Qingpu's proximity to downtown Shanghai means that it is a favourite playground for city dwellers, who are regular visitors to its parks, water villages and other sights.

The romance of Ming and Qing water villages such as **Zhujiajiao** are rapidly eroding with the onset of tourism. The original residents have moved out and are replaced by souvenir shops; shopping plazas now ring the historical areas and the narrow lanes are cheek-to-jowl with tourists.

Grand View Garden

Dàguānyuán 大观园
Address: 701 Qingshang Highway, Qingpu
Tel: 5926 2831
Opening Hrs: daily 8am–5pm
Entrance Fee: RMB 60 adults, RMB 30 children

Just off Qingshang Highway is a glimpse of ancient China at the **Grand View Garden** on the edge of Dianshan Lake (Dianshan Hu). A theme park based on the classic Chinese novel *Dream of the Red Mansion*, the garden's re-creations of the novel's buildings, set in a Suzhou-style garden, are enhanced by Chinese musicians and re-enactments of scenes from the book by actors in period garb.

CHONGMING ISLAND ⑥

Chongming Island (Chongming Dao) lies in silt-muddied waters at the mouth of the Yangtze River. China's third-largest island at 1,267 sq km (489 sq miles), the island is home to some 821,500 residents. Chongming's main business is agriculture, and it provides the fish, crabs and vegetables that feed Shanghai.

Chongming has doubled its size over the last half-century through land reclamation and the constant silting of the Yangtze River. And it continues to grow by about 5 sq km (1.9 sq miles) each year. With 30,000 hectares (74,130 acres) of beaches and a migratory bird conservation zone, the island has more wild creatures than people at certain times of the year. Plans are now under way to turn it into the world's first sustainable "green" island, beginning with the **Dongtan Eco-City** on the eastern tip of the island. It is also home to several organic farms where Shanghai urbanites take weekend drives to harvest their own fresh fruits and vegetables, plus a growing number of luxury resorts.

For most of its 1,300-year history, Chongming has battled the sea. The town has been relocated five times – and rebuilt six times – due to the flooding that destroys the sea walls.

Getting to Chongming

The Yangtze River Tunnel and Bridge Project connects Chongming with Pudong via Changxiang Island. It's an unfamiliar thrill to emerge from the underwater tunnel straight onto a

Making a splash at Happy Valley Amusement Park.

bridge. Metro Line 9 will also connect the island eventually, or you can get there the old-fashioned way, by boarding a ferry from one of Shanghai's three northeastern ports of Wusong, Baoyang and Shidongkou. Depending on which of Chongming's three gritty port towns you arrive at – Nanmen, Xinhe or Baozhen – head westwards for the island's main attraction – Dongping National Forest Park.

Dongping National Forest Park

Dōngpíng Guójiā Sēnlín Gōngyuán
东平国家森林公园

Out for a stroll, Chongming Island.

A great egret at Dongtan Nature Reserve. The species is under threat due to pollution, poaching and encroaching urbanisation.

Chongming Island's Dongtan Nature Reserve is a haven for rare bird species.

Tel: 5964 1841
Opening Hrs: daily 8am–5pm
Entrance Fee: RMB 60
Dongping National Forest Park covers 360 hectares (890 acres) of Chongming's western half. A boulevard of soaring cone-shaped deepgreen metasequoias fringe a canal leading to the entrance of eastern China's largest man-made forest.

The park began life as a tree farm in 1959 and has a fishing pond and lake. The myriad paths that criss-cross the interior, coupled with clean air and birdsong, are reasons enough to visit. However, Chongming's park administration is taking no chances: the lake is stocked with paddle boats, there is a Go-Kart track, a slightly grungy swimming pool (and a man-made beach), and downhill grass skiing. On the forest's edge is a modern hotel, the **Bao Dao Resort** (tel: 5933 9479).

Qianwei Ecology Village

Chóngmíng Qiánwèi Cūn 崇明前卫村
Tel: 5964 9261
Opening Hrs: daily 8.30am–10pm; accommodation and dining options also available
Entrance Fee: RMB 60

Most of Chongming's population is concentrated in the port towns, with the remainder in scattered villages. **Qianwei Ecology Village**, on the island's eastern edge, is a traditional village with restored Qing-era thatched roof farmhouses and farmers who practise ecologically sound cultivation. The farmers here grow organic vegetables, and some have turned their houses into bed-and-breakfast places. Qianwei encourages visitors to try out farm living and working in the fields.

Dongtan Nature Reserve

Dōngtān Hòuniǎo Zìránbǎohùqū 东滩候鸟自然保护区
Trekking into the remote marshes and mudflats at **Dongtan Nature Reserve** (daily 6am–6pm; free) on the island's eastern edge, is a highlight. Thousands of birds, sandpipers, terns, plovers, egrets and herons – 116 species and which represent one-tenth of the total species in China – flit among the shore grasses, shrieking and cooing, including migratory birds en route from Australia to Siberia. The birds, like everywhere else in China, are under threat due to pollution, poaching and urbanisation.

Giant metasequoia trees at Dongping National Forest Park on Chongming Island.

Sunrise over West Lake, Hangzhou.

EXCURSIONS FROM SHANGHAI

Suzhou and Hangzhou are perfect side trips for visitors wanting to escape the frenzy of Shanghai. There are also the water villages of Tongli, Zhouzhuang and Xitang, and for the more adventurous, the mist-shrouded mountain resort of Moganshan, near Hangzhou.

For almost a century, people from other parts of China have come to Shanghai to see what the West looks like. Even today, one is often reminded that urban Shanghai is not representative of China. Fortunately, some of the country's most famous classically Chinese sights are within a couple of hours of Shanghai. But even in these places, you can't really leave Shanghai behind. There are historical links and contemporary connections, as the spill-over from the Shanghai economic boom ignites growth and modernisation in these neighbouring cities, which once had more gravitas than Shanghai.

The combination of an efficient train system and high-speed highway makes getting out of the city easy. Only on China's two week-long holidays (Chinese New Year and National Day), when all transport routes are hopelessly jammed, does travelling become a major challenge.

SUZHOU ❶

Sùzhōu 苏州

The ancient city of **Suzhou**, just 80km (50 miles) northwest of Shanghai, has an intricate mosaic of canals and classical gardens that led Marco Polo to describe it as the "Venice of the East". Suzhou began to flourish after

the completion of the Grand Canal. Its prosperity soared further when neighbouring Hangzhou (and later, Nanjing) became the imperial capital of China. Silk production thrived, and imperial officials began laying out the famous classical gardens – almost 200 at its peak.

The city walls are now gone, but the moat that followed the wall's contours remains, as do almost 200 ancient humpback bridges. Today, the historic city is ringed by tomorrow: the Suzhou–Singapore industrial park

Main Attractions
Kunqu Opera Museum
Suzhou Silk Museum
Master of the Nets Garden
Tongli
Xitang
Gu Shan Island
Lingyin Temple
Tomb and Temple of Yue Fei
Moganshan

Maps
Pages 240, 242, 248

Moganshan mountain view.

Chinese gardens are more than what meets the eye: in the pavilions, rockeries, fish pools, gnarled trees and shrubs, and delicate blossoms are expressions of Chinese poetry, philosophy and art – a microcosm of the world. The pine trees, for instance, symbolise long life, the fat goldfish money, the peony blooms always nobility. Rocks and ponds always feature prominently because the Chinese word for landscape is *shanshui*, literally "mountain-water".

surrounds Old Suzhou, drawing it into a 21st-century world of fast food, modern industries and five-star hotels.

Suzhou's protected historical district, with its cobblestone streets and ancient stone dwellings, still retains its medieval character. But it is the tranquil gardens, now a Unesco World Heritage site, that are the soul of the city. Just 70 gardens remain; each with its own distinct personality, yet all a microcosm of the world, perfectly balanced in terms of harmony, proportion and variety.

Temple of Mystery Ⓐ

Xuánmiào Guàn 玄妙观
Address: 94 Guanqian Road
Opening Hrs: daily 7.30am–5pm
Entrance Fee: RMB 10

This 3rd-century Taoist temple, once the heart of an ancient-style Suzhou bazaar, is still a shopping magnet, today surrounded by a thriving street market. The temple has an Old China aura and an impressive scale: a great

The stage at Kunqu Opera Museum.

courtyard leads to the massive **San Qing Hall** (San Qing Tang), with its 60 magnificent red-lacquered columns, classic two-tiered roof with upturned

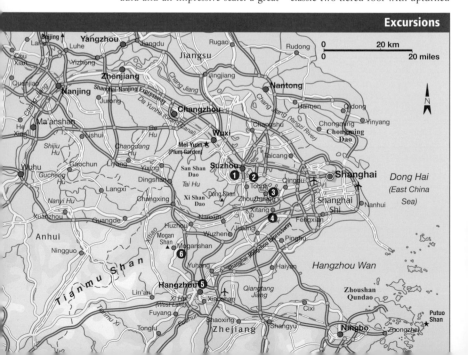

Excursions

eaves and vibrantly painted Taoist gods. The temple was badly damaged during the 19th century.

Kunqu Opera Museum B

Kūnqǔ Bówùguǎn 昆曲博物馆
Address: 14 Zhongzhang Jia Xiang
Opening Hrs: daily 8.30am–4.30pm
Entrance Fee: free

A 10-minute walk east, following the side of the canal, leads to the **Kunqu Opera Museum**, where Suzhou's own 500-year-old Kunqu opera tradition is chronicled. Pre-dating Beijing opera by 200 years, Kunqu, or Kūnjù, opera (see page 48) is still performed in this Ming dynasty building under a stunning wooden dome embellished with an intricate seashell-like whorl pattern. Across the courtyard, another building houses a display of costumes, opera masks, musical instruments – even a model orchestra – as well as documents on the opera's history.

Just next door, Suzhou's ancient storytelling song tradition called Pingtan (see page 48) comes alive each afternoon with performances (at 1.30pm daily) at the **Pingtan**

Museum (Pingtan Bowuguan). The performances, which are accompanied by Chines string instruments, are in the local Suzhou dialect.

Lion Grove garden.

Lion Grove C

Shīzi Lín 狮子林
Address: 23 Yuanlin Road
Tel: 512 6727 2428
Opening Hrs: daily 7.30am–5.30pm
Entrance Fee: RMB 40

It's a short taxi ride northwest to **Lion Grove**. A Buddhist temple

Temple of Mystery.

The Humble Administrator's Garden, the largest of the Suzhou gardens.

garden laid out in 1342, Lion Grove is a poem to the mountain. Encircled by a covered corridor, the garden has intricate piles of rocks taken from nearby Lake Tai – many lion-shaped – weathered by the elements and set among lakes and pavilions. Last owned by a branch of the well-known Chinese architect I.M. Pei's family, Lion Grove is said to be Emperor Qianlong's inspiration for Yuanmingyuan, the old Summer Palace on the outskirts of Beijing.

Suzhou Museum ⓓ

Sūzhōu Bówùguǎn 苏州博物馆
Address: 204 Dongbei Road;
www.szmuseum.com
Tel: 512 6754 1534
Opening Hrs: daily 9am–5pm
Entrance Fee: free

I.M. Pei, drawing on his family connection to Suzhou for inspiration, designed the landmark **Suzhou Museum** that opened in 2006, a short walk north of Lion Grove. The

US$40-million white and grey building reinvents traditional Suzhou architecture in a spectacular Modernist form. There is plenty of glass and light, and Chinese touches like a Chinese garden and footbridge. The massive museum features a collection of artefacts from early Suzhou, and includes a rare pearl stupa, porcelain, funeral relics unearthed from the mud of Dongshan Island, antique maps of Suzhou and the Grand Canal, and Song dynasty art and calligraphy.

Humble Administrator's Garden ⓔ

Zhuōzhèng Yuán 拙政园
Address: 178 Dongbei Road
Tel: 512 6751 0286
Opening Hrs: 7.30am–5pm
Entrance Fee: RMB 70/90

Just to the northeast is the **Humble Administrator's Garden**, whose name refers to a line of Jin dynasty poetry that says cultivating a garden is the work of a humble man. But this

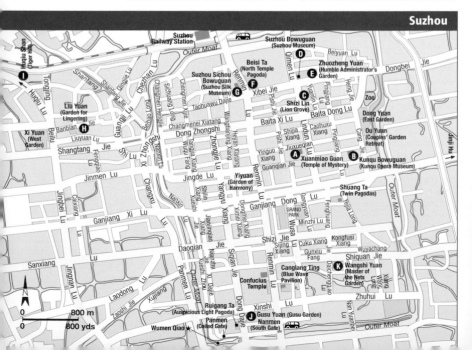

4-hectare (10-acre) garden, the largest of the Suzhou gardens, is far from a humble undertaking.

Laid out by retired Ming imperial official Wang Xianchen in 1513, the three main areas are thematically linked by water, used in pools and ponds of varying sizes. Twisting and turning rock-lined paths burst open onto a classical landscape: an expansive lotus pond crossed by zigzag bridges and pavilions perched on hillsides and in hollows.

North Temple Pagoda

Běisì Tǎ 北寺塔
Address: 652 Renmin Road
Opening Hrs: daily 8am–6pm
Entrance Fee: free

To the west, this 76-metre (250ft) high mustard and vermilion pagoda on the site of the Wu Kingdom ruler Sun Quan's childhood home, dominates the city. First built during the 3rd century and completely rebuilt in the 16th century, a climb to its summit offers spectacular views of the surrounding area, including the 17th-century **Nanmu Hall** on the grounds, with a teahouse just behind.

Suzhou Silk Museum

Sūzhōu Sīchóu Bówùguǎn 苏州丝绸博物馆
Address: 661 Renmin Road (opposite North Temple Pagoda)
Tel: 512 6753 1977
Opening Hrs: daily 9am–5pm
Entrance Fee: free

Across the street, the **Suzhou Silk Museum** recounts the history of silk in China. Especially interesting are the rare antique silk pieces, and the section on sericulture: one room has large woven pans holding wriggling silkworms (when in season) feasting on mulberry leaves, while on another shelf, silk cocoons sit neatly in rows. Weavers at the museum demonstrate how young girls ruined their hands in the old days by plunging them into boiling water to separate the cocoon threads into single strands. The big looms, strung with jewel-tone silk threads, bob up and down in the skilled hands of the weavers.

Garden for Lingering

Liú Yuán 留园
Address: 338 Liuyuan Road
Tel: 512 6533 7940
Opening Hrs: 7.30am–5.30pm
Entrance Fee: RMB 55

To the west, outside the city gates, is the Ming-era **Garden for Lingering**. Here, a 700-metre (2,300ft) walkway links the garden's four scenic areas. Laid out by Ming dynasty minister Xu Taishi, the corridor has inscribed tablets bearing flowery descriptions of the garden by poets and noted visitors. Its most famous pavilion, the **Mandarin Duck Hall** (Yuanyuang), has separate viewing rooms for men and women, both of which overlook the garden's pride: the 6.5-metre (21ft) 5,000kg (11,000lb) **Cloud Crowned Peak** (Junyun Feng), the largest rock from Lake Tai in any of the Suzhou gardens.

Tiger Hill

Hǔqiū Shān 虎丘山

A silk brocade jacket on display at the Suzhou Silk Museum.

The garden of North Temple Pagoda.

Address: 8 Huqiu Road
Tel: 512 6723 2305
Opening Hrs: daily 7am–6pm
Entrance Fee: RMB 60

A visit to Suzhou without seeing **Tiger Hill**, located far in the northwest of the city, would be incomplete, wrote Song poet Su Shi. Less formal and manicured than the others, Tiger Hill contains the tomb of Suzhou's ruler, the 6th-century BC Wu king He Lu. The garden gets its name from the mythical white tiger that appeared on the third day after his death to guard the grave. Archaeologists suspect it may be that grave, which lies beneath the seven-storey octagonal brick **Cloud Rock Pagoda** (Yunyan Ta) on the hilltop, that is causing the pagoda's severe tilt. Tiger Hill's **Thousand Men Rock** (Qian Ren Shi), at the foot of the hill, is reputedly the gruesome spot where the tomb builders were executed to keep secret the location of the tomb and its treasures, while **Sword Pond** (Jianchi) is said to be where the king's 3,000 swords were buried.

Gusu Garden ❶

Gūsū Yuán 姑苏园

Tiger Hill with Cloud Rock Pagoda in the background.

Address: 1 Dong Dajie
Opening Hrs: daily 7.30am–5pm
Entrance Fee: RMB 25

Head southeast to **Gusu Garden**, just south of the Sheraton Suzhou. Here you can climb the well-worn steps of **Five Gate Bridge** (Wumen Qiao), Suzhou's tallest bridge, for a vista of boats and barges sliding past the canal. **Pan Gate** (Pan Men), the only remaining stretch of Suzhou's 3rd-century city wall, is a short walk away. The climb up the 300 metres (980ft) of original city wall is rewarded with a view of fishing boats, arched bridges, graceful willows over canals and the 1,000-year-old **Ruigang Pagoda** (Ruigang Ta).

Master of the Nets Garden ❽

Wǎngshī Yuán 网师园
Address: 11 Kuojiatou Xiang
Tel: 512 6529 3190
Opening Hrs: 7.30am–5.30pm
Entrance Fee: RMB 40

The loveliest Suzhou garden is also one of the smallest: the exquisite **Master of the Nets Garden**. Dating from 1770, its name refers to the ambition of its retired court official owner, who longed to be a fisherman. The intimate garden's charm comes from

Master of the Nets Garden, depicted on tiles.

its delicate, scaled-down courtyards, pavilions and rockeries. Contained in its pavilions is some of Suzhou's most exquisite antique furniture, especially in the **Peony Study** (Dianchun Yi), which has been replicated at New York's Metropolitan Museum of Art. On summer nights, the beautifully lit pavilions are the setting for traditional performances – opera, music and dance – that transport the viewer to the days of the imperial court (daily 10-minute shows from 7.30–10pm; RMB 80). On moonlit nights, visitors may be given access to the **Moon Watching Pavilion** (Yue Dao Feng Lai Ting), where they can see the moon thrice over: in the sky, in the pond reflection, and in a mirror.

TONGLI ❷

Tónglǐ 同里
Tel: 512 6349 3027 for English-speaking guides from the Tongli Tourist Information Centre
Opening Hrs: daily 7.45am–5.30pm
Entrance Fee: entry to Old Town free; RMB 80 for entrance to major sights

The Song dynasty water village of **Tongli**, 20km (12 miles) southeast of Suzhou (and 80km/50 miles from Shanghai), is so pretty that it's often used as a backdrop for Chinese films and television shows. Be warned: it is touristy – residents no longer live here in the old houses – and it can get crowded during weekends and holidays.

Surrounded by five streams, Tongli is made up of seven islets, connected by ancient stone bridges. A boat trip on the canals is a pleasant way to get a perspective on the town. **Mingqing Street** (Mingqing Jie) is lined with wooden Ming and Qing dynasty houses, now occupied by tourist shops and restaurants. At the end of the street is the classical Chinese garden, the **Retreat and Reflection Garden** (Tuisi Yuan), built in 1886 and now a World Heritage site.

Also worth a visit are Tongli's old residences – **Gengle Hall** (Gengle Tang), **Jiayin Hall** (Jiayin Tang) and **Chongben Hall** (Chongben Tang) – all of which are open to visitors.

ZHOUZHUANG ❸

Zhōuzhuāng 周庄
Opening Hrs: daily 8am–7pm

Canal activity at Tongli.

Entrance Fee: RMB 110, includes admission to 16 sights

One of China's most famous water villages, 900-year-old **Zhouzhuang**, located about 80km (50 miles) southwest of Shanghai, has become a Chinese Disneyland of sorts. Listed as a World Heritage site "under preparation", Zhouzhuang was made famous by renowned Shanghai artist Chen Yifei, whose paintings of a pre-tourist Zhouzhuang were snapped up by the late Armand Hammer, the noted art collector. Now fronted by a shopping plaza and an endless supply of tour buses that ensures crowds at all times, Zhouzhuang's narrow, winding streets are lined with souvenir shops, restaurants, freshwater pearl shops and art galleries. Chen Yifei wannabes can be seen earnestly painting the sights, and tourists strike poses on the bridges, the most famous of which is the Ming dynasty **Double Bridge** (Shuangqiao).

A more worthwhile option is to visit the lesser-known water villages, which are also a little more challenging to reach by public transport, such as **Xinchang**, **Tongli** or **Xitang**. **Qibao** also merits a mention – now a convenient stop on Shanghai's

Atmospheric West Lake.

metro; and while its main alleys can be touristy and crowded, you can find respite in the less developed side lanes and whitewashed courtyards that time forgot.

XITANG ❹

Xītáng 西塘
Address: Jiashan county, Zhejiang province; www.xitang.com.cn
Entrance Fee: RMB 100 allows access to all sights in Xitang

Nine rivers converge in the charming water village of **Xitang**, located some 90km (56 miles) from central Shanghai. Xitang is still relatively quiet and authentic – especially when compared to more overexposed water

Xitang and its covered riverside walkways.

towns like **Zhouzhuang** (see page 246). Xitang's popularity received a boost in 2006 when it was featured in the film *Mission Impossible III*.

Xitang's riverside walkways are all covered and stretch for more than 1,300 metres (4,265ft); at night, the roofs are all strung up with pretty lanterns. Adding to the town's charm are some 122 lanes paved with slate meandering through the town, and more than 100 ancient bridges that connect the waterways.

Xi Yuan, the town's exquisite classical Chinese garden, was once the home of the Zhu family. Xitang's attractions include **Xue's House** (Xue Jia), the home of a wealthy merchant, the rear of the house facing the river, as well as **Zhongfu House** (Zhongfu Jia), dating from the Ming and Qing era, with its seven courtyards. Also worth visiting is the **Shang Tang Temple** (Shang Tang Miao), dedicated to the military hero of the same name.

HANGZHOU ❺

Háng zhōu 杭州

Located 185km (115 miles) southwest of Shanghai is **Hangzhou** – a classical Chinese beauty and the capital of Zhejiang province. Hangzhou was built on wealth, earned by its fortuitous position as the southern terminus of the Grand Canal (which connected all the way to the capital, Beijing), and by royal privilege as China's imperial capital during the Song dynasty. It quickly became an important centre for the silk industry and, as a favourite retreat for China's emperors, a place where the noble arts and leisure were cherished.

Today, Hangzhou is on an upswing again, as it grows as a centre for industry, pharmaceuticals and telecommunications. All this has given rise to a frenzy of construction in Hangzhou, mainly of hotels, office and civic buildings, and shopping malls.

West Lake ❹

Xīhú 西湖

Boat tours are an ideal way to see the famous 5.5-sq-km (2.25-sq-mile) freshwater **West Lake** and its attractions. Past **Mid-Lake Pavilion** (Huxinting) and **Ruan Yuan's Mound** (Ruangong Dun), most visitors disembark at **Xiao Ying Island**

A "dragon boat" moored at West Lake.

(Xiao Ying Dao) for views of the three 17th-century stone pagodas floating on the lake, known as the **Three Pools Mirroring the Moon** (San Tan Yin Yue). This is one of the 10 legendary views of West Lake.

Gu Shan Island

Gūshān Dǎo 孤山岛

The 1.5km (1-mile) **Bai Causeway** (Bai Di), named after the Hangzhou poet-governor Bai Juyi, cuts a path around the northern section of the lake, connecting Hangzhou's mainland to **Gu Shan**, the island on the lake's northwest shore. At

Zhejiang Provincial Museum.

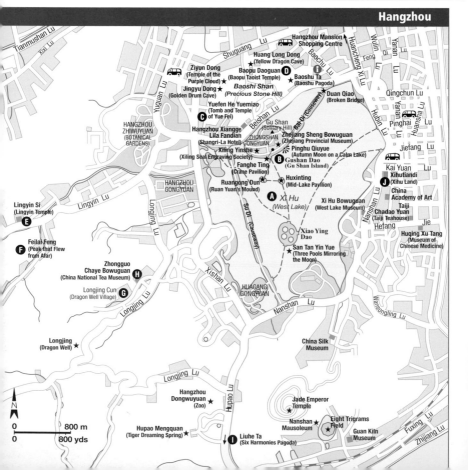

the entrance of Bai Causeway is **Broken Bridge** (Duan Qiao), so called because when winter snow on the bridge melts, it appears as if the bridge has been spilt into two. The bridge is famous as the setting for the Hangzhou folk tale *Lady White Snake*.

Further down the Bai Causeway is **Autumn Moon on a Calm Lake** (Pinghu Qiuyue), one of the traditional spots from which to view the lake, and, on a small road to the right, **Crane Pavilion** (Fanghe Ting), built in 1915 in memory of the Song poet Lin Hejing, who is said to have lived here alone with only a crane for company.

Zhejiang Provincial Museum

Zhèjiāng Shěng Bówùguǎn 浙江省博物馆
Address: 25 Gushan Road
Tel: 571 8797 1177
Opening Hrs: Tue–Sun 9am–5pm
Entrance Fee: free; audio guide RMB 10

On Gu Shan Island itself is **Zhejiang Provincial Museum**, built in 1929 on the grounds of the Emperor Qianlong's imperial palace. There are 100,000 cultural relics in its seven halls, including the famous Celadon Hall (Zhejiang was once the main producer of Chinese celadon).

Other sights on Gu Shan

The **Xiling Seal Engraving Society** (Xiling Yinshe; 8.30am–4.30pm; free), a short walk west, displays seal engravings on the walls of several pavilions strewn on the hillside.

A path to the rear leads gradually uphill, on whose summit is found the 11-storey unrestored **Pagoda of Avatamsaka Sutra** (Huayanjing Ta), built in 1924.

The **Sigillography Museum** (Zhongguo Yinxue Bowuguan; daily 8.30am–4.30pm; free), just before the bridge, recounts the history of the Chinese seal and has some lovely

exhibits. Displays range from rough clay shards to tiny carved seals with calligraphy to match.

Tomb and Temple of Yue Fei ⓒ

Yuèfén Hè Yuèmiào 岳坟和岳庙
Address: West of Beishan Road
Tel: 521 8798 6663
Opening Hrs: daily 7am–6pm
Entrance Fee: RMB 25

On the northwestern shore of the mainland is the **Tomb and Temple of Yue Fei**, a popular memorial to the 12th-century Song patriot commander who, despite his success against invaders from the north, was framed, arrested and killed with his son Yue Yun on trumped-up charges. He was exonerated and given a proper burial 21 years later in 1163. Yue Fei's temple was destroyed during the Cultural Revolution in 1966 and rebuilt in 1979. No longer a functioning temple, its main hall is dominated by a Yue Fei statue with a plaque that reads, "Recover our lost territories". Eight murals in the back tell the story of Yue Fei's life. Laid out as a Song dynasty garden, the temple is connected to the tomb grounds.

Grounds of the Seal Engraving Society.

Statue of Yue Fei at the temple named after him.

Rock carving of the Laughing Buddha, near Lingyin Temple.

Statuary at Lingyin Temple.

The back of the temple leads to the **Temple of the Purple Cloud** (Ziyun Dong), the oldest natural cave on the ridge. From here, it's a pleasant walk away from the tourists and into the peaceful surrounds of **Precious Stone Hill** (Baoshi Shan), where views can be enjoyed of the 10th-century **Baoshu Pagoda** (Baoshu Ta) to the east.

Baopu Taoist Temple **D**

Bàopǔ Dàoyuàn 抱朴道院
Opening Hrs: daily 6am–5pm
Entrance Fee: RMB 5

This lovely yellow-coloured temple, teetering over the rock face in nearby **Ge Hill**, is newly renovated but still retains an old-world charm. Black-clad nuns with tightly pulled buns can often be seen meditating in the temple. Originally built during the Jin dynasty (AD 317–420), the temple has been extended and restored several times. It is named after the Taoist master and alchemist Ge Hong, also known as Baopu, who was famous for producing the elixir of life.

Lingyin Temple **E**

Língyǐn Sì 灵隐寺
Opening Hrs: daily 5am–6pm
Entrance Fee: RMB 65

Found in the hills west of West Lake is **Lingyin Temple**, which translates as the Temple of the Soul's Retreat. This is Hangzhou's second-biggest attraction, as affirmed by the heaving crowds. **Liugong Pagoda** (Liugong Ta), the ancient hexagonal seven-storey pagoda at the entrance, contains the remains of the Indian monk Huili who built the temple in AD 326.

One of the five famous Chan (Zen) sect Buddhist temples of China, Lingyin Temple has been rebuilt several times since – at least 16 times according to one source. The temple was spared during the Cultural Revolution, and thus has retained treasured relics such as the 10th-century stone pagodas in front of the **Hall of the Four Heavenly Kings**. Inside is an image of the Maitreya (Future) Buddha, protected by an 800-year-old statue of Skanda, the Guardian of Buddhist Law and Order. Behind this building is the **Grand Hall** – accessed

via a courtyard – where a 20-metre (65ft) tall statue of Sakyamuni Buddha stands. Carved from 24 blocks of camphor wood in 1956, it is China's largest sitting Buddha and a replica of an original Tang dynasty statue.

Peak That Flew from Afar **F**

Fēilái Fēng 飞来峰

South of Lingyin Temple is the **Peak That Flew from Afar**, so named because the monk Huili exclaimed that it looked so much like the one in his native India that it must have flown here. Indeed, the peak – actually a cliff – is smaller than the surrounding peaks, and is the only one made of limestone, not sandstone.

The 470 **stone carvings** on the rockface, mostly intact, date from the 10th to the 14th century, with the oldest ones being the 10th-century Guanyin (Goddess of Mercy) in the **Deep Dragon Cave** (Longhong Dong) and the carvings in the **Shot of Gleam Cave** (Shexu Dong). Everyone's favourite carving is that of the famous jolly Laughing Buddha, as the crowds in front of it attest.

Dragon Well Village **G**

Lóngjǐng Cūn 龙井村

Southwest of West Lake is **Dragon Well Village**, where Hangzhou's famous tea of the same name is grown in nearby terraced plantations. Further southwest is **Dragon Well** (Longjing), the legendary spring after which the tea is named. What is unusual is that the two levels of springs that feed the pond create a line when the water is disturbed, instead of the usual concentric circles. Young girls often splash their faces with the cool water, believing that it will improve their complexion.

China National Tea Museum **H**

Zhōngguó Cháyè Bówùguǎn
中国茶叶博物馆

Address: Longjing Road
Tel: 571 8796 4221
Opening Hrs: Tue–Sun 8.30am–4.30pm
Entrance Fee: free

North of the village is the **Tea Museum of China**, which does an excellent job of documenting the history and culture of tea production in five linked buildings. One of its highlights is the re-creation of the tea rooms of different ethnic minorities.

Six Harmonies Pagoda **I**

Liùhé Tǎ 六和塔
Opening Hrs: daily 6am–6.30pm
Entrance Fee: RMB 30

About 3km (2 miles) southwest of West Lake is **Six Harmonies Pagoda**. Standing near the northern bank of the Qiantang River, it overlooks a large bridge. Built in 970 in the hope that it might control the river's mighty tidal waves, the seven-storey pagoda was last rebuilt in 1900, although its interior dates to 1123. The pagoda, its Song dynasty structure still intact, is the traditional spot to watch the river's famous tidal bore on the autumn equinox in mid-September.

Six Harmonies Pagoda along the northern bank of the Qiantang River. In mid-September, hundreds gather at the nearby bridge to watch the wall of water surging to as high as 6 metres (20ft), caused by the river's famous tidal bore.

Tea plantations near Dragon Well Village.

Lush bamboo forests at Moganshan.

Xihutiandi

Xihutiandì 西湖天地

Towards the east of West Lake is **Hangzhou City**, where a frenzy of construction is creating plazas and shopping malls, all concentrated around **Yan'an Road** and **Hubin Road.** There is plenty of brand-name shopping along landscaped Hubin Road, which has stores selling everything from Tag Heuer to Valentino.

South of Hubin Road, against a beautiful backdrop of historic buildings and the shores of West Lake, is **Xihutiandi**. Like its Shanghai sister, Xintiandi (see page 147), this is an upscale dining and nightlife complex.

Further south is **Hefang Street** (Hefang Jie), a shopping street dedicated to Chinese knick-knacks and local snacks in a Qing dynasty setting. **Taiji Teahouse** (Taiji Chadao Yuan), at No. 184, is one of the best places in town to enjoy a cup of the local brew.

Just off Hefang Street is the **Museum of Chinese Medicine** (Hu Qingyu Tang; daily 8.30am–5pm; RMB 10), a stunning Qing-era building that is a working pharmacy and clinic, one of the oldest in China. Continuing east is the **Drum Tower Antique Market** (Gulou Guwan

Waterfall at Moganshan.

Shichang), which has stalls selling reproductions and the occasional genuine article.

MOGANSHAN ⑥

Hangzhou makes a good base for exploring **Moganshan**, located some 65km (40 miles) north of Hangzhou and 195km (120 miles) west of Shanghai. An early start from Hangzhou allows a full day of exploration; if coming direct from Shanghai, an overnight stay is recommended.

Nestled in the mountains of north Zhejiang province, the highland

resort of Moganshan's cool evenings and summer temperatures – no higher than 27°C (80°F) – made it the ideal hill station for Concession-era foreigners longing for a more comfortable climate.

Before the first missionaries ventured here in the 1890s, there were only Chinese farmers living here, cultivating the bamboo that still grows thickly on Moganshan. Barely scraping a living, they were quite happy to rent their houses to the first foreigners who summered here. The frugal missionaries could only afford to rent houses, but later they were joined by wealthier citizens, some of whom even brought their architects from Shanghai to construct holiday villas using the grey stone quarried from the nearby hills. By the 1930s, there was a full-fledged summer community in Moganshan with post offices, two churches and nearly 160 houses.

Things to see

Today, Moganshan is experiencing a renaissance of sorts with many of the old villas restored as retreats, and it has become something of an escape for Shanghai urbanites, thanks to its quiet relaxing pace. Moganshan is best explored by wandering along its hilly paths, still paved with the stone laid a century ago, breathing the fresh mountain air and discovering the once-grand mansions tucked away in the hills and bamboo forests.

Start at Moganshan village, where along Yingshan Street is the **Bamboo Museum** (Zhuzi Bowuguan; daily 10am–5pm). It is amazing to see the many creative uses of bamboo for which Moganshan is famous.

Southwest of the village, on a grooved mountain road, is **No. 126**, a grey stone house with curved turrets and Gothic doors and windows, and framed against the pine and bamboo forest. Mao Zedong stayed in this house while he was working on China's Constitution in 1954.

Back on Yingshan Street, heading east up a steep hill above the post office and past the power station, is the former **Protestant church**. The parsonage next to it once served as a primary school. East of the church, thick bamboo pipes lead to the lonely stream-fed **swimming pool**, almost eerie in the swirling mists. The **tennis courts**, which once had Chinese pavilions for spectators, are just north of here on the hill.

Head back south on the main road, past the Moganshan Management Office, to the **Yellow Temple** (Huang Si), a simple Buddhist temple.

Part of the flourishing local scene of boutique hotels is **Naked Stables** (Shanghai office tel: 6431 8901; www.nakedretreats.cn), an eco-resort featuring mountainside villas and earth huts with horse riding, fine dining and spa facilities. Guests can avail themselves of activities that include hiking the many Moganshan trails, biking, tea-picking, yoga and massage.

Wuling Hotel, where Chiang Kai-shek once lived.

Waiting for the metro at Longyang Road.

下一站 世纪公园

Next stop   Century Park

龙阳
Longyang

TRAVEL TIPS
SHANGHAI

TRANSPORT

GETTING THERE AND GETTING AROUND

The boom in car ownership in Shanghai has meant that traffic congestion is a way of life, and getting around the city by car can be slow during peak hours. Still, this is a fairly compact city, and many of its neighbourhoods are easily (and best) seen on foot. Although taxis are inexpensive – flagfall begins at RMB 14 – they can be scarce during rush hour and when it rains, so some advance planning is required. As a backup, the metro is a fast, efficient option, but during peak times the carriages can get crowded. Uber has been bought by a Chinese company and doesn't operate on the international platform.

GETTING THERE

By air

Pudong International Airport

Most international flights arrive at the modern, designer-built **Pudong International Airport** (Pudong Jichang; tel: 9608 1388; www.shairport.com), located about 30km (18.5 miles) from the city centre. See Getting around for details on getting to the city.

The airport's two terminals handle about 38 million

passengers with a capacity of 80 million passengers annually in four connected halls – arrival halls are on the lower level, while departure halls are on the upper level.

Arriving passengers are quickly whisked through the terminal on a combination of travellators and escalators to immigration; after clearing immigration, proceed to baggage claim (carts are free) and customs.

The arrival hall is lined with hotel information desks, currency exchange facilities and ATMs, as well as the Tourist Information Centre and China International Travel Service (CITS) counters. Passages are clearly marked to the Maglev station, metro, bus stops, taxi queues and carpark.

Hongqiao Airport

Most domestic flights arrive at **Hongqiao Airport** (Hongqiao Jichang; tel: 5260 4620; www.shairport.com), located 13km (8 miles) from the city centre. See Getting around for details on getting to the city.

Hongqiao's second terminal opened in 2010, giving the 35 million travellers who come through a comfortable and efficient arrival and departure experience. Domestic arrivals at Hongqiao don't need to go through immigration and can proceed directly to baggage claim.

Two-wheeled transport.

It's important to note which terminal you require as Hongqiao's Terminal 1 and Terminal 2 lie a significant distance apart and can be accessed via different metro lines (line 10 connects both terminals but Terminal 2 can also be reached by line 2, which connects with Pudong International Airport at its eastern terminus). If you need to travel between Hongqiao's terminals allow sufficient time, as you'll need to take a bus, metro or taxi.

Key airline offices

Air China: Room 101B, Changfeng Centre, 1088 Yanan Road (W); tel: 5239 7227; www.airchina.com.cn.
British Airways: Room 703, Central Plaza, 227 Huangpi Road; tel: 6835 5633; www.britishairways.com.

BEIJING & HK TRAINS

Beijing – High-speed 'G' trains whizz between Shanghai Hongqiao Station and Beijing South Station, with several trains per hour. The journey takes around 4.5 hours. There are some overnight trains, taking around 12 hours, which can be a fun and convenient option for an early morning arrival.
Hong Kong – A comfortable train service runs on alternate days from Kowloon's Hung Hom Station to Shanghai – if you don't mind the journey time of 19 hours (see www.kcrcr.com for details). The Z100 departs from Kowloon at 3pm and the Z99 departs from Shanghai at 5.45pm. This route will also be connected to China's high-speed network in the future.

Book tickets directly at the Shanghai Railway Station, or contact a travel agent.

China Eastern Airlines: 1720 Huaihai Road (W); tel: 6247 5953; www.ce-air.com.
China North West Airlines: 258 Weihai Road; tel: 6267 4233; www.cnwa.com.
Dragonair: Suite 2103–4, Shanghai Plaza, 138 Central Huaihai Road; tel: 6375 6000/6375 6375; www.dragonair.com.
Northwest Airlines: Suite 207, East Podium, 1376 Nanjing Road (W); tel: 6279 8100; www.nwa.com.
Qantas: Room 3202, K. Wah Centre, 1010 Central Huaihai Road; tel: 6145 0188; www.qantas.com.au.
Shanghai Airlines: 212 Jiangning Road; tel: 6255 0550; www.shanghai-air.com.
Singapore Airlines: Room 1106, Tower 1, Plaza 66, 1266 Nanjing Road (W); tel: 6288 7999; www.singaporeair.com.
United Airlines: Room 3301, Central Plaza, 381 Central

Huaihai Road; tel: 3311 4567; www.ual.com.
Virgin Atlantic: Room 221, 12 Zhongshan No. 1 Road (E) (the Bund); tel: 5353 4600/5353 4605; www.virginatlantic.com.

By rail

The high-speed rail network, that now covers large tracts of the country, has changed domestic travel in China. The new high-speed trains are fast, modern, comfortable and run right on time – as opposed to air travel, which is regularly hampered by delays. Most fast trains (prefaced by the letters G and D) arrive and depart from the **Shanghai Hongqiao Railway Station** (near S20 Outer Ring Expressway), but be sure to check, as some trains arrive and depart from the **Shanghai Railway Station** (Xin Ke Zhan; 100 Moling Road; tel: 6317 9090, 6354 5358/3193) or **Shanghai South Railway Station** at 289 Laohumin Road (tel: 6404 1317, 6317 9090).

Same-day train tickets and up to a week in advance may be purchased at the railway stations or their satellite offices around the city. Hotel concierges and travel agencies will also book tickets for you. You'll need to show your passport when you buy the tickets and when you board the train. It's advisable to get your ticket a couple of days before you travel if possible as the trains do sell out.

The main hall of the Southern Railway Station.

Train classes

The high-speed trains offer first- and second-class carriages. Second class is comfortable but usually gets booked out quicker. Older trains have "hard" and "soft" classes.

Ying Zuo (Hard Seat) is the classic China train experience, with too many tickets issued for too few spaces (you may end up standing for the duration of the journey), cigarette smoke and a constant din.

Ruan Zuo (Soft Seat) is a less crowded, more comfortable experience. Comfortable soft-seat tourist trains run between Shanghai and the popular tourist destinations nearby – Hangzhou, Suzhou and Nanjing.

Ying Wo (Hard Sleeper) has two narrow three-tier bunks (six beds in total) to a compartment and no doors. Some trains have no air conditioning or heating. The lowest bunk is the most expensive – which converts into the communal train seat during the day. The top berth is the cheapest.

Ruan Wo (Soft Sleeper) has two bunks (four beds in total) in a closed-door compartment, with air conditioning.

By bus

High-speed highways linking Shanghai with its neighbours (Suzhou, Hangzhou, Nanjing etc.) make buses an efficient budget

option for linking up to nearby as well as long-distance destinations. For general bus inquiries, call: 9621 6800.

By sea

Luxury cruise liners stop in Shanghai, and there are also luxury ferries to S. Korea and Japan. There are two piers; ships from Hong Kong, S. Korea, Japan and beyond dock at the **International Cruise Terminal** (Guoji Keyun Matou) at 100 Yangshupu Road, tel: 6595 9259, just north of the Bund area. Domestic ships and ferries dock at the **Wusong Passenger Terminal** (Shanghai Gang Wusong Keyun Zhongxin) at 251 Songbao Road, tel: 5657 5500.

Tickets can be booked by travel agencies as well as directly from the ferry booking offices. General ticket information, tel: 6326 1261.

GETTING AROUND

From Pudong International Airport

Taxis

There is a well-organised taxi line outside the arrival hall (expect a long queue at peak hours, but it moves quickly). At the end of the

queue, tell the taxi handler your destination, or, better yet, hand him a piece of paper with your destination written out in Chinese characters (taxi drivers in Shanghai generally don't speak English). Taxis to the city centre in Puxi cost roughly RMB 150–200 (before 11pm; night rates are higher), and will take about an hour, depending on traffic conditions. Trips to downtown Pudong will cost a little less. Make sure the taxi meter is turned on at the start of your journey. Avoid touts who may approach you at the arrival hall – their rates are at least three times higher.

Airport buses

There are eight routes from the airport to different points in the city, and the pick-up point is between Doors 7 and 15 in the arrival hall. Tickets (which range from RMB 15–20) may be purchased at the airport-bus ticket counter (tel: 6834 6912) in the arrival hall or on the bus itself. The buses run from 6am until the last flight at night, and take about 75–90 minutes to reach the city centre.

Hotel shuttles

A private car transfer (expect to pay RMB 500 and above per trip) can be arranged when you book more upscale hotel accommodation. If so, either your

name or the name of your hotel will be prominently displayed by someone holding up a signboard. If you haven't arranged for a car transfer, most of the major hotels have counters at the airport that can arrange such transfers.

Maglev train

The high-speed Maglev (short for magnetic levitation) train runs from the airport to Pudong's Longyang metro (subway) station, a 30km (19-mile) journey that takes only eight minutes to cover, at up to a dizzying 430km (267 miles) an hour. Tickets are priced at RMB 50 for a single trip (RMB 40 if you have a ticket or boarding pass to show that you arrived or are departing by plane that same day). The trains run from 7am–9.30pm and tickets are available at the entrance gate. This is usually the fastest option to avoid traffic. Approximate journey time from Longyang Station is 20 minutes to downtown Pudong and 35 minutes to Puxi.

Metro

Metro Line 2 (located between Terminal 1 and Terminal 2) links Pudong International Airport with the heart of town and the metro network. The same line serves Hongqiao Airport Terminal 2 as well, which is around a two-hour journey. Fares start at RMB 3. It takes around 75-90 minutes from the airport to Lujiazui or downtown Puxi.

Inter-airport

The 40km (25-mile) distance between Pudong and Hongqiao airports is one of the longest taxi rides you can take in Shanghai, so take note if you have to make a connection from an international flight to a domestic one (or vice versa). There are regular airport shuttle buses between the two, costing RMB 30, while a taxi (60–90 minutes) will set you back by at least RMB 240. Metro line 2 connects the airports, taking two hours; a combination of Maglev and metro is a faster option.

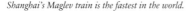

Shanghai's Maglev train is the fastest in the world.

The metro is a fast and convenient way of getting around.

From Hongqiao Airport

Taxi

The taxi line at Hongqiao Airport is notoriously long, but it moves quickly. Taxis to the city centre in Puxi cost approximately RMB 60 for the 30–45-minute ride. Avoid the taxi touts who hang around the arrival hall and invariably charge much more.

Airport bus

Hongqiao Airport's shuttle bus runs several routes from the airport to the city. The cost is RMB 5–7 and journey time is about 45 minutes.

Metro

Metro lines 2 and 10 extend to Hongqiao. Line 2 stops directly under Terminal 2 and then proceeds onto the Hongqiao Railway Station. Line 10 links Terminal 1, Terminal 2 and the Hongqiao Railway Station. Metro Line 2 serves Pudong International Airport as well, which is around a 2-hour journey. Fares start at RMB 3.

Inter-airport

See Pudong Airport (see page 256).

Orientation

The Huangpu River separates Pudong district, literally "east of the Huangpu", from the rest of Shanghai, or Puxi, "west of the Huangpu". The Suzhou Creek divides the thriving mid-section of Puxi (just after the Bund) from its quieter northern suburbs.

There are places to stay and things to do all over the city, but travellers will find the highest concentration of sights, restaurants, entertainment spots and hotels in the West Nanjing Road corridor in Puxi, anchored by the Shanghai Centre and continuing east to People's Square, after which it becomes East Nanjing Road, just a few blocks away from the Bund. This is where the majority of shopping, museums and attractions lie.

Pudong's Lujiazui area is largely made up of concrete and glass skyscrapers, and has much less soul. This is, after all, a designated economic zone. The places of interest lie mainly along or close to the banks of the Huangpu River. Travellers with business in Pudong have a wide range of hotels to choose from.

Overall, the streets in Puxi run north to south and east to west in a grid-like fashion, except for oval-shaped Old City and the old racetrack contours that ring People's Square. The major streets run the length of the city and have directional tags: for example, Huaihai Road (W) or West, Central Huaihai Road or Huaihai Road (E) or East (see box below left for translations).

The city is bisected from east to west by the Yan'an Road Elevated Highway and from north

USEFUL STREET TRANSLATIONS

Road signage in Shanghai is generally bilingual, with the Chinese characters first and their "pinyin" romanised equivalent written underneath. Young people on the street can generally speak some English, in case you need directions, but taxi drivers generally do not. Keep the following basic translations in mind when deciphering road signs:

English/Chinese
Central/Zhong
East/Dong
West/Xi
South/Nan
North/Bei

Road/Lu
Street/Jie
Da Dao/Avenue
One/Yi
Two/Er

Here are a few sample translations to give you a better idea.

English/Chinese
Central Huaihai Road/Huaihai Zhong Lu
Nanjing Road (E)/Nanjing Dong Lu
Nanjing Road (W)/Nanjing Xi Lu
Henan Road (S)/Henan Nan Lu
Henan Road (N)/Henan Bei Lu
Zhongshan No. 1 Road (E)/Zhongshan Dong Yi Lu
Ruijin No. 2 Road/Ruijin Er Lu

TRANSPORT

A – Z

LANGUAGE

to south by the North–South Elevated Highway.

Crossing Huangpu River to Pudong from Puxi can be done via ferry, metro, the Nanpu, Yangpu or Lupu bridges, or several tunnels.

Note: see also Addresses.

Public transport

Metro (subway)

Shanghai's slick metro system (*di tie*) is an efficient way to get around the city and avoid traffic jams, although the metro during rush hour has human jams of its own. The metro is fairly easy to navigate: entrances are identified by the letter "M"; there are metro maps, in English and Chinese, at the stations; and the ticket machines have an English-language option. Announcements on the train are made in both English and Chinese.

Single-journey metro tickets may be purchased at ticket machines or counters at all metro stations. Trains operate daily from 5.30am to 11pm.

Metro Hotline: 6318 9000/ 6437 0000 (no English spoken).

There are **14 lines** currently in operation and the city is aiming for 20 by 2020. For a map of the metro system, see back cover or check: www.exploreshanghai. com/metro.

Metro Line 1 runs a north–south path from Bao'an Highway, via the Shanghai Railway Station, to Xinzhuang in the southern suburbs.

Metro Line 2 runs an east–west axis from Pudong International Airport past Longyang Road (where a transfer can be made to the Maglev), via People's Square (where it intersects with Metro Line 1) to Hongqiao Airport and Railway Station, and finally to East Xujing in the west.

Metro Line 3 is a mostly elevated 36km (22-mile) line that runs from north to south from North Jiangyang Road to Shanghai South Railway Station.

Metro Line 4 forms almost a complete circle around the city. Along the way it intersects with multiple other lines, enabling convenient transfers.

Metro Line 5 runs from Xinzhuang, the terminal station of Metro Line 1 in the south, to the Minhang Development Zone in the southwest.

Metro Line 6 runs north–south between Gangcheng Road and the Oriental Sports Centre. Also called the Pudong Light Railway, it is located entirely within Pudong district.

Metro Line 7 links downtown Shanghai and Pudong with Baoshan district, running from Huamu Road to Meilan Lake. It connects with several downtown sights including Longhua Temple and Jing'An Temple.

Metro Line 8, the Yangpu Line, runs north–south from Shiguang Road (Yangpu District) to the China Art Museum and finally Shendu Highway.

Metro Line 9 runs east–west from Songjiang South Railway Station (Songjiang District) to Yanggao Central Road (Pudong).

Metro Line 10's main line runs from New Jiangwan Town to Hongqiao Railway Station, with a branch from Longxi Road to Hangzhong Road.

TRANSPORT CARD

If you're taking public transport, it is worth getting the **Shanghai Public Transport Card** (Jiaotong Ka), a stored-value contactless card that can be used for metro, bus and taxi rides. The card itself costs RMB 20 (which is refundable), and any denominations can be added. The card can be purchased at all metro stations and selected convenience stores. When the card is swiped on the sensor located at metro turnstiles or at scanners found in the bus and dashboards of taxis, the correct fee is automatically deducted.

Metro Line 11 has two lines: A, the main line, and B, the branch line. Line A starts at Jiading North and Line B starts from Huaqiao and connects with the Formula One racetrack, Shanghai International Circuit; the lines have the same route and stations after Jiading New City.

Metro Line 12 runs from Qixin Road to Jinhai Road, stopping in Nanjing Road and at the International Cruise Terminal, among other places.

Metro Line 13 runs an L shape from west to south, from Jiyun Road to Shibo Avenue.

Metro Line 16 runs from Longyang Road in Pudong to the Wild Animal Park and Dishui Lake.

Buses

Many of the downtown buses now have announcements and signage in English, but drivers and conductors only speak Chinese. During rush hour, buses can get very crowded, but otherwise are quite a pleasant way to get around – if you are not in a tearing hurry. Most buses run from 6am to midnight, while some special services operate 24 hours. Fares cost from RMB 2–5; tickets can be bought on board or use your stored-value Shanghai Public Transport Card (see box).

Taxis

Taxis are one of Shanghai's great deals – they can be hailed anywhere off the street, cost only RMB 14 (RMB18 between 11pm and 5am) at flagfall, and average RMB 14–35 for a journey in central Shanghai. The city's taxi drivers are also generally a reliable and honest lot – to the point of telling you if they don't know your destination. But as incomes rise, more and more people are taking taxis these days, making them scarce during peak times and in bad weather.

Taxi drivers generally speak only Chinese, so it is crucial that you have the name and address of your destination written out in Chinese, and, failing that, the name of the street and the cross-street in Chinese.

Taxis are metered and drivers usually turn it on as a matter of course. Fares cost RMB 14 (RMB18 between 11pm and 5am) for the first 3km (1.75 miles), and RMB 3.10 per additional km after that. Trips after 11pm start at RMB 16 for the first 3km, and revert to RMB 2.40 per additional km after that. Tips are not expected.

Payment is either by cash or by the stored-value Shanghai Public Transport Card (see box).

Rear seats rarely have safety belts, or else the belts seem stuck to the seat and are unusable. If this is a problem for you, sit in front. The back door on the driver's side is kept locked, so always board and alight on the other side.

Always ask for a printed receipt (*fa piao* in Chinese) which records the taxi number and the taxi company's telephone number; this will possibly help in the event you leave something behind in a taxi. With the exception of mobile phones, things are usually returned promptly. For complaints on taxi service, contact tel: 6323 2150.

Taxis can be booked in advance for a surcharge. They can also be hired for the whole day. The following taxi companies operate in Shanghai:

Da Zhong Taxi: tel: 800 6200 1688/6258 1688
Jin Jiang Taxi: tel: 6275 8800
Qiang Sheng Taxi: tel: 6258 0000
Shanghai Taxi: tel: 5481 1630, www.shanghai-taxi.com. This company only accepts pre-bookings.

Private car rental

Tourists are no longer expressly prohibited from driving in Shanghai, but neither are they encouraged – car-rental agencies generally recommend hiring a car with driver. Expect to pay RMB 600–800 a day. Petrol cost is usually included in the rates.
Shanghai Anji Car Rental (a joint venture with Avis), tel: 6229 1119, www.avischina.com.
Dazhong, tel: 6318 5666.

Trips out of Shanghai

The trips to the places covered in the Western Suburbs (see page 227) and Excursions (see page 239) chapters can be organised either on your own or with the aid of a good travel agency.

The cheap option is to use the special sightseeing buses that depart from several venues around town, but these are mainly used by domestic tourists and don't cater to foreigners (ie people who don't speak Chinese).

Trains are generally the fastest and easiest option for independent travel to Suzhou and Hangzhou; tickets can be booked through your hotel or directly at the railway stations or their satellite offices around town.

You could also arrange to hire a private car with a driver. This option gives you the most flexibility. Some travel agencies also have English-speaking guides who will accompany you – this is useful for translation purposes, but be aware that the "guide" may not know much about the destination itself. Places of interest in the Western Suburbs chapter like Jiading, Songjiang and Qingpu are easily covered in a day, depending on how many sights you wish to see. Expect to pay RMB 500 for a half-day car hire with driver and RMB 600 or more for a full-day's hire to these areas.

Some places (like Zhouzhuang and Suzhou) are standard day tours offered by travel agents. Some companies also sell a Hangzhou day trip, but this is a bit of a stretch. Ask about 2-day package tours to Hangzhou that include a night's accommodation and sightseeing.

Chongming Island

By ferry: Take a taxi to Baoyang port in northeastern Shanghai, where you can board the ferry to Nanmen port on Chongming; the boat ride takes 30–40 minutes. At Nanmen, take a taxi to your hotel or final destination.
Baoyang to Nanmen ferries run

13 times a day, with an additional trip at the weekends. Ferries run from 7.10am–5pm daily, tel: 5667 1205.
Nanmen to Baoyang ferries run from 6.30am–4.30pm daily, tel: 6961 2710/2711.
By car: The Yangtze River Bridge and Tunnel Project connects Chongming Island with Pudong via Changxiang Island (a journey of about 40 minutes).

Suzhou

By train: High-speed G and D trains run regularly between Shanghai Hongqiao Railway Station and Suzhou North Train Station. The journey is around half an hour.
By car: The expressway is the fastest way to travel to Suzhou, getting you there in just over an hour. A one-way car trip with driver will cost about RMB 420. A same-day return trip (with waiting time included) will cost around RMB 900.

Hangzhou

By train: High-speed G and D trains leave regularly for the Hangzhou East Train Station from Shanghai Hongqiao Railway Station. The trip takes just 45–60 minutes.
By car: The drive to Hangzhou via the expressway will take around double the time of the train, depending on road conditions. A one-way car trip with driver will cost about RMB 900.

Moganshan

By car: Moganshan is best done as a side trip from Hangzhou. From there, get a hired car or taxi. The ride from Hangzhou to Moganshan takes about an hour.

Tongli and Xitang

By car: Both of these water villages are more easily accessed from Suzhou. Enquire with the hotel desk in Suzhou about car rental cost. If going direct from Shanghai, a rented car with driver will cost about RMB 900 for a day trip to either of the villages. A combined trip to both villages will not cost much more.

A – Z

AN ALPHABETICAL SUMMARY OF PRACTICAL INFORMATION

A

Accommodation

Shanghai is an expensive place to bed down. There are plenty of options available in all the different price categories – but book early as demand is high at peak times and you can usually enjoy better prices when booking in advance. Rates, and occupancies, peak during the autumn and spring high season, and during major events and conferences.

Choosing your accommodation

Shanghai is mainly dominated by international four- and five-star hotels, but there is, increasingly, much more choice. Chinese hotel brands Hengshan and Jinjiang own and manage several key upmarket properties, and the number of mid-range hotels, particularly the international brands, is growing, although they are often not as centrally located as the five-star ones.

China's massive budget motel chains, like Motel 168, Home Inns, JJ Inns and GreenTree Inns, have opened throughout the city, but these can be difficult for non-Chinese speakers to navigate. Boutique hotels are a more recent, and welcome, addition to the scene.

Short-stay serviced apartments with kitchen facilities, maid services and security are ideal for those who are staying for a month or more. But they are also great for a few nights for families with children or people who just want more elbow room.

Discounts are usually available during the summer (July–Aug) and winter (Dec–Feb) months. Always ask if there are any special offers, packages or discounts available: hotels may not mention these if you don't ask. Reservations are usually best made by e-mail or via telephone; make sure you get a reservation number from the hotel, or a printout of the confirmation. Booking sites like China's english. ctrip.com and www.elong.net often offer the most competitive rates.

Hotel areas

Although there are hotels throughout the city, most are found in areas with the highest concentration of tourists and business travellers – like Jing'an, Fuxing Park area, the Bund, Hongqiao and Pudong. All these areas have a mix of both luxury and moderate options.

Jing'an is the traditional hotel district; the hotels in this area are mainly international five-stars, targeted at business and high-end leisure travellers.

Fuxing Park and surroundings have hotels that bear the character of the former French Concession – this is where you will find several of the city's historic hotels, some of them located in the mansions of old Shanghai tycoons.

The **Bund**, which until this century had no luxury lodgings except for the Peace Hotel, is now home to several brand-new and upmarket hotels as well as a few moderately priced ones.

Hongqiao, in the suburbs, was the first area in the city to open international hotels; the offerings here include state guesthouses, convention hotels as well as international five-star ones.

Pudong is the site of the some of the snazziest hotels in the city, whose profiles dominate its futuristic skyline.

Addresses

Buildings are usually sequentially numbered, odd numbers on one side of the street and even numbers on the other. Because the major streets often run the entire length of the city, it helps to know what the nearest cross-street is when trying to locate an address, such as Central Huaihai Road near *(kaojin)* Gao'an Road.

It's easier with newer buildings as the street address now indicates building numbers within an area, for example, Central Huaihai Road 1000–2000. See also Orientation and Useful street translations, page 259.

B

Budgeting your trip

Shanghai is as cheap or as expensive as you want it to be. Accommodation can cost from as little as RMB 100 for a dorm bed to upwards of RMB 3,000 for one of the city's deluxe five-star hotels.

Similarly, a meal in a simple Chinese restaurant can cost about RMB 50 per person, while you can easily pay RMB 500 at the one of the city's swankier Chinese or Western eateries. Local beer costs as little as RMB 25; imported beer is three times more. A glass of wine at an expensive restaurant costs RMB 40 and upwards.

The city's efficient public transport system is cheap – a bus or metro ride within the downtown area won't cost more than RMB 5. Taxi rides are also inexpensive, running about RMB 14–35 for trips within the city centre.

Entry fees to most attractions are under RMB 60, except for premier attractions that can cost around RMB 100.

Business hours

Shops generally open at 10am and close around 9pm, though some stay open until 10pm. Government offices are open from 9am to 5pm during weekdays with a 1–2-hour lunch break. Banks may stay open until 6pm or 7pm; some currency exchange desks are open around the clock; and ATMs are everywhere.

Most large malls and department stores are generally open daily from 9–10am to

Shopping on Maoming Road.

9–10pm. Smaller shops may have shorter hours, so call first. Keep in mind that small shops and restaurants usually close during Chinese New Year (see page 269). Banks close for three days during the week-long Chinese New Year holiday. Note that all big shopping malls stay open.

Business travellers

Business is the driving force in Shanghai, the Manhattan of China, and most things are set up for the needs of the business traveller. Most hotels – and not just the top end – are well equipped with business centres, hotel-wide Wi-fi, interpreter and support services. The city is also establishing itself as a key convention and exhibition centre, and is home to several international-standard venues.

The local Shanghai government is very pro-business. For more information on business and investing in Shanghai, see the website: www.investment.gov.cn. See also the chapter on **Business and economy** (see page 42).

C

Children

Shanghai loves children. There is not a museum, a restaurant or a

theatre where your child will feel unwelcome. The downside is a loss of privacy: your kids will be touched, stared at, talked to and photographed – just take a positive attitude about the whole thing and you'll meet new friends and gain fresh insights.

Hotels often allow children to stay with parents in a double room at no extra charge. Extra beds are available for a small surcharge. Reliable babysitters, called *ayi* (aunty), are easily available. If you're planning to be in Shanghai for any length of time, consider a serviced apartment with a kitchen (see Accommodation).

Climate

Shanghai has a northern sub-tropical monsoon climate with four distinct seasons. Rainfall is plentiful throughout the year, though most of it falls during the rainy season from June to September. Expect hot and muggy summers with temperatures hovering in the mid-30s°C (95°F) in July and August, and chilled-to-the-bone damp winters in December and January. January is the coldest month, although temperatures rarely dip below zero. Snow is rare in Shanghai, although there are the occasional late December/January flurries. Shanghai's mildest weather (and

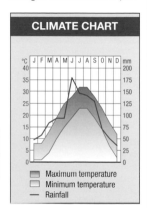

CLIMATE CHART

■ Maximum temperature
□ Minimum temperature
— Rainfall

best time to visit) is in spring (mid-March to May) and autumn (September to early November).

Clothing

Shanghai errs on the side of casual, but it is a city of unrelenting style: you'll be forgiven for not wearing a tie, but never for looking like a bumpkin. Light, breathable clothes work best in the hot, humid summertime, with a light wrap for the over-air-conditioned restaurants and offices. In winter, several layers of clothing is the key to staying warm. Savvy travellers always carry a foldable umbrella with them to protect against sudden showers.

Crime & safety

Shanghai is a relatively safe city, but petty crimes like pickpocketing do happen in crowded areas like train stations, markets and on busy streets. There is very little violent crime against foreigners, but tourists should be aware of scams.

It's a safe city for women, too, who are able to walk alone, even at night, safely and without being harassed – but again, you should be on your guard.

Every neighbourhood has its own police station or post, often labelled in English. This is the place to report any crime, although you might have to wait for the Public Security Bureau officer in charge of foreigners to handle your case. Otherwise, contact the **Public Security Bureau** directly. See right for a list of Emergency Numbers.

Customs regulations

Duty-free allowance per adult is as follows: two bottles of liquor (75cl each), 400 cigarettes, 50g of gold or silver, and perfume for personal use. On arrival, tourists have to fill out a baggage declaration form and hand it in to customs; be sure to retain the

duplicate copy to show upon exit. There is no limit to the amount of foreign currency that can be brought in; the unspent portion may be taken out. There is a long list of prohibited items, including animals, firearms, plant material and media deemed "detrimental" to China's social and political security. For up-to-date details see www.china.org. cn. Note: antiques require a government stamp in order to be exported; most reputable dealers can take care of the necessary paperwork.

D

Disabled access

Most of Shanghai's modern hotels, buildings and museums are all wheelchair-accessible, but older buildings and the myriad overpasses and underpasses are not. Newer metro stations all have wheelchair ramps, and the older ones are adding them.

Shanghai's wheelchair-bound use motorised wheelchairs to get around. **Bashi Taxi** (tel: 6431 2788) has several minivans that cater for those in wheelchairs.

E

Electricity

Local electricity is 220 volts; 50 cycles AC. Chinese-to-foreign conversion accessories – whether conversion plugs or voltage converters – are easily available at department stores and hotels.

Embassies & consulates

Australian Consulate: 22/F, citic Square, 1168 Nanjing Road (W); tel: 2215 5200; www.china. embassy.gov.au.
British Consulate: Suite 301, Shanghai Centre, 1376 Nanjing Road (W); tel: 6279 7650; www.uk.cn.

Tai chi on the Bund.

New Zealand Consulate: 1605–1607A, 989 Changle Road; tel: 5407 5858; www.nzembassy.com.
Singapore Consulate: 89 Wanshan Road; tel: 6278 5566; www.mfa.gov.sg/shanghai.
United States Consulate: 1469 Central Huaihai Road; tel: 6433 6880; also **American Citizen Services**: 8/F, Westgate Mall, 1038 Nanjing Road (W); tel: 3217 4650, after-hours emergencies tel: 6433 3936; http://shanghai. usconsulate.gov.

Emergency numbers

Public Security Bureau: 710 Hankou Road; tel: 6321 5380
Ambulance: 120
Fire: 119
Police: 110

Entry requirements

Passports should be valid for at least six months before you step out of your home country.

Most visitors to China require a visa. There are several ways of procuring one. The easy way is to use the services of a travel agent. There will be a commission charge on top of the visa-processing fee paid to the visa office of the Chinese embassy or consulate. If you are part of a group tour, the travel agent will issue a group visa for all the members of the tour party.

Individual travellers may also apply for a visa directly with the

Chinese embassy or consulate in their home country. For more details and to download a visa form, check the **Chinese Ministry of Foreign Affairs** website at www.fmprc.gov.cn/eng. To locate the relevant section, click on "About China" – "Travel to China" – "Visa Information".

Two passport-size pictures, the completed application form and the fee are required. There are additional requirements for first-time visa applicants who are foreign-born but of Chinese descent, or who were born in China but have migrated overseas.

It takes about 7–10 working days to process your China visa, so make sure you apply for one well before your intended departure. Visa fees vary by country, so check with the respective Chinese embassy or consulate. The fee also depends on the length of stay. The standard tourist visa is a single-entry 30-day visa. Multiple-entry and 60-day visas are also available at higher cost.

Business and student visas usually allow multiple-entry and come with three- to six-month validity. However, these require supporting documentation confirming your status. Travellers stopping through Shanghai can take advantage of the 72-Hour Visa Free Transit policy, allowing passengers from 51 countries to stay for up to 72 hours without a visa on a direct transit.

Visas in Hong Kong

As many people combine a trip to China's mainland with Hong Kong, another option is to get your mainland visa issued in Hong Kong. Many nationalities only require a valid passport for entry into Hong Kong. Once there, you can either apply for a visa directly with the local Chinese visa office, or use the services of a travel agent or the China Travel Service office (CTS).

Obtaining visas in Hong Kong is both inexpensive and speedy – most are issued within 2–3 working days and same-day service is available at premium rate.
Consular Dept of China's Foreign Ministry in Hong Kong: 7/F, Lower Block, China Resources Building, 26 Harbour Road, Wan Chai, Hong Kong; tel: 852 3413 2300; fax: 852 3413 23127; www.fmcoprc.gov.hk; Mon–Fri 9am–noon, 2–5pm.
China Travel Service: CTS House, 78–83 Connaught Road, Central, Hong Kong; tel: 852 2853 3533; fax: 852 2543 2671; www.chinatravelone.com. Check the website for branch locations.

Visa extensions

In Shanghai, tourist visas can be extended for a maximum of 30 days. To extend a business visa, a letter of sponsorship from a Chinese *danwei* (work unit) is required; student visa extensions must be accompanied by a letter from the school. The process usually takes three business days. All visa extensions require two passport-size photos and are processed at the **Public Security Bureau** in Pudong, No. 1500 Minsheng Road; tel: 2895 1900; nearest metro station: Science and Technology Museum; Mon–Sat 9am–5pm.

Etiquette

Bear in mind the following rules: Shoes should be removed when entering homes; sometimes slippers will be provided. Use both hands to present business cards at meetings. Tea should be offered when you visit someone, whether at home or in a business setting.

If you invite someone for dinner, you are expected to pay for the entire meal – Shanghainese generally do not go Dutch. Nevertheless, the Shanghainese are very forgiving

of foreigners when it comes to local rules of etiquette, so you will be excused of most gaffes.

The most serious breaches of etiquette tend to involve politics rather than manners.

Events & festivals

January–February
Spring Festival (Chun Jie, or Chinese New Year). A weeklong public holiday that takes place in either January or February, depending on the lunar calendar. In the lead-up to the festival, all transport around the country is totally overwhelmed as people travel to spend the festival with their families – prompting the largest human migration on the planet. The city gets dressed up in lucky red and gold and shops are filled with goodies ahead of New Year, but some shops and businesses close or operate shorter hours over the holiday days. This is the quietest time in Shanghai as many people are away for the duration of the holiday.
The Lantern Festival (Yuan Xiao Jie) is held on the 15th day of the new year, and celebrated with the eating of sweet rice balls and lantern displays – there's a pretty one at Yu Garden.

March
Shanghai International Literary Festival. China's biggest international literary event, the festival has attracted big names (like Gore Vidal, Amy Tan) as well as emerging local writers on China.

April
Formula One. The Shanghai International Circuit in Anting (in the outskirts of Shanghai) hosts this exciting race in April.
Qing Ming. A public holiday. The first week of April brings the "Clear and Bright Festival", known in English as the "Tomb-Sweeping Day". Chinese visit the graves of their ancestors bearing

gifts of food and fake paper money to be burnt for use in the afterlife.

May

Labour Day. A public holiday in honour of China's workers.

June

Dragon Boat Festival. A public holiday in honour of Qu Yuan (340–278 BC), a poet and patriot who drowned himself when he learnt that his home state had fallen to the enemy. People went out in boats, beating drums and tossing rice dumplings into the water so that fish would stay away from his body. *Zongzi*, the leaf-wrapped rice dumplings are eaten, and dragon boat races take place.

Shanghai International Film Festival. Attracts local celebrities as well as top Hollywood names.

September–October

Mid-Autumn Festival. A public holiday. The 15th night of the eighth lunar month, when the moon appears the roundest, is an occasion for people to celebrate with their families. After dinner, they share mooncakes filled with sweet red-bean or lotus-nut paste, with an egg yolk embedded in the centre.

October

National Day. A three-day holiday plus the weekend in celebration of the founding of the People's Republic of China on 1 Oct 1949 – expect another mass exodus of people and congested roads.

ATP World Tour Masters 1000 tournament. The Shanghai Rolex Masters brings the biggest names of men's tennis to Shanghai each October.

November

International Fashion Week. A showcase for the brightest domestic fashion designers, the festival also attracts international fashion names.

Shanghai Biennale. This event brings together some notable cutting-edge contemporary artists from both the Chinese and Western worlds.

Shanghai International Arts Festival. A month-long festival that features a programme of international as well as Chinese performing arts.

HSBC Champions Golf Tournament. Golf's top players compete in this tournament, held in Sheshan, just outside Shanghai.

December

Christmas and New Year. Decorations light up the shopping hubs along Nanjing Road and Central Huaihai Road. On New Year's Eve, the Longhua Temple fair has fireworks and lion dancing. New Year's Day is a public holiday.

Getting tickets

Tickets for most arts performances can be purchased either direct from the venue or from the **Shanghai Cultural Information and Booking Centre** (272 Fengxian Road; tel: 6217 2426; www.culture.sh.cn). The website has comprehensive listings for theatres and

Traditional Chinese tea.

performance spaces in town. 247collective is an English-language ticketing service: tel: 5456 2471.

H

Health & medical care

Healthcare is good in Shanghai, and improving all the time. There are Western-staffed clinics and designated foreigners' clinics in local hospitals with English-speaking personnel. For more serious and complicated issues, patients often return to their home countries or seek treatment in Hong Kong. Visitors to Shanghai should therefore have health insurance that includes repatriation expenses.

Similarly, all the medication you might need – over-the-counter and prescription – should be brought with you, as not all medication can be found in Shanghai.

Vaccines

Other than requiring a yellow fever vaccination certificate from travellers coming from tropical South America or sub-Saharan Africa, Shanghai does not require any immunisations.

The Centre for Disease Control (CDC) in Atlanta, US, recommends

the following vaccines for travellers to Shanghai. For more information, check its website: www.cdc.gov.

Be sure to consult your doctor at least 4 to 6 weeks before your trip so that there is sufficient time for the shots to take effect.

Hepatitis A – A food and water-borne viral infection of the liver.

Hepatitis B – An estimated 10 to 15 percent of the Chinese population carry hepatitis B, which is transmitted through bodily fluids and can lead to liver disease. The vaccine is recommended if you might be exposed to blood, have sexual contact with the local population, stay longer than six months, or risk exposure through medical treatment.

Japanese encephalitis – This is only recommended if you plan on visiting rural areas for four weeks or more, except under special circumstances, like an outbreak of the disease.

Rabies   Recommended if there is risk of exposure to wild animals.

Hospitals

Shanghai Huashan Hospital
Foreigner's Ward: 19th Floor, 12 Central Wulumuqi Road
Tel: 6248 9999, ext 1900
A mid-sized general hospital which offers most specialities except obstetrics and gynaecology, and paediatrics.

Pudong Children's Medical Centre
1678 Dongfang Road, Pudong
Tel: 5873 2020
A large, modern teaching hospital built as a Sino-US joint venture.

Ruijin Hospital
197 Ruijin No. 2 Road
Tel: 6437 0045, ext 8101 (outpatients and emergencies only); 6324 0090, ext 2101 (24-hour house calls)
Large teaching hospital with most specialities. The foreigners' clinic is located in Guang Ci Hospital, on the grounds.

Clinics

Parkway Health – Shanghai Centre Clinic
Suite 203, West Retail Plaza, Shanghai Centre, 1376 Nanjing Road (W)
Tel: 6445 5999
www.parkwayhealth.cn
Reputable clinic with overseas-trained and English-speaking doctors and staff. Offers a wide range of speciality clinics, including dentistry. Operates clinics throughout the city. For 24-hour assistance, call 6445 5999.

Shanghai East International Medical Centre
551 Pudong Road (S), Pudong
Tel: 5879 9999
www.seimc.com.cn
Opened in 2003, this international-class facility is operated by Shanghai East Hospital and a California-based healthcare company. Provides both outpatient and in-patient medical services.

Pharmacies

Parkway Health centres will fill prescriptions (see above).
Shanghai No. 1 Dispensary: 616 Nanjing Road (E), tel: 6322 4567; daily 9am–10pm.
Watsons: 789 Central Huaihai Road; tel: 6474 4775; daily 9am–10pm. Branches around the city.

Chinese medicine

At the core of Traditional Chinese Medicine (TCM) is the philosophy that disease is due to an imbalance of *yin* and *yang* in the body. Illness is cause by an interruption of the flow of energy *(qi)* through the channels, or acupuncture points, of the body. Restoring the body to health requires the correction of this imbalance or disruption through acupuncture and herbal medicines.

English-speaking TCM doctors run clinics at Parkway Health centres (see above). Body & Soul – The TCM Clinic (www.bodyand soul.com.cn) is another good

multilingual option under German management.

Internet & e-mail

Most business-class hotels either have in-room Wi-fi, rooms that are equipped with computer ports that allow for high-speed Internet connections, or a business centre where this facility is available for a fee. Most cafés across the city also offer free Wi-fi.

Left luggage

Luggage can be left at the airport and the train station.
Pudong International Airport: Arrival Hall, tel: 6834 6078; Departure Hall, tel: 6834 5035.
Hongqiao Airport: Arrival Hall, tel: 5114 4520. Rates depend on size of luggage.
Shanghai Railway Station: tel: 6354 3193 (RMB 80 per day).

Lost property

If you lose your passport, it's best to contact your consulate immediately. Some consulates have emergency 24-hour numbers for this. For items left in taxis, refer to the taxi receipt for the telephone number to call (the receipt also has the taxi number on it, which will help the company locate the vehicle).

Maps

Free tourist maps of Shanghai in English and Chinese are available at the concierge desks of most hotels. The maps sold at the bookshops are usually in Chinese. Recommended is the *Insight Fleximap Shanghai*, laminated for durability.

Media

Newspapers

Shanghai has two major daily English-language newspapers: the **Shanghai Daily** (www.shanghaidaily.com or http://english.eastday.com), published in Shanghai with a local perspective on information, is the choice for most people; the second paper, **China Daily** (www.chinadaily.com.cn) is published out of Beijing. *China Daily*'s Shanghai edition has two weekly supplements, one on business and the other on entertainment. The English edition of the Chinese-language **People's Daily** is available online at http://english.people daily.com.cn.

Overseas newspapers and publications are available from the city's four- and five-star hotels. One of the best sources is The Portman Ritz-Carlton Shanghai, which carries the *South China Morning Post*, *International Herald Tribune*, *Asian Wall Street Journal* and magazines like *Economist*, *Time* and *Newsweek*.

Magazines

Shanghai is awash with free English-language publications of varying quality, most with useful listings of restaurants, bars and entertainment spots. Among the best are **City Weekend** (www.cityweekend.com.cn), **That's Shanghai** (www.thatssh.com) and **Time Out** (www.timeoutshanghai. com), which provide insightful, timely articles as well as listings. Most of the magazines are available at bars and restaurants around town.

Television

Shanghai Broadcast Network (SBN) has the news in English at 10pm from Monday to Saturday; *Citybeat*, a cultural programme in English fills in the same time slot on Sundays. The news in English is also broadcast on **China Central Television** (CCTV) at 4, 7 and 11pm on weekdays and at noon on weekends.

Most four- and five-star hotels have cable channels with **Star World**, **CNN**, **HBO** and **ESPN**.

Radio

BBC World Service is accessible on radio. English-language programming is on FM 101.7 and FM 103.7.

Money

Chinese currency

The Chinese yuan (CNY) is also known as renminbi (RMB). One yuan or renminbi (colloquially called *kuai*) is divided into 10 jiao (or *mao*); one jiao is divided into 10 fen. RMB bills are in the following denominations: 5, 10, 20, 50 and 100. Coins come in denominations of 1 RMB, 1, 2 and 5 jiao and 1, 2 and 5 fen. These days, fen isn't used much.

Exchanging money

At the time of press, US$1 was roughly equivalent to RMB 6.65 while £1 bought about RMB 8.69.

All rates are uniform regardless of whether you exchange money at a bank or hotel. Major currencies can be changed at hotels – but you must be a registered guest – as well as at banks. The same applies for traveller's cheques.

Convertibility

When you change money, you'll receive a foreign exchange receipt, showing the amount exchanged. Any unused RMB can be changed back into foreign currency at the end of your visit, but you must show the foreign exchange receipt.

In theory, because the Chinese RMB isn't convertible, you won't be able to exchange it back into foreign currency (or vice versa) outside of China. However, in practice, many countries that share borders with China or have business contacts with China are likely to have RMB. Check with banks and money exchange outlets in your country.

Chinese renminbi notes.

Credit cards are widely used in Shanghai.

Emergency money

Western Union, a reliable international money-transfer agency, will wire money through the China Courier Service Corp. Identification is required for collection, tel: 6356 6666; or visit the website www.western union.com.

Cash points

If you find yourself short of cash, international credit cards and bank cards (Cirrus, Plus, Visa, MasterCard, American Express) can be used to withdraw local currency from ATMs, which are found throughout the city.

The Bank of China will issue credit card cash advances with a 3 percent commission in US$ or RMB. The following are helpfully located ATMs:
Bank of China, Hongqiao Airport Arrival Hall; Pudong International Airport Arrival Hall; 139 Ruijin No. 1 Road; and 1377 Nanjing Road.
Citibank, Pudong International Airport Arrival Hall; and Zhongshan Road (next to Peace Hotel).
Hongkong and Shanghai Bank, Ground Floor, West Retail Plaza, Shanghai Centre, 1376 Nanjing Road (W); Hong Kong Plaza, 282 Central Huaihai Road; at the Bund, 15A Zhongshan No. 1 Road (E).

Credit cards

International credit cards are accepted at major hotels and most restaurants.
American Express Hotline: 6279 7183. Daily 9am–5.30pm.
MasterCard Hotline: 10-800 110 7309.
Visa Hotline: 10-800 110 2911.

Foreign banks

For a comprehensive list of banks in Shanghai, check the **Shanghai Banking Association** website: www.sbacn.org.

Post offices

The main **Shanghai Post Office** is at 395 Suzhou Road (N), tel: 6393 6666 – just across Suzhou Creek from the Bund. The international mail section is open daily from 8am to 10pm.

Every neighbourhood in Shanghai city has a post office, open 8 to 12 hours a day depending on the area. Post offices in the busiest areas, ie Sichuan Road, Central Huaihai Road, Nanjing Road and Xujiahui, are open 14 hours, while the Luwan district post office is open 24 hours.

In addition to mailing and selling stamps, post offices also deliver local courier packages. Most large hotels will post letters to international destinations for you.

Overseas courier services

DHL-Sinotrans: Shanghai International Trade Centre, 2200 Yan'an Road (W), tel: 6275 3543; and 303 Jinian Road, tel: 6536 2900, www.dhl.com.
FedEx: 10/F, Aetna Building, 107 Zunyi Road, tel: 6275 0808, www.fedex.com.
UPS: Room 1318, Central Plaza, 318 Central Huaihai Road, tel: 6391 5555, www.ups.com.

Local courier services

Express Mail Service (EMS): Offices at the following locations: 1337 Central Huaihai Road, tel: 6437 4272; 431 Fuxing Road, tel: 6328 3322; 2 Century Boulevard, Pudong, tel: 5047 2288; 146 Gao Qiao Shi Jia Road, Pudong, tel: 5867 5114.

Public holidays

The list of public holidays is as follows (*denotes holidays determined by the lunar calendar):
New Year's Day: 1 Jan
Spring Festival: Jan/Feb*
Qing Ming: Apr*
Labour Day: 1 May
Dragon Boat Festival: June*
Mid-Autumn Festival: Sept/Oct*
National Day: 1 Oct
Note that **Spring Festival** (or Chinese New Year) and **National Day** are weeklong holidays. Schools and government offices are open the weekend before or after the one-week holiday.

The seven-day holiday is meant to encourage domestic travel, and as a result, not only are Shanghai's tourist spots busy during the holidays, so are all forms of transport in and out of the city. This is especially true during Spring Festival, when Shanghai's migrants return to their hometowns for the festivities. Try to avoid travelling

Offering prayers.

from place to place within China during these periods.

Public toilets

Public toilets are plentiful, but toilet paper is sometimes in short supply – so always carry a pack of tissues with you. Payment – usually a few jiao – is occasionally required. If you are squeamish, head for a nice hotel or shopping mall, where the public facilities are almost always user-friendly.

R

Religious services

China has five official religions: Buddhist, Taoist, Catholic, Protestant and Islam. Shanghai's 140,000 Chinese Catholics look to the local Catholic Patriotic Association as their head.

Catholic

Dongjiadu Cathedral
175 Dongjiadu Road
Tel: 6377 5665

Chinese-language Sunday mass only at 7.30am.
St Ignatius Cathedral
158 Puxi Road
Tel: 6469 0930
Sunday mass (in Shanghainese) at 7am and 10.30am, and 6pm. Foreigners may attend.
St Peter's Catholic Church
270 Chongqing Road (S)
Tel: 6467 8282
English-language Sunday mass at Shanghai's expatriate's church is at 10.30am; Saturday evening mass is at 5pm.

Protestant

Shanghai Community Church
53 Hengshan Road
Tel: 6437 6576
English-language service for foreigners is at 4pm on Sunday.

Jewish

The Shanghai Jewish Centre
Shang-Mira Garden Villa No. 2, 1720 Hongqiao Road
Tel: 6278 0225
For times of Shabbat services and to make reservations for Shabbat

meals, check its website at www.chinajewish.org.
Chabad Jewish Centre of Pudong
Yanlord Garden, Apt 2B, Building 11, Alley 99, Puming Road, Pudong
Tel: 5878 2008
www.jewishpudong.com

Muslim

Xiaotaoyuan Mosque
52 Xiaotaoyuan Street (off Fuxing Road (E) at Henan Road)
Tel: 6377 5443
Daily 8am–7pm.

Buddhist

Jing'an Temple
1686 Nanjing Road (W)
Daily 7.30am–4pm.
Jade Buddha Temple
170 Anyuan Road (at Jiangning Road)
Daily 8am–noon, 1–5pm.

S

Shopping

Shanghai's shopping runs the gamut from brand-name designers on the Bund to streetside tailors and sprawling markets where virtually everything imaginable is on sale. Some of Shanghai's best buys are unique to the city: boutiques selling contemporary products that feature local design; antiques from the Concession era; propaganda posters from the 1960s; and custom-designed clothes, jewellery and furniture. The Shanghainese love to shop, so you'll have plenty of company, especially at weekends and during the run-up to Chinese New Year.

Nanjing Road (W), Central Huaihai Road, Xujiahui and Pudong are the city's major shopping areas, filled with large shopping centres, department stores and brand-name designer shops. One-of-a-kind boutiques are mainly found along Maoming Road, Taikang

Road, Fumin Road and in Xintiandi (see page 74).

Most large malls and department stores are generally open daily from 9–10am to 9–10pm. Smaller shops may operate shorter hours, so call first.

T

Taxes

Four- and five-star hotels add a 15 percent tax – really a service charge in disguise – to their bills. Some high-end restaurants also add a service charge. Tipping is becoming more common in upscale restaurants but isn't expected.

Telephones

The **country code** for China is **86**; the **city code** for Shanghai is **021**. When calling Shanghai from **overseas**, drop the prefix zero. When making a **domestic** call from one province to another in China, dial the city code first (including the prefix zero). **Local** calls within Shanghai do not require the city code.

To make an **international direct dial** call from Shanghai, dial the international access code: 00, followed by the country code, the area code and the local telephone number.
Local directory assistance: 114
International operator: 116

The following are city codes of places covered in the Excursions section of this guidebook:
Hangzhou 0571
Moganshan 0572
Suzhou 0512

Mobile phones

Most mobile phone users with roaming will be able to hook up with the GSM 900 network that China uses. The exceptions are users from Japan (unless they have a tri-band phone). Check with your service provider before leaving home.

To save on expensive mobile phone charges, consider using a local prepaid phone card. These are available in denominations of RMB 100 and up at magazine stands and convenience stores throughout the city. You will be given a SIM card and a local number to use. Incoming and outgoing calls are charged by the minute. The main service providers are **Shanghai Telecom**, **Shanghai Mobile** and **China Unicom**.

Note: local mobile numbers begin with 13 or 15.

Public telephones

Most public telephones in China use prepaid phone cards, which can be used for local, long distance and international (IDD) calls. Prepaid phone cards are available in amounts of RMB 20, RMB 30, RMB 50 and RMB 100.

Call charges are RMB 0.20 for three minutes, while a call exceeding three minutes is charged RMB 0.10 for every six seconds (or RMB 0.60 for the fourth minute). For some strange reason, it becomes more expensive after the third minute, presumably because the authorities don't want users hogging public phones.

Reading the paper.

International long-distance call rates vary, but are usually fairly expensive, over RMB 10 a minute. Discounted rates often apply on public holidays.

Time zones

Shanghai (and all of China) is on Beijing time, which is 8 hours ahead of Greenwich Mean Time (GMT). There is no daylight saving.

Tipping

Locals do not tip, but many tourists do, probably because they are used to doing so back home. For taxis and many restaurants, you needn't tip, but in international restaurants it is becoming accepted. RMB 10 per day is reasonable for a tour guide.

Tourist information

Local tourism offices

A **Tourist Hotline** (tel: 962 020) operates daily from 10am to 9pm. Information can be patchy depending on who you get on the line. Be sure to ask for an operator who speaks English.

The **Shanghai Tourist Information and Service Centre** (http:// lyw.sh.gov.cn/en) operates branches in each of Shanghai's districts, including one at the ground level of the arrival hall of Pudong International Airport. They are geared towards Chinese-speaking travellers and are seldom of much use to foreign travellers – the level of English spoken by the counter staff varies from one service centre to another. Hotel concierges in five-star hotels and local tourist magazines and websites are generally the best source of current information. *City Weekend* (www.cityweekend.com. cn) has a useful text-messaging service that sends addresses in Chinese to your mobile phone.

Following are some of the more centrally located info centres:

Jingan District Tourist Information & Service Centre: 699 Nanjing Road (W); tel: 3214 0042.

Luwan District Tourist Information & Service Centre: 127 Chengdu Road (S); tel: 5386 1882.

North Huangpu Tourist Information & Service Centre: 518 Jiujiang Road; tel: 6350 3718.

South Huangpu Tourist Information & Service Centre: 159 Jiujiaochang Road; tel: 6355 5032/5033.

Pudong New Area Tourist Information & Service Centre: Super Brand Mall, 168 Lujiazui Road (W); tel: 3878 0202.

If you're in **Xintiandi**, stop by the **Shanghai Information Centre for International Visitors** at No. 2, Lane 123, Xinye Road (tel: 6384 9366), just round the corner from the Shikumen Open House Museum. It has a good range of free brochures and maps, and if you're lucky, English-speaking counter staff.

Overseas tourism offices

The **China National Tourism Offices** abroad are useful sources for maps, brochures and travel information. Check its website at www.cnto.org. It's likely that the CNTO branches will recommend that you book your holiday packages with its affiliated CITS – **China International Travel Service** (www.cits.net) or the CTS – **China Travel Service** (www.ctsho.com), both of which are government-run travel agencies. They handle tours, hotels, flights (international and domestic) and train tickets. You can opt to use CITS or CTS agencies even before you set foot in Shanghai. Or you can fly to Shanghai and then book your

trips locally, either with the CITS or CTS office in Shanghai or a privately run travel agency.

Because language makes independent travel in China a bit of a challenge, package tours are a good option for the less adventurous.

Below are addresses of key CNTO offices abroad:

CNTO Australia: 19th floor, 44 Market Street, Sydney, NSW 2000, Australia; tel: 61-2 9299 4057.

CNTO Canada: 480 University Avenue, Suite 806, Toronto, Ontario, M5G1V2, Canada; tel: 1-416 599 6636.

CNTO Singapore: 7 Temasek Boulevard, 12–02, Suntec Tower One, Singapore 038987; tel: 65-63372 220.

CNTO UK: 4 Glentworth Street, London, NW1 5PG, UK; tel: 44-20 7935 9787.

CNTO USA: **New York**, 350 Fifth Avenue, Suite 6413, Empire State Building, New York, NY 10118, US; tel: (toll free) 1-888 760 8218; **Los Angeles**, 550 North Brand Boulevard, Suite 910, Glendale, CA 91203, US; tel: (toll free) 1-800 670 2228, tel: 1-818 545 7507.

W

Websites

The following websites provide a variety of information on travel-related subjects on Shanghai.
General Information
www.china.org.cn
China Foreign Ministry
www.fmprc.gov.cn/eng
Shanghai Government
www.shanghai.gov.cn
www.investment.gov.cn
Health Matters
www.worldlink-shanghai.com
Banks in Shanghai
www.sbacn.org
Airport Information
www.shanghaiairport.com

A street vendor.

Government Travel Services
www.cits.net; www.ctsho.com;
www.cnto.org; www.cnta.gov.cn
Local Media
www.shine.cn/
www.shanghaidaily.com
http://english.eastday.com
www.chinadaily.com.cn
http://english.peopledaily.com.cn
Entertainment and Events
www.cityweekend.com.cn
www.thatsshanghai.com
www.smartshanghai.com
www.timeoutshanghai.com
Hotel Bookings
english.ctrip.com
www.elong.net

Weights & measures

China uses the metric system of weights and measures. Traditional Chinese measurements like *jin* (0.5 kg) and *chi* (1/3 metre) are commonly used, particularly in the local markets and more traditional shops.

LANGUAGE

UNDERSTANDING THE LANGUAGE

GENERAL

Mandarin is the official national language of China. In addition to Mandarin, known as *putonghua*, most Chinese speak local dialects. In Shanghai, the dialect is Shanghainese, or *Shanghaihua*.

Written Chinese uses characters based on pictograms, which are pictorial representations of ideas. The standard Romanisation system for Chinese characters is known as *hanyu pinyin*. It has been in use since 1958, and is used throughout this book.

Some 6,000 to 8,000 characters are in regular use; 3,000 characters are sufficient for reading a newspaper. In China's mainland, simplified characters *(jianti zi)* are used, while in Hong Kong and Taiwan, complex characters *(fanti zi)* are used.

BASIC RULES

Tones make it difficult for foreigners to speak Mandarin correctly, as different tones give the same syllable completely different meanings. Take the four tones of the syllable *ma*, for instance: the first tone *mā* means "mother"; the second tone *má* means "hemp"; the third tone *mǎ* means "horse"; and the fourth tone *mà* means "to scold". There is also a fifth "neutral" tone.

There is a standard set of diacritical marks to indicate which of the four tones is used:
mā = high and even tone
má = rising tone
mǎ = falling then rising tone
mà = falling tone

SHANGHAI DIALECT

Most Shanghainese prefer to speak their own dialect, *Shanghaihua*. A lilting language that sounds almost Japanese, *Shanghaihua* is unintelligible to speakers of Mandarin and other dialects. It is derived from the Wu region, south of the Yangtze River.

PRONUNCIATION

The pronunciation of the consonants in *hanyu pinyin* is similar to those in English: b, p, d, t, g, k are all voiceless; p, t, k are aspirated; b, d, g are not aspirated. The i after the consonants ch, c, r, sh, s, z, zh is not pronounced; it indicates that the preceding sound is lengthened.

PINYIN/PHONETIC/SOUND

a/a/f**a**r
an /un/r**un**
ang/ung /l**ung**
ao/ou/l**oud**
b/b/**b**ath
c/ts/ra**ts**
ch/ch/**ch**ange
d/d/**d**ay
e/er/d**ir**t
e (after i,u,y)/a/tr**a**m
ei/ay/m**ay**
en/en/wh**en**
eng/eong/**ng** has a nasal sound
er/or/h**o**nour
f/f/**f**ast
g/g/**g**o
h/ch/lo**ch**
i/ee/k**ee**n
j/j/**j**eep
k/k/ca**k**e
l/l/**l**ittle
m/m/**m**onth
n/n/**n**ame
o/o/b**o**nd
p/p/tra**pp**ed
q/ch/**ch**eer
r/r/**r**ight
s/s/me**ss**
sh/sh/**sh**ade
t/t/**t**on
u/oo/sh**oo**t
u (after j,q,x,y)/as in German ü
u+/mu+de
w/w/**w**ater
x/sh/as in **sh**eep

y/y/**y**ogi
z/ds/re**ds**
zh/dj/**j**ungle

Greetings

Hello **Nǐ hǎo** 你好
How are you? **Nǐ hǎo ma?** 你好吗?
Thank you **Xièxie** 谢谢
Goodbye **Zài jiàn** 再见
My name is… **Wǒ jiào…** 我叫…
My last name is **Wǒ xìng** 我姓…
What is your name? **Nín jiào shénme míngzì?** 您叫什么名字?
What is your last name? **Nín guìxìng?** 您贵姓?
I am very happy… **Wǒ hěn gāoxìng…** 我很高兴…
All right **Hǎo** 好
Not all right **Bù hǎo** 不好
Can you speak English? **Nín huì shuō Yīngyǔ ma?** 您会说英语吗?
Can you speak Chinese? **Nín huì shuō Hànyǔ ma?** 您会说汉语吗?
I cannot speak Chinese **Wǒ bù huì hànyǔ** 我不会汉语
I do not understand **Wǒ bù dǒng** 我不懂
Do you understand? **Nín dǒng ma?** 您懂吗?
Please speak a little slower **Qǐng nín shuō màn yìdiǎn** 请您说慢一点
What is this called? **Zhège jiào shénme?** 这个叫什么?
How do you say…? **…Zěnme shuō?** …怎么说?
Please **Qǐng** 请
Never mind **Méi guānxi** 没关系
Sorry **Duìbuqǐ** 对不起

Pronouns

Who/who is it? **Shuí?** 谁?
My/mine **Wǒ/wǒde** 我/我的
You/yours (singular) **Nǐ/nǐde** 你/你的
You/yours (respectful) **Nín/nínde** 您/您的
He/his/she/hers **Tā/tāde/tā/tāde** 他/他的/她/她的
We/ours **Wǒmen/wǒmende** 我们/我们的
You/yours (plural) **Nǐmen/nǐmende** 你们/你们的
They/theirs **Tāmen/tāmende** 他们/他们的

Travel

Where is it? **Zài nǎr?** 在哪儿?
Do you have it here? **Zhèr… yǒu ma?** 这儿有… 吗?
No/it's not here/there aren't any **Méi yǒu** 没有
Hotel **Fàndiàn/bīnguǎn** 饭店/宾馆
Restaurant **Fànguǎn** 饭馆
Bank **Yínháng** 银行
Post office **Yóujú** 邮局
Toilet **Cèsuǒ** 厕所
Railway station **Huǒchēzhàn** 火车站
Bus station **Qìchēzhàn** 汽车站
Embassy **Dàshǐguǎn** 大使馆
Consulate **Lǐngshìguǎn** 领事馆
Passport **Hùzhào** 护照
Visa **Qiānzhèng** 签证
Pharmacy **Yàodiàn** 药店
Hospital **Yīyuàn** 医院
Doctor **Dàifu/yīshēng** 大夫/医生
Translate **Fānyì** 翻译
Bar **Jiǔbā** 酒吧
Do you have…? **Nín yǒu… ma?** 您有…吗?
I want to go to… **Wǒ yào qù…** 我要去…
I want/I would like **Wǒ yào/wǒ xiǎng yào** 我要/我想要
I want to buy **Wǒ xiǎng mǎi…** 我想买…
Where can I buy it? **Zài nǎr néng mǎidào?** 在哪儿能买到?
This/that **Zhège/nàge** 这个/那个
Ticket **Piào** 票
Postcard **Míngxìnpiàn** 明信片
Letter **Yì fēng xìn** 一封信
Airmail **Hángkōng xìn** 航空信
Postage stamp **Yóupiào** 邮票

Shopping

How much? **Duōshǎo?** 多少?
How much does it cost? **Zhège duōshǎo qián?** 这个多少钱?
Too expensive, thank you **Tài guì le, xièxie** 太贵了,谢谢
Very expensive **Hěn guì** 很贵
A lot **Duō** 多
Few **Shǎo** 少

Money, hotels, transport, communications

Money **Qián** 钱

Chinese currency **Rénmínbì** 人民币
One yuan/one kuai (10 jiao) **Yì yuán/yí kuài** 一元/一块
One jiao/one mao (10 fen) **Yī jiǎo/yì máo** 一角/一毛
One fen **Yì fēn** 一分
Traveller's cheque **Lǚxíng zhīpiào** 旅行支票
Credit card **Xìnyòngkǎ** 信用卡
Foreign currency **Wàihuìquàn** 外汇券
Where can I change money? **Zài nǎr kěyǐ huàn qián?** 在哪儿可以换钱?
I want to change money **Wǒ xiǎng huàn qián** 我想换钱
What is the exchange rate? **Bǐjià shì duōshǎo?** 比价是多少?
We want to stay for one (two/three) nights **Wǒmen xiǎng zhù yì (liǎng/sān) tiān** 我们想住一(两、三)天
How much is the room per day? **Fángjiān duōshǎo qián yì tiān?** 房间多少钱一天?
Room number **Fángjiān hàomǎ** 房间号码
Single room **Dānrén fángjiān** 单人房间
Double room **Shuāngrén fángjiān** 双人房间
Reception **Qiántái/fúwùtái** 前台/服务台
Key **Yàoshi** 钥匙
Clothes **Yīfu** 衣服
Luggage **Xíngli** 行李
Airport **Fēijīchǎng** 飞机场
Bus **Gōnggòng qìchē** 公共汽车
Taxi **Chūzū qìchē** 出租汽车
Bicycle **Zìxíngchē** 自行车
Telephone **Diànhuà** 电话
Long-distance call **Chángtú diànhuà** 长途电话
International call **Guójì diànhuà** 国际电话
Telephone number **Diànhuà hàomǎ** 电话号码
Computer **Diànnǎo** 电脑
Check e-mail **Chá yóujiàn** 查电邮
Use the Internet **Shàngwǎng** 上网

Time

When? **Shénme shíhou?** 什么时候?
What time is it now? **Xiànzàijǐ diǎn zhōng?** 现在几点钟?

How long? **Duōcháng shíjiān?** 多
长时间?

One/two/three o'clock **Yìdiǎn/
liǎng diǎn/sān diǎn zhōng** 一
点/两点/三点钟

Early morning/morning
Zǎoshàng/shàngwǔ 早上/上午

Midday/afternoon/evening
Zhōngwǔ/xiàwǔ/wǎnshang 中
午/下午/晚上

Monday/Tuesday **Xīngqīyī/
Xīngqī'èr** 星期一/星期二

Wednesday/Thursday
Xīngqīsān/Xīngqīsì 星期三/星期
四

Friday/Saturday **Xīngqīwǔ/
Xīngqīliù** 星期五/星期六

Sunday **Xīngqītiān/Xīngqīrì** 星期
天/星期日

Weekend **Zhōumò** 周末

Yesterday/today/tomorrow
Zuótiān/jīntiān/míngtiān 昨天/
今天/明天

This week/last week/next week
**Zhège xīngqī/shàng xīngqī/
xià xīngqī** 这个星期/上星期/下
星期

Hour/day/week/month **Xiǎoshí/
tiān/xīngqī/yuè** 小时/天/星
期/月

January/February/March **Yíyuè/
èryuè/sānyuè** 一月/二月/三月

April/May/June **Sìyuè/wǔyuè/
liùyuè** 四月/五月/六月

July/August/September **Qīyuè/
bāyuè/jiǔyuè** 七月/八月/九月

October/November/December
Shíyuè/shíyīyuè/shí'èryuè 十
月/十一月/十二月

Eating out

Attendant/waiter/waitress
Fúwùyuán/xiǎojiě 服务员/小姐

Eat **Chīfàn** 吃饭

Breakfast **Zǎofàn** 早饭

Lunch **Wǔfàn** 午饭

Dinner **Wǎnfàn** 晚饭

Menu **Càidān** 菜单

Chopsticks **Kuàizi** 筷子

Knife **Dāozi** 刀子

Fork **Chāzi** 叉子

Spoon **Sháozi** 勺子

Cup/glass **Bēizi/bōlibēi** 杯子/玻
璃杯

Bowl **Wǎn** 碗

Plate **Pán** 盘

I want… **Wǒ yào…** 我要…

I do not want… **Wǒ bú yào…** 我不
要…

I did not order this **Zhège wǒ méi
diǎn** 这个我没点

I am a vegetarian **Wǒ shì chī sù
de rén** 我是吃素的人

I do not eat any meat or fish **Wǒ
suǒyǒude ròu hé yú dōu bù chī**
我所有的肉和鱼都不吃

Please fry it in vegetable oil **Qǐng
yòng zhíwù yóu lái chǎo** 请用植
物油来炒

Beer **Píjiǔ** 啤酒

Liquor **Bái jiǔ** 白酒

Red/white wine **Hóng/bái pú táo
jiǔ** 红/白葡萄酒

Mineral water **Kuàngquánshuǐ** 矿
泉水

Soft drinks **Yǐnliào** 饮料

Green tea/black tea **Lǜchá/
hóngchá** 绿茶/红茶

Coffee **Kāfēi** 咖啡

Tea **Cháshuǐ** 茶水

Fruit **Shuǐguǒ** 水果

Rice **Mǐfàn** 米饭

Soup **Tāng** 汤

Stir-fried dishes **Chǎocài** 炒菜

Beef/pork/lamb/chicken
Niúròu/zhūròu/yángròu/jīròu
牛肉/猪肉/羊肉/鸡肉

Vegetables **Shūcài** 蔬菜

Spicy/sweet/sour/salty **Là/tián/
suān/xián** 辣/甜/酸/咸

Hot/cold **Rè/liáng** 热/凉

Can we have the bill, please
Qǐng jié zhàng/mǎidān 请结
帐/买单

Numbers

One/two/three/four/five **Yī/ér/
sān/sì/wǔ** 一/二/三/四/五

Six/seven/eight/nine/ten **Liù/
qī/bā/jiǔ/shí** 六/七/八/九/十

Eleven/twelve/twenty/thirty/
forty **Shíyī/shíèr/érshí/
sānshí/sìshí** 十一/十二/二十/
三十/四十

Fifty/sixty/seventy/eighty/ninety
**Wǔshí/liùshí/qīshí/bāshí/
jiǔshí** 五十/六十/七十/八十/九
十

One hundred **Yībǎi** 一百

One hundred and one **Yībǎi língyī**
一百零一

Two hundred/three hundred
Liǎng bǎi/sān bǎi 两百/三百

Four hundred/five hundred **Sì
bǎi/wǔ bǎi** 四百/五百

One thousand **Yìqiān** 一千

TRANSPORT

A – Z

LANGUAGE

FURTHER READING

HISTORY

Life and Death in Shanghai by Nien Ching, HarperCollins, 1995. A beautifully written account of a privileged woman's ordeal during the Cultural Revolution in Shanghai.

Red Azalea by Anchee Min, Berkeley Publishing Group, 1995. An honest memoir of growing up during the Cultural Revolution in Shanghai, chronicling the injustices and torments through the eyes of a teenage girl.

In Search of Old Shanghai by Lynn Pan, Joint Publishing Co., 1982. Meticulously researched and the best historical account of Old Shanghai.

The Soong Dynasty by Sterling Seagrave, Vintage, 1992. Well-researched book that reads like a novel on the Soongs, Old Shanghai's "first family", whose rise parallels China's story in the first half of the 20th century.

Strangers Always: A Jewish Family in Wartime Shanghai by Rena Krasno, Pacific View Press, 1992. Krasno, born and raised in Shanghai, used her diaries and letters as the basis for this account of wartime Shanghai.

ARCHITECTURE

Building Shanghai: The Story of China's Gateway by Edward Denison and Ren Guangyu, Wiley, 2006. A captivating account of the evolution of the city's architecture – beautifully illustrated with archival maps and photographs.

A Last Look: Western Architecture in Old Shanghai by Tess Johnston and Deke Erh, Old China Hand Press, 2003. Shanghai's legacy of Western architecture – some of it already gone – captured over 25 years by historian Johnston and photographer Erh.

Phantom Shanghai by Greg Girard, Magenta Foundation, 2007. A photographic documentation of the architectural destruction and reinvention of Shanghai.

Shanghai Art Deco by Tess Johnston and Deke Erh, Old China Hand Press, 2006. Johnston and Erh document Shanghai's signature Art Deco style in architecture, interior design and objects. Archival photographs and maps are also included.

CONTEMPORARY CHINA

Chinese Lessons: Five Classmates and the Story of New China by John Pomfret, Henry Holt & Co., 2006. Former *Washington Post* Beijing bureau chief Pomfret insightfully relates the experiences of his five classmates from Nanjing University, and through them, examines the dramatic changes in recent Chinese history.

Country Driving: A Journey Through China from Farm to Factory by Peter Hessler, Harper-Collins, 2009. The former *New Yorker China* correspondent's final chapter in his trilogy of a changing China: Hessler drives through China, chronicling the human side of the China boom.

Factory Girls: From Village to City in a Changing China by Leslie Chang, Spiegel & Grau, 2008. *Wall Street Journal* correspondent Chang tells the story of the exodus of China's rural population through the lives of two teenage girls. A remarkable portrait of a side of China that is often hidden.

One Billion Customers: Lessons from the Front Lines of Doing Business in China by Jim McGregor, Free Press, 2005. Journalist-turned-businessman McGregor's clear-eyed account of two decades of doing business in China.

Operation Yao Ming: The Chinese Sports Empire, American Big Business and the Making of an NBA Superstar by Brook Larmer, Gotham Books, 2005. Former *Newsweek* journalist Larmer chronicles the rise of Shanghai boy Yao Ming. Vividly illustrating the strictures of the sports system and modern Chinese society.

The Where's Where of the Who's Who of Old Shanghai by Tess Johnston, Historic Shanghai, 2016. The final edition of a much-loved walking guide series uncovers the colourful characters who once lived, loved and worked in Shanghai's historic buildings.

SHANGHAI STREET ATLAS

The key map shows the area of Shanghai covered by the atlas section. An index of street names and places of interest shown on the maps can be found on the following pages. For each entry there is a page number and grid reference.

Map Legend

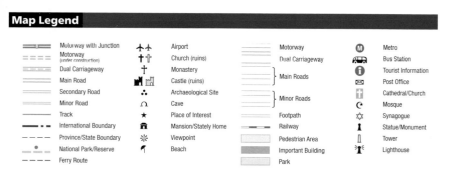

Motorway with Junction	✈ ✈ Airport	Motorway	Ⓜ Metro
Motorway (under construction)	✝ ✝ Church (ruins)	Dual Carriageway	🚌 Bus Station
Dual Carriageway	✝ Monastery	Main Roads	❶ Tourist Information
Main Road	🏰 🏚 Castle (ruins)		✉ Post Office
Secondary Road	⁘ Archaeological Site	Minor Roads	✝ Cathedral/Church
Minor Road	∩ Cave		☾ Mosque
Track	★ Place of Interest	Footpath	✡ Synagogue
International Boundary	🏛 Mansion/Stately Home	Railway	⍐ Statue/Monument
Province/State Boundary	✳ Viewpoint	Pedestrian Area	⍾ Tower
National Park/Reserve	↟ Beach	Important Building	⍾ Lighthouse
Ferry Route		Park	

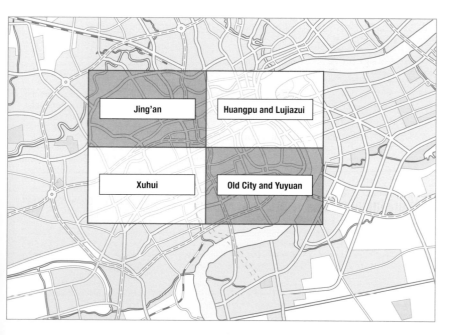

Jing'an

Huangpu and Lujiazui

Xuhui

Old City and Yuyuan

A   B

Guangfu Road W. (Guangfu Xilu)
Suzhou Creek (Wusong)
Macao Rd
Shaanxi Rd North
CHANGSHOU PARK
Yichang Road (Yichang Lu)
Xikang Road
Jiangning Road
Changhua Road
Xinhui Lu
Xisuzhou
Changde Road
Peng
(Changshou Lu)
(Xikang Lu)
(Shaanxi Beilu)
Anyuan Road
Yu Fo Si (Jade Buddha Temple)
(Changhua Lu)

1

Jiaozhou Road
Guihuayi
CHANGSHOU ROAD
常熟路站
Xinhui
Road
(Anyuan Lu)
Renhe Road
Shaanxi Road North
Jiangning Lu
(Haifang
JIANGNING ROAD
江宁路站
Huai

Changshou Road
(Changde Lu)
(Jiaozhou Lu)
Xikang Road
Haifang Road
JING'AN
静安区
Shaanxi Lu

2

Anyuan Road
WUNING ROAD
武宁路站
(Yuyao Lu)
Yanping Road
Jiaozhou Road
CHANGPING ROAD
昌平路站
(Changping Lu)
(Kangding Lu)
Xikang

Changping Road
Kangding Road
Changde

3

Yuyao Road
WUNING ROAD SOUTH (Wuning Jielu)
(Kangding Lu)
Wuding Road
(Wuding Lu)
Kangding Road
Xinzha Road
Changde
(Xinzha Lu)
Shan Child Hosp

Kangding Road
Wanhangdu Road
Wuding Road
(Wuding Xilu)
Yanping Road
Nanjing Lu
Jiaozhou Lu
Beijing Road West

Wanhangdu Road (Wanhangdu Lu)
(Yuyuan Lu)

4

Jiangsu Road
Wuding Road West
(Wanhangdu Lu)
Zhenning Road
Wulumuqi Road North
Yuyuan Road
Jiu Gong City Plaza
Reel Mall
Jing Ke Cer

CHANGNING
长宁区
Jingan Si (Jing'an Temple)
JING'AN TEMPLE
静安寺站
Huashan
JINGAN GONGYUAN (JING'AN PARK)
Yan'an Freeway

N
JIANGSU ROAD
江苏路站
Yuyuan Road (Yuyuan Lu)
Nanjing Road West
Shi Shaonian Gong (Municipal Children's Palace)
Zhenning Road
Road
Cai Yuanpei (Cai Yuanpei's former resider

0   500 m
0   500 yds

A   B

ZHABEI
闸北区

Chang'an Road
Yutong Rd
Puji Road
Hengfeng Road (Hengfeng Lu)
Gonghe Road (Gonghe Lu)
Minli Road
Meiyuan
Huasheng Rd
Haichang Rd
Datong Rd
Nanjing Road
Xinjiang Road
Jinyuan
Menggu Road
Guoqing
Qufu Road
Tibet (Xizang) Rd N

Hengfeng Road Bus Interchange
Hanzhong Lu
Hengtong Rd
(Chang'an Lu)
Wuzhen Road

HANZHONG ROAD
漢中路站

QUFU ROAD
曲阜路站

Chang'an Road (Guangfu Lu)
Suzhouhe Road
Guangfu Road
North-South Freeway (elevated)
Xinyou Road
(Guangfu Lu)
(Suzhouhe Lu)
Xinzha Road

Suzhou Creek (Wusong)
(Suzhou Lu)
Dalian Road
Shanghaiguan Road
Chengdu Road North (Chengdu Beilu)
Xinchang Road
Hanjine Road
Wenzhou Rd
Xinzha Road

Kangding Lu
Shimen No.2 Road (Shimen 2-Lu)
(Xinzha Lu)
XINZHA ROAD
新閘路站
Beijing Road East
Guling Road

Jiangning Road
Changhua Road
Kangding Road
Wuding Lu
Taixing Road
Cixi Road
(Dajian Lu)
(Beijing Xilu)
Chengdu Road North (Chengdu Beilu)
Beijing Road East
PEOPLE'S SQUARE
人民廣場站

Xinzha Road
Zhangjiazhai Road
SHANGHAI NATURAL HISTORY MUSEUM
自然博物館站
Shanghai Ziran Bowuguan (Natural History Museum)
Fengyang Lu
Daguangming Dian Ying (Grand Cinema)

Jiangning Road
(Shanxi Lu)
Taixing Lu
Fengyang
Beijing Road West
(Nanjing Xilu)
Nanjing Road West
Xinchang Road
Huangpi Road West

Youtai Jiaotang (Ohel Rachel Synagogue)
Majestic Theatre
Nanhui Road
Beijing Road West
Road
Ming Tien Guangchang (Tomorrow Square)

(Beijing Xilu)
Westgate Mall
Taixing Road
Wuliang
NANJING ROAD (W.)
南京西路站
Qinghai Road
Jiangyin Road
Chongqing
Central Plaza

Nanyang Rd
CITIC Square
Maoming Road North
Shimen No.1 Road (Shimen 1-Lu)
Shanghai Dianshitai (TV Station)
Weihai Road
Wusheng Rd (Wusheng Lu)
Huangpi Road North

Shanghai Jiangcheng (Shanghai Centre)
Plaza 66
Shaanxi Rd N.
Nanhui Road
Nanhui Road
(Weihai Lu)
Weihai Road (Weihai Lu)
Road North
(Dagu)

Shanghai Zhanlan Zhongxin (Shanghai Exhibition Centre)
Weihai Road
Maoming Beilu
Dagu Road

Yan'an Chengdu Interchange
Chongqing Road South (Chongqing Beilu)

(elevated)
Central Yan'an Road (Yan'an Zhonglu)

Hengshan Male Bieshu (Hengshan Moller Villa)
Shaanxi Road South
Maoming
Rujin No.2 Road (Rujin 2-Lu)
Julu Road
Chengdu Rd S.
Julu Road

(Julu Lu)
Jinxian Road
Lanxin Daxiyuan (Lyceum Theatre)
Changle Road
Road
Xing'an Rd

Julu Road
Changle Road
(Changle Lu)
Changle Road South
South
Central Huaihai Road
Isetan

HONGHOU
虹口区

Qufu Rd
Tiantong Rd
QUFU ROAD
曲阜路站

Guoqing Road

Tiantong Rd
TIANTONG ROAD
天潼路站

(Wusong)

Shanghai Waitan Meishuguan
(Rockbund Art Museum)

No. 1 Wa
(forme
Cons

Peni
Sha

Zhongguo Yinh
(Bank of C

Dianchi R

Zhejiang Road North
Suzhouhe Road
Beisuzhou Road
Fujian Road North
Shanxi Road North
Suzhouhe Rd

Suzhou Creek
(Suzhouhe Lu)
(Beisuzhou Lu)

Central Henan Road
Central Jiangxi Road
Yuanmingyuan Rd

Road

Xiamen
Xinzha Road
Wenzhou Rd
Huanghe

Beijing Road East

Guling Road

Zhejiang Rd N.
Central Yunnan Road

Tibet (Xizang) Beilu

Huangpu
Theatre

Zhongguo
Theatre

Niuzhuang Road
Ningbe Road

Guangxi Road
Guizhou Road

Tianjin Road

(Beijing Donglu)

Central Fujian Road

HUANGPU
黄浦区

(Tianjin Lu)

NANJING
ROAD (E.)
南京東路站

Heping Fanc
(Fairmont Peace

Heping Huiz
Fa
(Swat
Peace

Tianjin Road

(Nanjing Donglu)

Nanjing Road Pedestrian Mall

Jiujiang Lu

Hong Miao
(Holy Trinity,
Red Temple)

Hankou R
Laohaig
(Customs Hou

Shanghai Nº1
Department
Store

Nanjing Road East

(Jiujiang Lu)

Shanxi Rd
Rd

Pudong Fazhan Yi
(Pudong Development

Huaxia
M on the

Raffles City

Jiujiang

(Hankou Lu)

Foreign Languages
Bookstore

Central Shandong Road
(Henan Zhong Lu)

Fuzhou
Road

Mu'en Tang
(Moore Church)

Renmin Grand
Stage Theatre

Hankou
Rd

Guangx

Central
Zhejiang

Hubei

(Fuzhou Lu)

Guangdong
Road

PEOPLE'S
SQUARE
人民广场站

PEOPLE'S PARK
(RENMIN GONGYUAN)

Chengshi Guihua
Zhanlan Guan
(Shanghai Urban
Planning Exhibition
Centre)

PEOPLE'S SQUARE
人民广场站

(Guangdong Lu)

Fengyang

Daguangming
Dian Ying
(Grand Theatre
Cinema)

Shanghai
Dangdai
Yishu Guan
(Museum of
Contemporary
Art, MOCA)

Xinchang Road

Nanjing Rd West

Shanghai Pao
Ma Zong Hui
(former Shanghai
Racing Club)

Shanghai Renmin
Zhengfu
(City Hall)

Yifu Wutai
(Theatre)

Beihai Road

Jiujiang

Guang'an

Zhejiang

Fuzhou Road

Central (Xizang) Tibet Road

(Yan'an

Jiangn

Ruose
(St Jose

Jiangyin Rd

Shanghai Dajuyuan
(Grand Theatre)

Renmin Guangchang
(People's Square)

Zhonghu
North

Yan'an Freeway (elevated)

Shenze Road
Ningyhai Road E.
Fujian Rd S.
Shandong Rd S.

Henan Road South

YUYUAN GARD
豫园站

Central
Plaza

Weihai Rd

Huangpi Road East

People's Avenue (Renmin Da Dao)

Shanghai Bowuguan
(Shanghai Museum)

Da Shijie
(Great World)

Yongshou Road

Yunnan Road South
Guang'an Road South
Ningyhai Rd S.
Jinling Road

Fuyou Road

Ruose
(St Jose

Wusheng Road

Wusheng Road

Shanghai
Yinyueting
(Concert Hall)

DASHIJIE
大世界站

Tibet (Xizang) Road South

(Huaihai Zhonglu)

Luxiangyuan

Fuyou Lu Qingzhensi
(Fuyou Rd Mosque)

Chenxi
(N

Chongqing Rd North

Dagu Road

Yan'an Road East

PEOPLE'S PARK
(RENMIN GONGYUAN)

Shanghai
Cybermart

Times
Square

(Huaihai Zhonglu)

Pu'an Road

Central Jinling Road

Yunnan
Nanlu

(Renmin Lu)

Dongganglian St

Dajingge
(Dajing Tower)

Wanzhu St

Baiyun Guan
(Taoist Temple)

Dajing

Jiucang St

Shizi St

Road

(Fangbang Zhonglu)

Zihua St

Cang Bao Lou
(Can Bao Bldg)

Henan Nanlu

Songyue Lu

Central Huaihai Road

Hong Kong
Plaza

HUANGPI ROAD (S.)
黄陂南路站

Shui On
Plaza

Jinling Road West

HUAIHAI
GONGYUAN

Songshan Road

Taoyuan
Road

Dongtai Lu
Shichang
(Antiques Market)

Shouning Road

Dongtai Road

Kuaiji

Central Fangbang Rd

Oinglian St

LAOXIMEN
老西门站

Fuxing Road East

Qindan St

Jinjia Fang
Kongjia Long

Xiaotao
Qingzh
(Peach Or
Mosqu

Chongqing Rd South (Chongqing Beilu)

Central
Plaza

Xing'an Rd

Taicang Road

Danshui Road

Xintiandi

Xing'an Road (Xing'an Lu)

Chongde Road

Liuhekou Road (Liuhekou Lu)

Jin

Zizhong Road

Shanghai Wanshang
Huaniaoi Shichang
(Wanshang Bird & Flower Market)

TAIPINGQIAO
GONGYUAN

Jingxiu St

Huangpu

Renmin Yingxiong Jinianbei (Monument to the People's Heroes)

gpu Rd
du Bridge
du Qiao)

NGPU
GYUAN

Shanghai Daziran Yesheng Kunchong (Natural Wild Insect Kingdom)

MINGZHU GONGYUAN

Shanghai Haiyang Shuizuguan (Ocean Aquarium)

Shanghai Guoji Huiyi Zhongxin (SICC) (International Convention Centre)

Dongfang Mingzhu Guangbo Dianshui (Oriental Pearl Tower)

Shanghai Shi Lishi Bowuguan (Municipal History Museum)

aitan Canguang Sui Dao und Sightseeing Tunnel)

Fenghe Road

LUJIAZUI 陆家嘴站 Ⓜ

LUJIAZUI 陆家嘴

Bank of India Shanghai HQ

Xijian Rd Tunnel

Yincheng Road North

Dongguang Rd

Yincheng Road East

Yincheng Road

Pudong Road South (Pudon Nanlu)

Dongchen Rd

RIVERSIDE PARK

Zhen Da Guangchang (Super Brand Mall)

IFC Mall

LUJIAZUI GONGYUAN

Chen Guichun Jiuzhai (Chen Guichen's House)

Lujiazui Road East

Century Boulevard

Shanghai Zhengjuan Jiaoyisuo (Stock Exchange Building)

Yan'an Road East Tunnel

Fucheng Road

Yincheng Road West

Käfer

Zhendan Yishu Bowuguan (Aurora Museum)

Huayuanshiqiao Road

Jinmao Dasha (Jin Mao Tower)

(Shi Ji Da Dao)

Shanghai World Financial Center

Shanghai 21

Yincheng Rd

Shanghai Tower

e on und

Jinling Dong Lu Ma Tou (Jinling Pier)

mer i Club Astoria nd, Heritage

Yincheng Road South

Pucheng Road

Dongchang Road

P U D O N G 浦东

onglu)

nyong'an Rd

min Road

Zhongshan No.2 Road East

Dangfeng Road

Renmin Road Tunnel

Pumin Road (Pumin Lu)

(Fucheng Lu)

Sangcheng Road

Qixin Road

GUCHENG GONGYUAN

Shillupu Wharf

ng St
an Shangchang rden Bazaar)

UAN

Gangu St

(Anren Jie)

Wutong Road

ashe ouse)

Chenghuang Miao (Temple of the Town God)

bang Rd

(Fangbang Zhonglu)

Shiliu Puhong Qixlang (Cloth Market)

Dong Street

Zhonghua Road

Zhongshan Road South (Zhongshan Nanlu)

Waikansha

Laotaiping Long

Xinmatou St

Fuxing Road Tunnel (E.)

Huangpu

Zhoujin Road

Xueyuan Road (Xueyuan Lu)

(air chuang)

Xiyaojie Long

apu Rd 南
Rd

Wangun Road

Guangjia Road South

Meijia St

Lingli St

Penglai Rd

Xipldao Street

(Zhonghua Lu)

Miezhu Road

Fuxing Road E.

Laoxin St

Doushi Street

Waima Road (Waima Lu)

THE OLD CITY

(Fuxing Donglu)

Maojia Road

0   500 m

0   500 yds

N

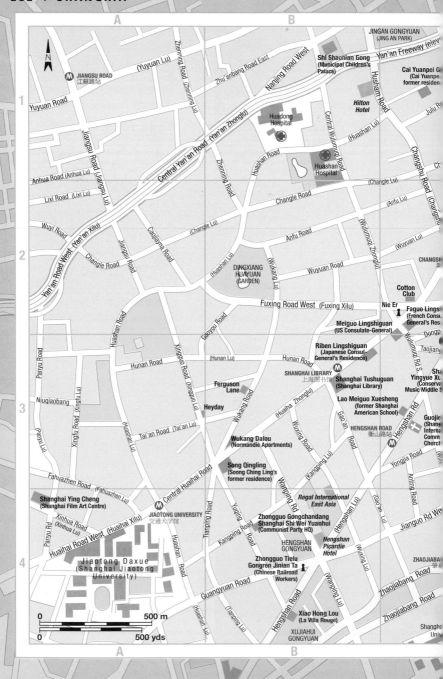

A

B

N

1

JINGAN GONGYUAN
(JING AN PARK)

Yan'an Freeway (elev

Ⓜ JIANGSU ROAD
江蘇路站

(Yuyuan Lu)

Zhenning Road (Zhenning Lu)

Zhu'anbang Road East

Nanjing Road West

Shi Shaonlan Gong
(Municipal Children's
Palace)

Husham Road

Cai Yuanpei G
(Cai Yuanpe
former residen

Julu Ro

Yuyuan Road

**Hilton
Hotel**

Huadong
Hospital

Central Wulumuqi Road

(Huashan Lu)

Changshu Road (Changshu

Ch

Anhua Road (Anhua Lu)

Jiangsu Road (Jiangsu Lu)

Central Yan'an Road (Yan'an Zhonglu)

Zhenning Road

Huashan Road

**Huashan
Hospital**

(Changle Lu)

Lixi Road (Lixi Lu)

Changle Road

(Anfu Lu)

Wuyi Road

(Changle Lu)

Anfu Road

(Wulumuqi Zhonglu)

(Wuyuan Lu)

2

Yan'an Road West (Yan'an Xilu)

Changle Road

Jiangsu Road

Caojiayna Road

(Huashan Lu)

**DINGXIANG
HUAYUAN
(GARDEN)**

(Wukang Lu)

Wuyuan Road

CHANGS

Fuxing Road West (Fuxing Xilu)

**Cotton
Club**

Huashan Road

Caoyou Road

Xingguo Road (Xingguo Lu)

Nie Er ⚓

**Faguo Lings
(French Consu
General's Res**

Wulumuqi Rd S

Dongp

Meiguo Lingshiguan
(US Consulate-General)

Panyu Road

Hunan Road

(Hunan Lu)

Hunan Road

Riben Lingshiguan
(Japanese Consul-
General's Residence)

Taojian

3

Huashan Road (Huashan Lu)

SHANGHAI LIBRARY
上海图书馆

Shanghai Tushuguan
(Shanghai Library)

Sha
Yingyue Xu
(Conserva
Music Middle S

**Ferguson
Lane**

Wukang Road

Lao Meiguo Xuesheng
(former Shanghai
American School)

Niuqiaobang

Xingfu Road (Xingfu Lu)

Huaihai Road (Huaihai Zhonglu)

Heyday

Gao an
Road

Hengshan Rd

**Guojie
(Shan
Interna
Comm
Com**

Ⓜ

HENGSHAN ROAD
衡山路站

Tai'an Road (Tai'an Lu)

Wuxing Road

Huashan Lu

Kangping Lu)

Ⓜ

Yongjia Road

Anting Road

Fahuazhen Road (Fahuazhen Lu)

Wukang Dalou
(Normandie Apartments)

Song Qingling
(Soong Ching Ling's
former residence)

Wanping Rd

Panyu Rd

Shanghai Ying Cheng
(Shanghai Film Art Centre)

Xinhua Road (Xinhua Lu)

Ⓜ JIAOTONG UNIVERSITY
交通大学馆

**Regal International
East Asia**

(Hengshan Lu)

Jianguo Rd We

Gao an Lu

Zhaojiabang Road

Central Huaihai Road (Huaihai Xilu)

Tianping Road

Yuqing Road

Kangping Road

**Zhongguo Gongchandang
Shanghai Shi Wei Yuanhui**
(Communist Party HQ)

**Hengshan
Picardie
Hotel**

Wuxing Lu

Zhaojiaba
王

ZHAOJIABA

4

Huaihai Road West (Huaihai Xilu)

Huashan Road

**Jiaotong Daxue
(Shanghai Jiaotong
University)**

**HENGSHAN
GONGYUAN**

**Zhongguo Tielu
Gongren Jinian Ta**
(Chinese Railroad
Workers)

Wanping Lu

Zhaojiabang Road

Guangyuan Road

(Zhenning Lu)

Huashan Lu

Hengshan Lu

Xiao Hong Lou
(La Villa Rouge)

**XUJIAHUI
GONGYUAN**

Shangha
Uni

0 ——————— 500 m

0 ——————— 500 yds

A

B

D

E

(Julu Lu)

Jinxian Road (Jinxian Lu)

(Change Lu)

Lanxin Daxiyuan
(Lyceum Theatre)

Changle Road

Xing'an Rd

Central Huaihai Road

Chongqing Road South (Chongqing Beilu)

Chongqing Road South

Yandang Entertainment Street

Chongqing Road North (Xiangyang Beilu)

Xiangyang Road North (Xiangyang Beilu)

Maoming Road South

Ruijin No.2 Road

Isetan

1

Xinle Road

HUAIHAI
ROAD (M)
淮海中路站

Mansion
Complex

Baisheng Gouwu
Zhongxin
(Parkson Department
Store)

Guotai Dianyingyuan
(Cathay Cinema)
Jinchen
Hotel

New Hualian
Commercial
Building

Nanchang

Xinle Road

XIANGYANG
GONGYUAN

Zhonglu

Sheng Nigulasi Jiaotang
(former St Nicholas
Church)

FUXING
GONGYUAN

Donghu Road

(Huaihai

(Nanchang Nanlu)

Gaolan Road

Shaanxi Road South (Xiangyang Nanlu)

Xhongguo Lanyin
uabu Guan
Chinese Printed Blue
ankeen Exhibition Hall)

iapm
Mall

SHAANXI
ROAD (S.)
陕西南路站

Maoming Nanlu

Sun Zhongshan Guju
(former Residence of
Sun Yat-sen)

Shan Road

Central Fuxing Road

Xiangshan
Road

Central Huaihai Road

Yinyue Xueyuan
(Conservatory
of Music)

Nanchang Road

(Fuxing Zhonglu)

Zhou Enlai Guju
(former Residence
of Enlai)

Ilefei Rd

North-South Freeway (elevated)

2

ng Lu)

Fenyang

Intercontinental
Shanghai Ruijin
(former Ruijin
Guesthouse)

Shan Lu

Ruijin No.2 Road

entral Fuxing Road

Shanghai Gongyi
Meishuguan
(Arts & Crafts Museum)

Damuqiao Road

Wenhua
Guangchang
(Shanghai Culture
Square)

Yongjia Road

Ruijin Yi Yuan
(Ruijin Hospital)

Fenyang Rd

Yongkang Road

Shaanxi Road South

Jiande Road

ushkin
riangle

Shaoxing Road (Shaoxing Lu)

Central Jianguo Road

Shan Rd

♟ Puxijin
(Pushkin)

Yongjia Lu

Tianzi Fang

Taikang Road

(Xiangyang Nanlu)

Taiyuan Road

Jianguo Road West

Ruijin 2-Lu

DAPUQIAO
打浦桥站

Xujiahui Road (Xujiahui Lu)

Dapu Road

3

(Yueyang Road)

(Jianguo Xilu)

(Damuqiao Road)

Shaanxi Nanlu

Zhaojiabang Road

(Taiyuan Lu)

JIASHAN ROAD
嘉善路站

Zhaojiabang Road

Xietu Road

(Zhaojiabang Lu)

Shanghai Gongan Bowuguan
(Museum of Public Security)

(Zhaojiabang Lu)

Damuqiao Road

(Pingjiang Lu)

(Yixueyuan Lu)

(Qingzhen Lu)

Xietu Lu

Ruijin Branch

Ruijin Road

(Dapu Lu)

4

Pingjiang Road

Fenglin Road (Fenglin Lu)

Xiaomuqiao Road

Qingzhen Road

Xiaomuqiao Lu

(Damuqiao Lu)

Yixueyuan Road

Zhongshan
Hospital

♟ Pediatric
Hospital

Xietu Road

Chaling Road

Quxi Rd

(Quxi Lu)

D

E

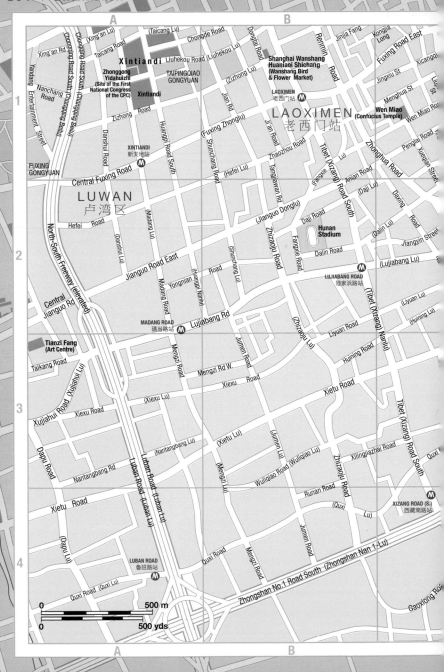

Yandang Road

Xing'an Rd

Nanchang Road

Chongqing Road South (Chongqing Beilu)

Chongqing Road South (Chongqing Beilu)

Entertainment Street

FUXING GONGYUAN

(Xing'an Lu)

(Taicang Lu)

Taicang Road

Xintiandi

Zhonggong Yidahuizhi (Site of the First National Congress of the CPC)

Xintiandi

Zizhong Road

Danshui Road

XINTIANDI 新天地站

Chongde Road

Liuhekou Road (Liuhekou Lu)

TAIPINGQIAO GONGYUAN

Huangpi Road South

Jian Rd

(Fuxing Zhonglu)

Shunchang Road

(Hefei Lu)

Central Fuxing Road

Dongtai Road

Renmin

(Zizhong Lu)

Jinjia Fang

Kongjia Long

Fuxing Road East

Xicanggi

Jingxiu St

Menghua St

Wen Miao Rd

Pengtai Road

Xueqian Road

Zhonghua Road

Shanghai Wanshang Huaniaoi Shichang (Wanshang Bird & Flower Market)

LAOXIMEN 老西门站

LAOXIMEN 老西门站

Jian Road

Jian Road

Zhaozhou Road

Tanglawan Rd

Fangxie

Wen Miao (Confucius Temple)

Tibet (Xizang) Road South

Anlan Road

(Daji Lu)

LUWAN 卢湾区

Hefei   Road

Danshui Lu

Madang Lu

Jianguo Road East

Shunchang Lu

Yongnian   Road

Madang Road

(Huangpi Namlu)

(Jianguo Donglu)

Zhizaoju Road

Fangxie Road

Daji Road

Hunan Stadium

Dalin Road

Dalin Road

Daxing

Road

(Dalin Lu)

Jiangyin Street

LUJIABANG ROAD 陆家浜路站

(Lujiabang Lu)

(Liyuan Lu)

(Huning Lu)

North-South Freeway (elevated)

Central Jianguo Rd

MADANG ROAD 码当路站

Lujiabang Rd

Zhizaoju Lu

Liyuan Road

Huning Road

Tibet (Xizang) Nanlu

Tianzi Fang (Art Centre)

Taikang Road

Xuijiahui Road (Xujiahui Lu)

Xiexu Road

Dapu Road

Nantangbang Rd

Luban Road (Luban Lu)

Luban Road (Luban Lu)

Mengzi Road

(Xiexu Lu)

(Nantangbang Lu)

Mengzi Rd W.

Xiexu   Road

Jumen Road

Xietu Lu

(Xietu Lu)

Jumen Lu

(Mengzi Lu)

Xietu Road

Wuliqiao Road (Wuliqiao Lu)

Zhizaoju Road

Xilingjiazhai Road

Runan Road

(Quxi Lu)

Tibet (Xizang) Road South

XIZANG ROAD (S.) 西藏南路站

Xietu   Road

(Dapu Lu)

LUBAN ROAD 鲁班路站

Quxi Road (Quxi Lu)

Quxi Road

Mengzi Road

Jumen Road

Zhongshan No.1 Road South Zhongshan Nan 1-Lu)

Gaoxiong Road

0   500 m

0   500 yds

THE OLD CITY

Wangyun Road

Guangqi Road South (Guangqi Nanlu)

(Penglai Lu)

Ninghe Road

Meijia St

Lingii St

Fuxing Rd East

Penglai Rd

Xundao Street (Xundao Jie)

Laoxin St

Dousil Street

Zhonghua Road (Zhonghua Lu)

Miezhu Road

Wallangjiaqiao Street

Zixia Road

Maojia Road

Xinmatou Street

Waima Road

n South

Qiaojia Road

1

Wangjiazuijiao Street

Beishija St

Zhuhangmatou

Huayi Long

St

St

Zhongshan Road South (Zhongshan Nanlu)

(Waima Lu)

ngwen Road

XIAONANMEN
小南门站
Yujia Long

Wangjiamatou Road

(Wangjiamatou)

St

Miezhu Road

Huangjia Road

Waicang-
giao St

Wanyumatou

St

(Henan Nanlu)

(Zhonghua Lu)

Dongjiadu Road (Dongjiadu Lu)

Wanyu St

Gongyimatou

St

Dongjiadu
Tianzhutang/
(Dongjiadu
Cathedral)

Waima Road

HUANGPU
黄浦區

(Jiangyin Jie)

Sangyuan Street

Xigouyu Road

Nangu St

Laiyimatou Rd

Luxi Street

DONGJIADU
董家渡

Lujiabang Road

Dongjiangyin Street

(Dongjiangyin Jie)

Nancang Street

Duojia Road

2

(Huining Lu)

Liushi Road

Xuejiabang Rd

nzhushan Rd

Puyu Road West

Road
East

Hainan Long W.

South Bund
Fabric Market

(Duojia Lu)

Haichao Road

(Waima Lu)

Huangpu

Xietu Road East (Xietu Donglu)

Caoyeyuan Road

NANPU BRIDGE
南浦大桥站

Youchematoue
St

Chezhan Road East

Nanjiang St

(Quxi Lu)

Puyu

Chezhan Rd
West

hezhan Rd

3

njian Shoucangpin
Chenlieguan/
Sanshan Huiguan
(Museum of Folk Art)

Miaojiang Rd

Nanpu Qiao (Nanpu Bridge)

PUDONG
浦东

LAI
UAN

Zhongshan Road South (Zhongshan Nanlu)

Miaojiang Rd

Baolun Rd

Tangnan Road

Power Station
of Art

Nanmatou Road

Jianan Road

Pudong Road South

Bansongyuan Road

Wangda Rd

Sanliqiao Road East

Nanmatou Road East

4

Yinan Road

(Yinan Lu)

Nanmatou Lu

Pusan Rd

STREET INDEX

A
Anfu Road (Anfu Lu) 282 B2–C2
Anhua Road (Anhua Lu) 282 A1
Anian Road 284 B2–B1
Anping Street 280 C3
Anren Street (Anren Jie) 280 C3
Anting Road 282 C3–C4
Anyi Road 278 C4
Anyuan Road (Anyuan Lu) A2–C1

B
Baisheng Gouwu Zhongxin (Parkson Department Store) 282 D2
Baiyun Guan (Taoist Temple) 280 B4
Bansongyuan Road (Bansongyuan Lu) 284 C4–D3
Beihai Road 280 B3
Beijing Road East (Beijing Donglu) 278 E2, 280 A2–C1
Beijing Road West (Beijing Xilu) 278 B3–C3, C3–D2
Beishija Long 284 D1–E1
Beisuzhou Road (Beisuzhou Lu) 280 A1–B1, C1
Bund Centre 280 C2
Bund, The 280 C2

C
Cai Yuanpei Guju (Cai Yuanpei former residence) 278 C4
Cang Bao Lou (Can Bao Building) 280 C4
Caojiayna Road 282 A2
Caonitang Road 280 E4
Caoxievan Road 284 D3–D2
Central (Xizang) Tibet Road 280 A2–A3
Central Fangbang Road (Fangbang Zhonglu) 280 B4–C4, C4
Central Fujian Road (Fujian Zhonglu) 280 B1–B2
Central Fuxing Road (Fuxing Zhonglu) 282 C2–E2, 284 A2–B1
Central Henan Road (Henan Zhong Lu) 280 B1–B2
Central Huaihai Road (Huaihai Zhonglu) 280 A4–E3, 282 A4–B3, C2–E3
Central Huaihai Road 278 E4

Central Jianguo Road 282 E3–E2
Central Jiangxi Road (Jiangxi Zhonglu) 280 B1–C2
Central Jinling Road 280 A4–B3
Central Plaza 280 A3
Central Shandong Road 280 B2
Central Sichuan Road 280 C2–C3
Central Wulumuqi Road (Wulumuqi Zhonglu) 282 B1–B2
Central Yan'an Road (Yan'an Zhonglu) 278 D4, 282 A1–B1
Central Yunnan Road (Yunnan Zhonglu) 280 A2
Central Zhejiang Road 280 B2–B3
Century Boulevard (Shi Ji Da Dao) 280 E2
Chaling Road 282 E4
Chang'an Road (Chang'an Lu) 278 C1–E1
Changde Road (Changde Lu) 278 A1–C4
Changhua Road (Changhua Lu) 278 B1–C1, C2–D2
Changle Road (Changle Lu) 282 A2–C1, C1–E1
Changping Road (Changping Lu) 278 A3–B3, C2
Changshou Road (Changshou Lu) 278 A2–B1
Changshu Road (Changshu Lu) 282 C1–C2
Chen Guichun Jiuzhai (Chen Guichen's House) 280 E2
Chen Yi 280 C1
Chengdu Road North (Chengdu Beilu) 278 E2
Chengdu Road South 278 E4
Chenghuang Miao (City Temple of Shanghai) 280 C3
Chenxiangge (Nunnery) 280 C3
Chezhan Road East 284 C3
Chezhan Road West 284 C3
Chongde Road 280 A4–B4
Chongqing Road North 278 E3
Chongqing Road South (Chongqing Beilu) 278 E4
CITC Square 278 D3
Cixi Road 278 D2
Cotton Club 282 C2

D
Da Shijie (Great World) 280 B3
Dagu Road (Dagu Lu) 278 E4–E3
Daguangming Dian Ying (Grand Cinema) 280 A2
Daji Road (Daji Lu) 284 B2
Dajing Road 280 B4–C3
Dajingge (Dajing Tower) 280 B4
Dalin Road (Dalin Lu) 284 B2–C2
Damuqiao Road (Damuqiao Lu) 282 D2–D4
Dangfeng Road 280 C3
Danshui Road (Danshui Lu) 284 A1–A2
Dapu Road (Dapu Lu) 284 A3–A4
Datian Road (Datian Lu) 278 D1–D2
Datong Road 278 E1
Daxing Road 284 C2
Dianchi Road 280 C1
Dong Street 280 D4
Dongchang Road 280 E3
Dongfang Mingzhu Guangbo Dianshui (Oriental Pearl Tower) 280 D1
Donghu Road 282 C1
Dongjiadu Road (Dongjiadu Lu) 284 D2
Dongjiadu Tianzhutang (Dongjiadu Cathedral) 284 E2
Dongjiangyin Street (Dongjiangyin Jie) 284 D2
Dongmen Road 280 D4–D3
Dongping Road 282 C3–C2
Dongqinglian Street 280 B3
Dongtai Lu Shichang (Antiques Market) 280 B4
Dongtai Road (Dongtai Lu) 280 B4, E3
Dongyuang Road 280 E1
Doushi Street 280 D4
Duojia Road (Duojia Lu) 284 D2–E2

F
Faguo Lingshiguan (French Consul-General's Residence) 282 C2
Fahuazhen Road (Fahuazhen Lu) 282 A3–A4
Fangxie Road (Fangxie Lu) 284 B2–B1
Fenghe Road 280 D1
Fenglin Road (Fenglin Lu) 282 C4–D4
Fengyang Road (Fengyang Lu) 278 D3–E2

Fenyang Road (Fenyang Lu) 282 C2–D2
Ferguson Lane 282 B3
Fucheng Road (Fucheng Lu) 280 D2–D3
Fujian Road North 280 B1
Fujian Road South 280 B3
Fumin Road 282 C1
Fumin Street 280 C3
Fuxing Road East (Fuxing Donglu) 280 C4, C4–D4, 284 C1, D1
Fuxing Road East Tunnel 280 E4
Fuxing Road West (Fuxing Xilu) 282 B2
Fuyou Lu Qingzhensi (Fuyou Road Mosque) 280 C3
Fuyou Road (Fuyou Lu) 280 C3
Fuzhou Road (Fuzhou Lu) 280 A2–C2

G
Gangu Street (Gangu Jie) 280 C3–C4
Gao'an Road (Gao'an Lu) 282 B3–C4
Gaolan Road 282 E1
Gaoxiong Road 284 C4
Gaoyou Road 282 A3–B2
Gonghe Road (Gonghe Lu) 278 D1
Gongyimatou Street 284 E2
Grand Nation 280 B2
Guangdong Road (Guangdong Lu) 280 B3–C2
Guangfu Road (Guangfu Lu) 278 C1–E1
Guangfu Road West (Guangfu Xilu) 278 A1
Guangqi Road South (Guangqi Nanlu) 284 C1
Guangxi Road 280 A2
Guangxi Road North 280 B2–B3
Guangxi Road South 280 B3
Guangyuan Road 282 B4
Guizhou Road 280 A2
Guling Road 280 A2
Guoji Fandian (Park Hotel) 280 A2
Guojie Jiaotang (Community Church) 282 C3
Guoqing Road 278 E1
Guotai Dianyingyuan (Cathay Cinema) 282 D1

H
Haichang Road 278 D1–E1
Haichao Road 284 D3–D2

Haifang Road (Haifang Lu) 278 B2–C1
Hainan Long West 284 D2
Hankou Road (Hankou Lu) 280 A2–C2
Hanzhong Road (Hanzhong Lu) 278 D1
Hefei Road (Hefei Lu) 284 A2–B1
Henan Road North 280 B1
Henan Road South (Henan Nanlu) 280 C3–C4, 284 C1–C1
Hengfeng Road (Hengfeng Lu) 278 D1
Hengshan Male Bieshu (Hengshan Moller Villa) 278 D4
Hengshan Road (Hengshan Lu) 282 B4–C3
Hengtong Road 278 D1
Heping Fandian (Fairmont Peace Hotel) 280 C1
Heping Huizhong Fandian (Swatch Art Peace Hotel) 280 C1
Hong Kong Plaza 280 A4
Hong Miao (Holy Trinity, Red Temple) 280 C2
Houjia Road 280 C3
Huai'an Road (Huai'an Lu) 278 C1, C1
Huaihai Road West (Huaihai Xilu) 282 A4
Huanghe Road 280 A2
Huangjia Road 284 C1–D1
Huangpi Road North (Huangpi Beilu) 280 A3–A4
Huangpi Road South (Huangpi Nanlu) 284 A1–A2
Huangpu Theatre 280 A1
Huashan Road (Huashan Lu) 282 A4–B1
Huasheng Road 278 D1
Huating Road (Huating Lu) 282 C1–C2
Huaxia Bank 280 C2
Huayi Road 284 D1
Huayuanshiqiao Road 280 D2–E2
Hubei Road 280 B2
Huiguan Street 284 E2
Huining Road (Huining Lu) 284 B3–C2, C2
Hunan Road (Hunan Lu) 282 A3–B3
Huqiu Road 280 C1
Huxinting Chashe (Teahouse) 280 C3

I–J
International Financial Centre 280 D2
Isetan 282 E1

ART AND PHOTO CREDITS

INDEX

INSIGHT ⊙ GUIDES
OFF THE SHELF

Since 1970, **INSIGHT GUIDES** has provided a unique perspective on the world's best travel destinations by using specially commissioned photography and illuminating text written by local authors.

Whether you're planning a city break, a walking tour or the journey of a lifetime, our superb range of guidebooks and phrasebooks will inspire you to discover more about your chosen destination.

INSIGHT GUIDES

offer a unique combination of stunning photos, absorbing narrative and detailed maps, providing all the inspiration and information you need.

PHRASEBOOKS & DICTIONARIES

help users to feel at home, when away. Pocket-sized with a free app to download, they go where you do.

CITY GUIDES

pack hundreds of great photos into a smaller format with detailed practical information, so you can navigate the world's top cities with confidence.

EXPLORE GUIDES

feature easy-to-follow walks and itineraries in the world's most exciting destinations, with our choice of the best places to eat and drink along the way.

POCKET GUIDES

combine concise information on where to go and what to do in a handy compact format, ideal on the ground. Includes a full-colour, fold-out map.

EXPERIENCE GUIDES

feature offbeat perspectives and secret gems for experienced travellers, with a collection of over 100 ideas for a memorable stay in a city.

www.insightguides.com

INSIGHT ⦿ GUIDES
SHANGHAI

This new edition of *Insight Guides City Guide Shanghai* was updated on behalf of and in cooperation with Shanghai Municipality

Distribution

UK, Ireland and Europe
Apa Publications (UK) Ltd
sales@insightguides.com

United States and Canada
Ingram Publisher Services
ips@ingramcontent.com

Australia and New Zealand
Woodslane
info@woodslane.com.au

Southeast Asia
Apa Publications (SN) Pte
singaporeoffice@insightguides.com

Worldwide
Apa Publications (UK) Ltd
sales@insightguides.com

Special Sales, Content Licensing and CoPublishing
Insight Guides can be purchased in bulk quantities at discounted prices. We can create special editions, personalised jackets and corporate imprints tailored to your needs. sales@insightguides.com; www.insightguides.biz

Printing
Printed in China by CTPS

All Rights Reserved
© 2018 Apa Digital (CH) AG and Apa Publications (UK) Ltd

First Edition 2003
Fifth Edition 2018

www.insightguides.com

ABOUT THIS BOOK

This new edition of *City Guide Shanghai* was updated in cooperation with the Information Office of Shanghai Municipality, building on previous editions updated by Shanghai experts including **Amy Fabris-Shi, Tina Kanagaratnam, Abby Lavin, Rebecca Pasquali** and **Ye Beidi**.

The book was edited by **Catherine Yu**.

Earlier editions of the guide were worked on by **Graham Earnshaw, Sheila Melvin, Ceil Bouchet, Lisa Movius, Andrew Field** and **Patrick Cranley**.

Most of the striking images that bring the city to life were taken by photographers **David Shen Kai** and **Ryan Pyle**.

The book was indexed by **Helen Peters**.

Thanks to the **Information Office of Shanghai Municipality** for their support with the project.

SEND US YOUR THOUGHTS

We do our best to ensure the information in our books is as accurate and up-to-date as possible. The books are updated on a regular basis using local contacts, who painstakingly add, amend, and correct as required. However, some details (such as telephone numbers and opening times) are liable to change, and we are ultimately reliant on our readers to put us in the picture.

We welcome your feedback, especially your experience of using the book "on the road". Maybe you came across a great bar or new attraction that we missed.

We will acknowledge all contributions, and we'll offer an Insight Guide to the best letters received.

Please write to us at:
Insight Guides
PO Box 7910, London SE1 1WE
Or email us at:
hello@insightguides.com

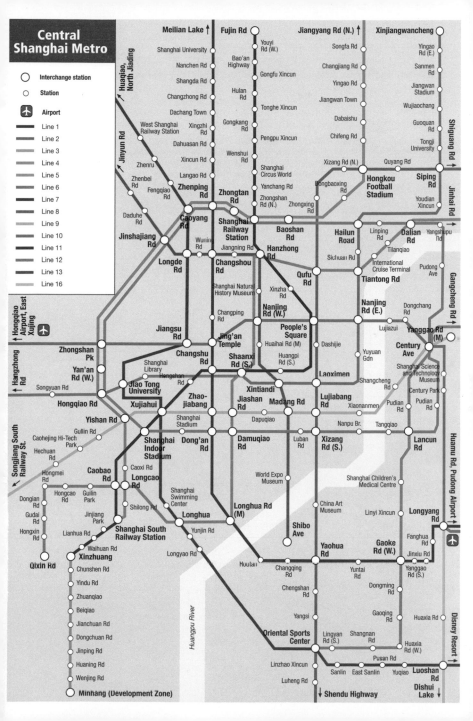